D1617114

Film Consciousness

Film Consciousness

From Phenomenology to Deleuze

SPENCER SHAW

McFarland & Company, Inc., Publishers
Jefferson, North Carolina, and London

LIBRARY OF CONGRESS CATALOGUING-IN-PUBLICATION DATA

Shaw, Spencer.
    Film consciousness : from phenomenology to Deleuze /
Spencer Shaw.
        p.   cm.
    Includes bibliographical references and index.

    ISBN: 978-0-7864-3334-6
    softcover : 50# alkaline paper ∞

    1. Deleuze, Gilles, 1925–1995.   2. Motion pictures — Philosophy.
3. Phenomenology.   I. Title.
B2430.D454S53   2008
791.4301— dc22   2007050797

British Library cataloguing data are available

Cover photograph ©2007 Shutterstock

Manufactured in the United States of America

McFarland & Company, Inc., Publishers
  Box 611, Jefferson, North Carolina 28640
  www.mcfarlandpub.com

For Birgitte, Sarah and Tristan

Acknowledgments

My interest in scholarship and philosophy in particular first began when I had the privilege of studying under Dr. Walter Isaacson. I would like to thank Frank Henriksen, at Copenhagen University, for the original inspiration to work in phenomenology and hermeneutics. At the University of Southern California, Alan Casebier, Marsha Kinder and the late Professor Beverle Houston were generous in their support, as was Daniel Dayan at the Annenberg School for Communication. Finally, for research into Deleuze I am indebted to the guidance of Professor Keith Ansell-Pearson at Warwick University, UK.

Contents

Preface

This work is the first major expression of the notion of film consciousness. As such there was a clear need to be highly selective about the many theorists who could have contributed towards an understanding of the notion. What we are left with is a group of thinkers and schools of thought that show the various stages in a consciousness that is unique, in terms of perception, memory and understanding. Film consciousness emanates from a technical medium with repercussions both for the way we see and experience reality, and for the significant contribution of an art form to that reality. The theorists who have been chosen to populate this somewhat complex mosaic have been picked for their landmark contribution to the evolution of a techno consciousness. Others could have worked, but there seemed to be some continuity in starting with phenomenology and Husserl and working through to Merleau-Ponty, Benjamin, Bergson and Deleuze. Early phenomenology did not deal with film as such, while Merleau-Ponty and Bergson made references to film without a specific focus. Benjamin and Deleuze, however, made major contributions as both saw its importance to modernity and postmodernity respectively. Hopefully, it will be apparent that there are substantial links between all the various schools of thought but without those links appearing overly reductive.

Introduction

Film Consciousness first attempts to understand the elements of the film experience and its concomitant consciousness through the descriptive tools of phenomenology. Starting with phenomenology and ending with Deleuze resulted in this book, to all intents and purposes, being divided into two parts. The first "does phenomenology," a descriptive pursuit in which, as much as possible, one immerses oneself in an experience to analyze and understand it. Though it has rarely been applied to the film experience, phenomenology is a perfect conduit, as it is a philosophy very much concerned with the constitution of consciousness — the intentionality that comprises the subject/object correlation. The technical apparatus of photography and film acts as an incursion into the lifeworld, producing a change in consciousness both in relation to reality and the aesthetic experience. The various concepts phenomenology uses to understand this phenomenon range from the reduction, époche, transcendental subjectivity and the concretized lifeworld. They all help us categorize a film experience we intuitively understand but rarely formalize philosophically. The second half of the book develops the idea of film consciousness as a unique vision of the world and as a change to human sensibility. It should not, however, be considered separate from the first part. Hopefully, through the descriptive tools that are used an evaluative and critical stance will be detected, one which is a prelude to Benjamin and Deleuze. It should also be apparent that the transition from the descriptive to the evaluative is aided by probably the key transitional figure of twentieth-century philosophy, Merleau-Ponty, and mention of his notions of depth, embodiment, invisibility and flesh should ease theoretical development.

Phenomenology helps us describe and delineate the stages of the film experience from the act of filming itself, or the photographic reproduction of reality, to its collective reception in the cinema. In this way, the work draws a distinction between filming, the recording of raw materiality, and the film work, the edited artwork. Both phases impact the final aesthetic experience, individually and collectively and both have implications for perception. Clearly, phenomenology's intentionality is a core concept, as it has to do with the structure of experience and consciousness. Different forms of consciousness have different intending objects; they are seen in various noetic guises, such as perceiving, doubting or expecting. This helps us understand what it is to intentionally be conscious of reality and the challenge, or displacement, thrown down to the perceptual mindset of an anchored subjectivity from the filter of a camera lens. This puts into perspective, by processes of exploration and questioning, the nature of representation as expressed through film. The influence of intentionality, the noetic consciousness of the viewer and the way objects and situations come to givenness, force us to reconsider the status of an image. We do not merely see through an image to something beyond but have to focus on the perception of the image itself, before it is interpreted. Furthermore, with all intentional acts we get a concurrent inner time-consciousness of the act, indeed, phenomenological subjectivity is, as such, self-temporalizing, part of a streaming continuum. Chapter three takes up the notion of phenomenological time and compares it to film time, or rather the experience of film, bearing in mind Husserl's notions of retention, protention and primal impression. Again, this is crucial to the understanding we have of time in film consciousness, both as a direct experience and thematically in criticism or reflection. Once acts are thematized they can be constituted as objects. Husserl and Merleau-Ponty have been chosen as the main representatives of the phenomenological school. Though Merleau-Ponty is frequently taken to be a Heideggarian "corrective" to Husserl's transcendental idealism, this is clearly a distortion of the facts. "Given Merleau-Ponty's persistent and rather enthusiastic (though by no means uncritical) interest in Husserl ... this unwillingness among Merleau-Ponty scholars to take his Husserl interpretations seriously is somewhat astonishing."[1] For example, the concepts of épochè and reduction are discussed in chapter two. Nowhere is it suggested that in carrying out the change of attitude necessary for these procedures the real world should be somehow deserted or negated, as many commentators insist on seeing it: "Quite to the contrary, the purpose of the épochè and reduction is exactly to enable us to approach the world in a way that will allow for a disclosure of its true sense."[2] This is what makes the procedures interesting in terms of film consciousness, for to focus only on the transcendental would be to deconcretize film's inbuilt materiality and visuality. If Merleau-Ponty is at odds with Husserl's position here it becomes a challenging foray into the meaning of body and embodiment as to how social intercourse is expressed and intersubjectivity explored. Indeed, the tension between the emphasis on transcendental subjectivity as an anonymous, superior ego, comparable to the supra human camera eye, and Merleau-Ponty's more inferior, impersonal version of the transcendental brings out interesting tensions that film consciousness reflects. In addition, Husserl's expansion of the transcendental sphere into transcendental intersubjectivity is an area also ignored by theorists who take no account of Husserl's later work.

This is not to say there are no differences between Merleau-Ponty and Husserl, certainly, "both Merleau-Ponty and Husserl had insights that cannot be found in the other" and the recasting of subject and object we find in Merleau-Ponty's *The Visible and Invisible* "went further than Husserl ever did."[3] But the readings of Husserl by Merleau-Ponty are highly instructive; for example, Merleau-Ponty's comments on inner-time consciousness that immediately show a move away from idealism into the forces of the lifeworld: "Husserl uses the terms protentions and retentions for the intentionalities which anchor me to an environment. They do not run from a *central I*, but from my perceptual field itself, which draws along in its wake its own horizon...."[4] Most importantly, Merleau-Ponty emphasizes that retention is not voluntary memory: "Husserl introduced the notion of retention, and held that I still have the immediate past in hand ... but I do not posit the past.... I reach it in its recent, yet already elapsed, thisness."[5] However, where Husserl's emphasis, though not implication, is still within the transcendental, Merleau-Ponty clearly links this expansive, unconscious memory to the body and makes this even clearer in his remarks on Proust. It is this same, direct reference to Proust's mémoire involuntaire that Benjamin used to explore the past and film's particular, optical unconscious.

One could claim that although the notion of film consciousness is not unknown to film theory and aesthetics, it has only gained currency as an important aspect of thought with the publication of Deleuze's two volumes on cinema in English. Before this, a more formidable area of study in relation to consciousness and film was within the analytic tradition that includes film cognition. The present work, however, draws on the continental tradition of philosophy. The dialectic, for example, has Hegel, and Marx behind Benjamin's own interpretation. The phenomenology of Husserl should also be considered in the light of Hegel and Kant. And Heidegger is, perhaps, the figure who touches upon all the modern theorists in one way or another. Though a detailed analysis of his influence would take us beyond the remit of the present study, some mention should be made of his relationship to Benjamin's critical theories.

It has been said that Benjamin worked under the "shadow" of Heidegger, "we can approach Benjamin's work in what might be called the 'shadow' of Heidegger's writing."[6] But the shadow that relates to the Benjamin-Heidegger relationship, is one that is cast from Heidegger's *The Age of the World-Picture* on to Benjamin's "Work of Art in the Age of Reproducibility", and is not a darkness but more like the veil Benjamin discusses with regards to the traditional work of art. "Everyday opinion sees in the shadow only the lack of light.... In truth, however, the shadow is a manifest, though impenetrable, testimony to the concealed emitting of light."[7] Once the configuration in the world as picture is established, with the human as subject and the world as picture, an invisible shadow is cast over things and the world itself becomes shadow. The activity of mankind, for Heidegger in the modern age, was characterized by negation, with the shadow suggestively pointing to "something else," a truth that escaped the plans of total representation. "But man will never be able to experience and ponder this that is denied so long as he dawdles about in the mere negating of the age."[8] The only way around this impasse and to get to know the incalculable was through reflection and creative questioning, "reflection transports the man of the future into that 'between' in which he belongs to Being...."[9] And, it is this "in-between" that leads Weber to conclude that the thinker more than any other, save Heidegger, who "explored the relation of the 'age' to the in-between, was Walter Benjamin."[10]

The scientific influence of film's technological instrumentality played a significant part in the writings of philosophers like Adorno and Heidegger, though their focus was not specifically aimed at film. Technology was the main human aid in controlling and ordering nature and film's instrumentality could be seen to mirror this process in action. The tendency was to believe everything could be subsumed under universal concepts and whatever was unknowable could ultimately be co-opted by science. As a reflection of this, the film frame could be seen as a synecdoche for the whole gamut of technological perception. For Heidegger, everything outside the frame was excluded, everything within, the "enframed" (ge-stell) was all that was knowable. The enframed became a version of reality connected to the world-view of technology in general and the age of the world picture in particular. Enframing frustrated us experiencing "the thing" in its worldly character and we also missed our own essence as belonging to the finitude of the world. In the modern age, everything encountered was mere human construct, lacking the originary finitude of presencing. It was expressed through a view of the world as representation: "The fundamental event of the modern age is the conquest of the world as picture. The word 'picture' now means the structured image that is the creature of man's producing which represents and sets before."[11]

For Heidegger, without distance all is lost. Enframing forced what is framed to drop out of presence, fall into a temporal hiatus and the spatial oblivion of distanceless. From this point of view, filming would be judged to characterize the illusion of presence by the continual creation of absent beings, the mechanical shadow reality of reproduction, the technological configuration of Being seen as infinite substitution, without presencing of actuality. For Heidegger, the whole of the modern age was characterized by technological consciousness and it was symptomatic of a major change in the essence of humanity. Modern technology was not seen as a desire for the making present of anything but a flight from any worldly presence through a curious, aggressive, subjective-seeing appropriation. Holding-in-vision by a play of distance through approach and retreat was linked to modern techne as a desire to control and make all that was visualized conform, an attitude that invariably hindered the "letting-be" of Being. The dynamic of technology, then, was a modern transformation of the desire to see, an ironic desire for absence, a withdrawal from the temporality of the world and its finitude. In this context, a constructed film work, one representing the world, would be an external force, a shedding-of-light-on, making it manipulative and extraneous.

Benjamin's assessment of film and technology should be seen against this background, though he comes to different conclusions. Benjamin's ideas on popular culture differed from Heidegger's, though he employed similar concepts, including flashing imagery, disclosure, constellation, concealment and an ambiguous attitude to Erlebnis. Benjamin, at different times, supported an anti-bourgeois form of art that replaced ideal use-value by leaving art and media experiences to the market place as an exchange-value linked to supply and demand. It was anti-élitist and placed faith in the collective to act as critic and judge according to their needs and desires, a faith that aroused skepticism in Adorno. The intimacy and cult values linked to traditional works were replaced by the openness and exhibition values characterized most markedly in the film experience.

Shock effect played a key role for both thinkers but Heidegger's experience of the shock of art was connected to death. Just as the work of art was a new opening into Being, as an historical event, so Benjamin's dialectical image was also an historical event that shocked us. Heidegger's *Stoss* suspended the familiarity of the world and Benjamin's intoxication associated with drugs or surrealist imagery also suspended the familiar. Though the two experiences are related to different artworks and different media, they emphasize feelings of disorientation in shock.

Both thinkers allied the momentary to the experience of vision and both argued its elusiveness. For Heidegger, nothing could occur inside a moment of vision because it leapt away before it could be acknowledged. That is to say, cognition of the moment and the sensation of the moment could never inhabit the same moment. If sensation and cognition cannot inhabit the same space then the present is always lost. One cannot recognize the category of the present because it is only sensed non-consciously as we always follow it. Recognition arrives after the present of presence. But such a falling into being lost has its own form of redemption, one that is reliant on valuing the sensual and pre-rational. In also recognizing this, Benjamin suggested the best way to experience such temporal aporia was through dialectical imagery.

Heidegger went on to describe how the claim of technological presencing could, positively, turn towards human beings in such a way as to grant them explicit insight into presencing. To accomplish this, there would have to be a sudden "gestalt" switch, a change, in fact, of consciousness, "once we realize ... that we receive our technological understanding of being, we have stepped out of the technological understanding of being, for we then see that what is most important in our lives is not subject to efficient enhancement."[12] Only in this way will we catch sight of the event of finitude, Ereignis, as that which technological desire otherwise conceals when it sets up presencing as standing reserve. Here we can intimate the constructive potential for filming through a consciousness that is not the adversely technological, "we whose hearing and seeing are perishing through radio and film under the rule of technology"[13] but, on the contrary, can oppose the danger of the essence of technology, with an-other consciousness, or what Heidegger preferred to describe as an — other "thinking" — originary thinking as a form of praxis. The first inkling of this change was the lightning-flash, as Being appeared, out of the stillness,[14] for both Benjamin and Heidegger.

With Deleuze's impact on the development of film consciousness, Bergson becomes a pivotal figure, not least of all for the contribution to film time and his notion of élan vital. Renewed interest came with *Bergsonism*, published in 1966, and the focus on his work in Deleuze's two volumes on cinema. In my study, Bergson is used mostly to link Deleuze's notion of time with Phenomenology. From this, however, it should not be assumed that Bergson was an outright phenomenologist. Sartre had repeatedly criticized Bergson's phenomenology in his early works for its lack of intentionality: "Thought, irreducible to sensation, becomes defined by meaning and intentionality.... But in Bergson we seek in vain for a positive description of the intentionality that constitutes it. Such is the constant ambiguity of the Bergsonian dynamism: melodic syntheses — but without a synthetic act."[15] Yet, in that "Bergson appeals to immediate experience" and "to intuition," Bergson had a close affiliation to phenomenology.[16] There are, however, marked differences with regards to perception, "perception is not an immediate experience.... Nor does perception occur in the service of knowledge, it pertains ... to action. Finally, in Bergson, it is never a question of self-presence, not even in the act of intuition."[17]

In some ways Bergson escapes Derrida's critique of Husserl even though he skirts similar themes of duration and constitutionality. Derrida was mostly concerned with the antinomy of indication and expression in Husserl's theory of language. He emphasized Husserl's metaphysics of self-thinking, the dual function within inner time-consciousness, as a mode of presence, even though he admitted Husserl was still radical and performed a critique of metaphysics, "do not phenomenological necessity, the rigor and subtlety of Husserl's analysis, the exigencies to which it responds and which we must first recognize, nonetheless conceal a metaphysical presupposition?"[18] Levinas, Husserl's student, early interpreter and avowed phenomenologist was someone who could still not accept what he saw to be Husserl's insistence on representation and adequation in intentionality. Nonetheless, in praising Bergson's notion of intuition as a radically new, unceasing creation, Levinas still pointed out close affinities with Husserl, "The Husserlian analysis of time answers to this essential message of Bergson on time, in a way that is a meeting of two independent minds. In Husserl, too, there is a rupture with the static notion of the separable instant.... There is also the absolute novelty of the proto-impression occurring without genesis."[19]

Bergson is especially important to film consciousness for his description of élan vital, the germinal life-force that is most apparent in *Creative Evolution* and *Creative Mind*. Deleuze picks up on the perpetual creation of new forms and his philosophy has an affinity to Bergson's "vital impulse." The vital impulse is beyond science. In terms of Bergson's intuition of pure change, the vital that arises out of the indivisibility and continuity of the inner flow of life is the impulse for growth and change. The vital impulse is such that "it has driven life to greater and greater risks of complexification towards its goal of ever higher and higher efficiency." Though this is essentially "a spiritual thing and 'impregnated with spirituality,' it is not deterministic."[20]

Although it may seem the vital impulse is a "metaphysics of presence in which 'man' is the privileged life-form," there are, in fact, "resources for a non-organismic mapping of evolution which will take us well beyond any residual perfectionism and anthropocentrism."[21] Ansell-Pearson argues for a revision of Darwin through Bergson's influence, a move that has been theorized in the works of geneticist, Richard Dawkins, as well as Deleuze. Dawkins' notion of the extended phenotype opens up the enclosure of the individual body into the world at large, "genetic action" at a distance: "An animal's behavior tends to maximize the survival of the genes 'for' that behavior, whether or not those genes happen to be in the body of the particular animal performing it."[22] Dawkins ideas on the extended phenotype come close to "what Deleuze and Guattari mean by transversal communication, communication of matter and information across phyletic lineages...."[23] The gene, or germ-line replicator, "travels wherever it can, far or near.... Through a variety of physical and chemical media it radiates out beyond the individual body to touch objects in the world outside, inanimate artifacts and even other living organisms."[24] Breaking the conventional boundaries of evolution and going beyond the confines of the organism capture the significance of what Deleuze and Guattari mean by the "machinic phylum in which evolution takes place via modes of symbiosis and contagion"[25] and lays a theoretical foundation for Deleuze's discussion of machinic thought in his cinema studies. With specific reference to the brain, Deleuze explodes the notion of self-containment and internalization. For Deleuze, it was Bergson who "proposed a new conception of the brain" and "introduced a profound element of transformation: the brain was now only an interval, a void, nothing, nothing but a stimulation and response."[26]

Film Consciousness tunes into the fact that in its filming phase it catches the flow of life in an imperceptible way, something Kracauer constantly returns to through filming's materiality, and Bazin in a more spiritual connection. Bergson is important to Deleuze because of his contribution to the notion of virtuality and memory, where memory "is to be understood neither as a drawer for storing things away nor as a faculty. Whereas a faculty works only intermittently, switching on and off as it pleases, the reality of the past is a deep and productive unconscious that evolves automatically."[27] This productivity is ceaseless; an eternal flow of becoming that resists completed identity. Film consciousness achieves an intrusion into self-perpetuating matter and registers its own identity, as unique spatio-temporal perspective and optical unconscious. The intrusion of film consciousness is both an outer and inner relationship, an image of but also an image in. Film, as movement and time itself, substantiates the pulsing life force and creation of new forms within creative evolution. In this way, film consciousness keeps up with, or keeps a track of, the past as a dynamic, virtual process within film's own temporal unfolding as imagery.

For Deleuze and Benjamin, the dialectic is an important process and they grapple with it in both a positive and negative way; both oppose Bergson to Hegel's own interpretation of the dialectic. Deleuze in particular "finds in Bergson ... a philosophical alternative to Hegel."[28] In Deleuze's analysis of Bergson's concept of difference we find why Benjamin could not totally agree with Bergson: "Consciousness in Bergson is not at all historical; history is just the only point where consciousness re-emerges, having traversed matter."[29] For Benjamin, however, consciousness is always historical. But, Deleuze continues, there are rare occasions when Bergson also relates consciousness to history. Referring to *The Two Sources of Morality and Religion*, Deleuze points out Bergson returns to the process of differentiation, where it is now not only couched in terms of biology but also history. Normally, in biology, original forms have an inherent limitation, "the material form they (the species) have assumed prevents them from reuniting to bring back again ... the original tendency."[30] But, on the level of history, it is "in the same individual and in the same society that the tendencies which have constituted themselves by disassociation evolve."[31] This is one of the "rare texts" where Bergson directly referred to the historical in relation to élan vital. In self-consciousness, consciousness of difference becomes historical, a fact that Deleuze explores in his historical spheres that enlace the movement and time image. The relevance regarding Benjamin is that if history reanimates consciousness "it is only because this consciousness identical to life was asleep, numbed in matter, annulled consciousness, not no consciousness at all."[32] Benjamin echoed this in his description in the Arcades Project of the dream sleep from which the collective must awaken, or come back to consciousness.

Deleuze is equally interested to point out that not only is Bergson's method not the dialectical method, but there is no contradiction or external determination and negation to the method at all. Rather, even though differentiation comes from "the resistance life encounters in matter ... it comes first and above all from the internal explosive force that life carries in itself."[33] In film consciousness, too, there is first the image of resistance, as filming is the other of reality, its outer skin, but then dissociation from this reality. It still has the spatial traces and imprint of duration but it becomes self-differentiation, with its own élan vital, as it establishes its own, specific force: "[E]ach line will also find certain apparati, certain identical organ structures obtained by different means."[34]

To clarify this further, we can turn to Deleuze's comment on the time-image where he compares sheets of the past memory events to points locked within an age. These ages are multifaceted, they can relate to territories, lines of flight or blockages, different social conditions or literally, past ages. Points of the past make no sense without their ages. Moreover, these ages, locked within virtual memory, transcend individuals, "memory for two, memory for several, memory-world, memory-ages of the world."[35] Each age has its own potential transformation, where its shape and division of points alter; not being fixed, they are in a constant state of rearrangement. Ultimately, the continuum of a sheet of the past will fragment and form another continuum. The point being, film consciousness works by breaking down predictable time patterns and the representational markers traditional narratives use. Resnais, for example, "conceives of cinema not as an instrument for representing reality but as the best way of approaching the way the mind functions."[36] When we inhabit sheets of the past, we draw on the virtuality of pure recollection and choose a point to actualize. It becomes, in film consciousness, the recollection-image that constitutes the present of film experience. As we inhabit preformed ages we seek associated memories to become recollection-images, images that may come from different ages, all of which make for the variety and peculiarity of independent consciousnesses. What may be most interesting is when we combine points or events from different sheets or ages, so that images reform the continuum or are superimposed on each other transversally. Again, redolent of Benjamin's faith in the shock of montage or the superimposition of Surrealism, the result may be "incoherent dust"[37] or, equally, a lavish ground to explore productive possibility, possibilities that mostly relate to feelings. Film consciousness, as the mode of thought, or its analogous work of art, can show the crossing of "coexistent ages," in an "excess" that can transform the "ages of memory or the world," constituting a "magnetic operation (that) … explains montage."[38] Film consciousness characterizes the transversal quality of feelings constituted by points of the past and the impending future. The brain, the screen itself as the cerebral membrane, is the dynamic determinant, the facilitator of open systems and transversal complexity "preventing them from halting and becoming fixed in a death-position."[39]

Deleuze's intention throughout his cinema studies is to sustain the groundwork he has laid in his previous, inventive, philosophical works by creating a slew of new, specifically cinematic concepts. He can do this because cinema studies are a continuation of philosophy, "Cinema's concepts are not given in cinema. And yet they are cinema's concepts, not theories about cinema. So that there is always a time, midday-midnight, when we must no longer ask ourselves, 'What is cinema?' but 'What is philosophy?'"[40] The cinema studies are a response to several previously raised issues. For example, in *Difference and Repetition* Deleuze introduces the notion of imagery in a negative way, criticizing the image of thought as that thought which represents doxa and presuppositions. There are two kinds of presuppositions, objective, concepts explicitly presupposed by another pregiven concept, and subjective, the implicit presuppositions of opinion.[41] Thought is always associated with a natural capacity for finding truth. In a common sense way, the natural image of thought has an affinity with the true; "it formally possesses the true and materially wants the true."[42] It is this image that underpins what it is commonly believed to think; that thought can know what is true, that everyone naturally knows what it is to think and that there is an identity of consciousness that does the thinking. Deleuze calls this a transcendental model of thought, "this image presupposes a certain distribution of the empirical and the transcendental, and it is this distribution or transcendental model implied by the image that must be judged."[43] This model is characterized by recognition, when a particular human faculty such as perception, or imagination can relate objects to each other in identity, as being the same or similar. There is also agreement between the faculties, or rather a unity of the thinking subject which "reflects the subjective identity" and "provides a philosophical concept for the presupposition of a common sense."[44] To challenge this image, as Deleuze believes is necessary, there cannot be the opposition of mere contrary facts, what is necessary is the overturning of the very principle of the image of thought. It is necessary to find thinkers who base their thought neither on representation nor on predetermined concepts.

The problem of overturning the image of thought is exacerbated because "nothing assures us that thought can, in effect, begin to think."[45] To activate thought it needs the unknown, an encounter with otherness: "Something in the world forces us to think. This something is an object not of recognition but of fundamental *encounter.*... It is not a quality but a sign. It is not a sensible being but the being *of* the sensible."[46] For thinking to be activated and start thinking the new it must be "a thought without image."[47] But by the time Deleuze comes to his cinema work, the notion of images in *Difference and Repetition* has been displaced. True, clichéd images abound in the cinema and Deleuze devotes space to argue for their dismantling, but he is more concerned with the new images and the shock effect they can produce to the human sensorium, just as Benjamin. The first step is to achieve a consciousness of clichés, the clichés that both internally and externally enshroud us, disabling and disillusioning. Godard asked "if images have become clichés, internally as well as externally, how can an image be extracted from all these clichés?"[48] Deleuze shares this question and also the implied solution; that it is imagery of a special kind that will bring light to the end of the tunnel.

New images are needed as film consciousness partakes in the thought of the time-image. In cinema, images are now to be the ally of thought; the great figures in cinema are great thinkers and they think with movement and time images: "Cinema's images can liberate movement and time themselves."[49] Film consciousness directly relates to Deleuze's notion of immanence but in different guises. Certainly, on one level, as part of the plane of immanence that is perpetually modifying, it is part of the univocity of being, without equivalence of substances and with no transcendence. But with the sense of alienation characteristic of post World War II mentality, "the idea that cinema as the art of the masses, could be supremely revolutionary ... (was) compromised." Rather than the masses becoming "subject," they became "subjected."[50] The world had become "intolerable," the expression of the sensorimotor image and actions in the interval suggested that no differences could really be made. Now "trapped"[51] thought looked for a subtle way out, not as a transcendent escape to another world but within immanence, here on earth. The issue was to believe "not in a different world, but in a link between man and the world."[52] Deleuze believed that if there is a leap here to reinsert all within immanence, it is to be achieved by an act of faith, a belief that cinema can be both revolutionary and Catholic.[53] The cinematographic image offered possibilities "either in the direction of a transformation of the world by man, or in the discovery of an internal and higher world than man himself was.... It cannot be said that these two poles of cinema have weakened: a certain Catholic quality has continued to inspire a great number of authors, and revolutionary passion has passed into Third World Cinema."[54] On the one hand, one could intervene between culture and nature to remake perceptions through revolution and in the process remake the world. On the other, spiritualizing humanity "in the name of" Catholicism could involve new images of thought that question film ontology in order to resurrect belief in *this* world. There is a conviction that cinema can make a difference, that there can be a conversion of faith, but to do so these new images, or the cinema of purely optical and sound situations, must "retrace the path from the crisis of the action-image ... back to its cause."[55] This cause will be recognized as the broken link between humans and the world and salvation will lie, not in another world, or God beyond this world, but in the belief that "it is still *our* world and the world needs faith."[56]

A photograph as Barthes described it, "cannot be transformed (spoken) philosophically, it is wholly ballasted by the contingency of which it is the weightless, transparent envelope."[57] And if we take Benjamin's advice seriously, we must resolutely refuse the concept of "timeless truth," admit it is differential, and that history is dialectical in the sense of eruptive and image-full. We are then forced to consider each technological development in its conditioning context: "For the historical index of the images not only says that they belong to a particular time; it says above all, that they attain to legibility only at a particular time.... Every present day is determined by the images that are synchronic with it."[58] In this way, it may be necessary to reassess Benjamin's messianic time, as well as Deleuze's film images in terms of digital imagery, which are "capable of morphing in cyclic rhythms and in infinite supplementarity."[59] Unlike Barthes' photographs, digital images "do not circumscribe the unloving, the mourned or the mortified as photographs have always done — instead, they affirm vitality and the joyful intoxication of a constant alterability."[60] The road that Benjamin's technical reproducibility leads to may be an unexpected one — the clone. With the destruction of aura different kinds of reproducibility vie for contention. "Cloning a fragment of DNA allows indefinite amounts to be produced from even a singular original molecule. (A clone is defined as a large number of cells or molecules all identical with an ancestral cell or molecule.)"[61] This iteration and reciprocity between original and reproduction, and ultimate redundancy of the original can be characterized in Benjamin's terms as a displacement of the originality of the unique.

Analog photographs literally adhere, stick to the reality from which they emanate through mechanical reproduction, digital images, on the other hand, "are fabricated through layers of algorithmic computer processing with no trace of the materially mimetic qualities of film."[62] The influence of the machine as prosthetic accoutrement to brain power and source for another development in consciousness has taken many facets. Cyborg films, for example, have led to the exploration of hybrid identity in terms of the nature of human identity, as well as questioning our general relationship to technology. This is interesting in terms of Deleuze's discussion of the mechanical and machinic, but definitive insights have been hard to find: "Despite emanating from a scientific worldview that sought to make humans increasingly knowable, the cyborgs appear to have produced a pronounced uncertainty with regard to identity."[63] The debate on embodiment, however, has been rekindled: "Cyberspace developers foresee a time when they will be able to forget about the body. But it is important to bear in mind that virtual community originates in, and must return to the body."[64] Questions concerning embodiment have especially foregrounded the female body and feminist identity. As Benjamin foretold, the impact of new technologies on collective and individual identities, in terms of cognition and consciousness, is far-reaching. With cyborg consciousness there is a realization that everyone is somewhat cyborg, as we benefit from advanced technologies and implants in medicine, and interface with a plethora of screens and delve into myriad virtual realities. Unquestionably, the attempt to determine identity is infinitely complex, and the areas of debate have spilled over into questions of gender and race. The questions raised have invoked the same doubts about divisions, categories and popular assumptions Deleuze raises philosophically, with speculation over whether technology "refutes or simply reinforces such distinctions."[65] Benjamin noted that technology could be both a liberating or oppressive force and "it is in recognizing this joint potential that the cyborg offers a new means of orientation."[66] Cinema can be considered a machine that defines the sense of self, or equally displaces it. But experiencing cyborg films stimulates cyborg consciousness as "a means of understanding how specific agencies work upon the subject."[67] Cyborg consciousness serves as a means of thinking through technology's impact on human identity, the relation of mind to body and the vital flux of a posthuman world.

Deleuze's special use of the machinic is best seen in terms of considering humans as desiring machines, not propelled by an unconscious in which desire is contained or restrained, but an unconscious which is itself desire. Humanity comprises an interrelated network of desiring machines through which material flows. But, under the requirements of representation "the unconscious ceases to be what it is, a factory, a workshop, to become a theatre.... The psychoanalyst is the director of this private theatre ... instead of being the engineer or the mechanic that puts together the units of production."[68] Deleuze was not an avowed theorist of cybernetics but was concerned with the mechanical and machinic. He expressed his perspective on machinic thinking through the rhizome. Rather then the tree image, which is rooted and grows from its foundation, rhizomes can grow from any points, as if with no beginning or end. "The tree is filiation, but the rhizome is alliance, uniquely alliance. The tree imposes the verb 'to be,' but the fabric of the rhizome is the conjunction, 'and ... and ... and.' *Between* things does not designate a localizable relation ... but a perpendicular direction, a transversal movement ... without beginning or end."[69] To this, Deleuze adds that "our current inspiration doesn't come from computers but from the microbiology of the brain: the brain's organized like a rhizome, more like grass than a tree, 'an uncertain system.'"[70]

Deleuze's system establishes a decentered film consciousness that promotes singularity, multiplicity and immanent difference, but there can be other approaches that accommodate new technology, in the form of digital consciousness, which also explore and manage to pose questions for which the answers are not assumed in advance. Manovich, for example, begins his definition of digital cinema in terms relating to Benjamin's insight into pre–Second World War technology and the importance of film animation for hybrid identity. For Manovich: "Digital Cinema is a particular case of animation that uses live-action footage as one of its many elements."[71] In the information age, Manovich sees all media objects as being composed of digital code, originating in mathematical form and subject to algorithmic manipulation, "they can exist in potentially infinite versions thanks to techniques of transcoding."[72] Mark Hansen takes issue with some of Manovich's observations. He agrees that the user has an opportunity to be a co-creator of a reality rendered by data that is fully manipulable and unique, unlike previous media of print, photography or television. However, what is questionable is arguing for a certain continuity of media in a deterministic way within technology. The reference to traditional animation within the digital is, for example, perceptive but also a somewhat self-serving way of sustaining continuity from cinema's early roots into the new technological age and bit information. Emphasis should be on a unique medium, which is perpetually self-differing, with no natural physical support. As such it is "necessary" to foreground embodiment "to transform its endless self-differing into a *concrete* experience of today's informational (post-medium) environment."[73] Touch functions to bring the body to life, to facilitate the body's experience of itself, and "not just (as cinema proper) to embody the illusion of the image," but also to "bring into play a supplementary element of bodily stimulation."[74] There has always been an element of manual actions from the early cinema days, from the thaumatrope to the stroboscope, and onwards, either through literally touching equipment and being a participant in creating effects or to an implied "sense" of touch in 3D. This sense of participation and bodily movement is not tangential to digital consciousness but is its core element. Referring to the neuroscientist, Franco Valera, we find that the capacity of the embodied mind "to adapt quickly to new virtual realities demonstrates the plasticity of the nervous system and the operative role of bodily motility in the production of perception."[75]

Hansen is determined to obviate the inclination of some theorists to see ultra formalism introduced into digital art as the universal and limitless inter-conversion of data, rendering "obsolete" the role of human perception and body; in other words, consciousness. Hansen turns to Benjamin for his emphasis on the shock effect of art, since it acted to relocate the impact of the artwork back into experience. The result of Benjamin grounding aura was that it was transformed rather than negated in modernism: "If the shock-effect relocates the impact of the work squarely in the domain of experience, this is all in the service of a redemption of embodied experience ... the source for a new, more or less ubiquitous form of aura: the aura that belongs to *this* singular actualization of data in embodied experience."[76]

Perhaps, most interesting for our purposes is the reappraisal of the Deleuze-Bergson relationship. Hansen sees in Bergson's theory of perception an emphasis on embodiment (taken to include the cognitive activity of the brain), as the "center of indetermination within an acentered universe."[77] When, for example, Bergson insists in *Matter and Memory* that "My body is the aggregate of the material world, an image which acts like other images, receiving and giving back movement"[78] this makes him a theorist of embodied perception: "Bergson correlates perception with the concrete life of the body."[79] In utilizing Bergson for his film analysis, Deleuze also incorporated Bergson's center of indetermination as the body into his notion of the interval, where the montage cut and the action of body perception are made homologous in the act of "framing." But in doing so, Hansen argues, Deleuze "brackets Bergson's embodied conception of affection," placing it in the regimen of the movement-image, defined "exclusively by the protracted interruption of the sensorimotor circuit."[80] This act of disembodiment is also carried through to the time-image as the apotheosis of the universal flux of images, again divorcing perception from embodiment.

To reinsert the body, Hansen takes issue with Deleuze's interpretation of the body's role in Cinema 1, rejecting the description of the sensorimotor body as a passive correlate of linkages between images. The corrective, for Hansen, comes through the very indeterminacy of the body in the interval, as it must constitute an excess over itself by dint of motion. It is motion that triggers affection, in the same creative way as Deleuze, but now as an active modality of bodily action. "I shall call this 'affectivity': the capacity of the body to experience itself as 'more than itself' and thus to deploy its sensori-motor power to create the unpredictable, the experimental, the new."[81] Rather than interrupt action, or, as in the affection-image, bring forth expression, affection should be seen as Bergson originally intended; an independent bod-ily modality in its own right: "The affective body is the 'glue' that underpins consciousness and connects it with subperceptual sensorimotor processes."[82] In the information age, dislocation, in the sense of malfunction, as well as ultra dissemination, characterize the radical disembodiment of perception and the changed status of the image. Images proliferate and are articulated by an other logic than the traditional. Disembodiment is correlated with automated vision and within the all-inclusiveness of imagery; personal vision dissipates into the machinic. In terms of Deleuzean immanence and the outside being intrinsic to the inside, no possible personal distance is feasible "for the digi-tal image there is no outside, only the vast telecommunications networks that support it and in which it is instantiated as data."[83] This can either mean visual automation completely replaces human vision, or human vision reacts to the challenge and reconstitutes itself in terms of both intelligence and affection.

The importance of embodiment, affection in perception and the tactile are the cornerstones that support a digital consciousness based on an inter-active aesthetic. In this way the virtual, instead of being the "transcendental condition for thought ... becomes the quasi — or inframepirical catalyst for the 'real' genesis of a bodily spacing, which is, not surprisingly, nothing other than the virtualization of the body itself."[84] Under such conditions, one is tempted to go full circle and think again of Benjamin's comments on the physical, aesthetic experience of walking through, and absorbing buildings where architecture is seen as the prototype of an artwork received in a state of distraction: "Not a disembodied eye, but an active, tactile and optical per-ception, one which results in a profound change to apperception."[85] Expanded consciousness led to an expanded sense of space, one that involved not only optical means but also the tactile. All in all, we are getting close to an other form of film consciousness, camera consciousness that discerns self-represen-tation and the lifeworld in much the same ecstatic way as contemporary vir-tual creations, "then came film and exploded this prison-world with the dynamite of the split second, so that now we can set off calmly on journeys of adventure among it far-flung debris."[86] The developments in glass and iron represented, for Benjamin, by virtue of labyrinth connections and spatial transparency, a breakdown of divisions. Now there were ubiquitous linkages and the distinction between home and street, interior and exterior was dissipating, both socially and psychologically. In contemporary terms, there is an equal breakdown of life spheres through information technology and simulacra. But we would not want to equate new media technology with the artificial constructs of a simulated virtual reality. Rather, it is much closer to the bodily sensations we find cultivated in the creation of new spaces through digital imagery which transform previous spatiotemporal notions and demand an equal effort from human perception.

1

Phenomenology and Film

Origins

The notion of film consciousness is one that has played around various film and philosophical discourses without every really surfacing as a cogent theory. Only in the work of Gilles Deleuze and his two volumes on Cinema has such a notion begun to take shape and here, more in terms of Deleuze's own philosophy than as a principle of film theory. To understand what film consciousness comprises, we need to look at fundamentals and by far the best descriptive tool for this purpose is phenomenology. I use phenomenology notwithstanding the fact that phenomenology and Deleuze make strange bedfellows. Deleuze has consistently criticised both the modern phenomenological movement as well as earlier Hegelianism, a phenomenology that had considerable influence on later developments. However, as I will try to show, some of the critique is reductive and does little justice to the pioneering works of Husserl and Merleau-Ponty. In addition, by way of one of Deleuze's favored philosophers, Bergson, we find a clear phenomenological link. Both Bergson and phenomenology use a scientifically based philosophy to challenge a worldview itself based on science. Their purpose is not to discard rational laws of nature and behavior but rather use rationality to understand behavior in a fuller, less linear sense. While science furthers our knowledge of the world, it is also used to mathematize it, seeking prediction and ultimate control of action. This is apparent in Bergson's critique of abstraction. Abstraction divides movement into artificial components, something that goes beyond the human experience of space and time. Major phenomenological thinkers take the scientific worldview seriously but at the same time undermine its objective tenets in favor of the movements of consciousness.

Theories directly linking phenomenology and film have been uncommon. This is surprising as there is an inbuilt similarity between the two areas.[1] Film, like phenomenology, carries within it an intentional act of perception. The primordial recording of the concrete world by the camera is both a view of the world and a temporal recording of it while the projection of the final film is a re-view of this world, configured into a meaningful mode of aesthetic consciousness. Interpreting film imagery and interpreting real life imagery have a close but distinct correspondence, one more easily understood through the wide array of concepts phenomenology provides.

The various modes of consciousness we use in our every day life such as daydream, recollections or wish fulfilments are used constantly in film as part of its narrative armoury. But, whereas in life the quality of the act is determined by a whole range of human emotions to do with imagining, doubting and wishing, in film, consciousness is determined by the "as-if," a suspension of disbelief. We accept we are watching the fiction of film's reproduction but we lay-aside that knowledge in order to experience the film as-if it were real. Naturally, this state of mind is nuanced by whether we believe we are watching a documentary or pure fiction film, but generic divisions are not crucial for understanding the mechanics of how we experience film and how consciousness and spatio-temporal awareness in film are engendered. As a study of the essence of the film experience, phenomenological description applies to all film types and genres.

Film accommodates a wide range of productions none of which changes the initial conditions of its formation. Its itinerary is wide, a vista moving from "neutral" news reportage with minimal manipulative treatment and sense of propriety towards the real, to a formalized and intentionally abstracted montage of Avant-Garde or Surrealism. Phenomenological description does not argue in favor of a particular style or genre or for cinema as social institution. It rather looks, in a presuppositionless way, at what filming would mean in order for it to be subsequently viewed cinematically.

Phenomenology helps bridge the classical gap between the formalist bias on film's unique expressive qualities and realism, which favors film's revelatory capability for depicting nature and the empirical world. Indeed, the phenomenological approach serves as an account of the way this bridge is built. Phenomenological film analysis confronts theories of film spectatorship that statically divide the film experience between a viewing subject and an object viewed. Contrary to this dualism, phenomenology's immanent correlation of consciousness rather makes film experience reciprocally alive, eliding fixity. Film's phenomenological aesthetic takes shape as a metacritique, an intricate dialectic of a consciousness of consciousness and a perception of the perceived. This makes the film experience a subject-object correlation that switches back and forth like a fusing mirror, a Janus-face alternation between spatio-temporal awareness and spatio-temporal perspectives. An intricate interplay of reflection takes place expressed as an exchange of perspectives. Traditional ways of describing film spectatorship in terms of escapist identification or voyeurism are clearly not radical enough to understand spectatorship in the presuppositionless way demanded by phenomenology.

As a showtime, film is dialectic grounding for the initial phase of recording as a natural and positive component of ontology prior to the processes of montage and postproduction. Rather than dichotomize two kinds of film approaches into realist and idealist, emphasizing either the inviolable world-outside or formal aesthetic shaping, it is preferable to acknowledge these two phases as reciprocally inclusive rather than mutually exclusive. By doing so, we are able to include phenomenological concepts that likewise look at interrelated stages in consciousness formation and components of perception. We can combine Husserl's transcendental phenomenology with Merleau-Ponty's existential embodiment to assess film, both in terms of placement in the lifeworld and displacement in the aesthetic world. In practice, both phases merge within spatio-temporal movement to comprise a unique dialectic.

As a regional ontology, filming can never be categorized as a hermetically sealed experience because the camera begins from the material world. As an embodiment in the lifeworld, it is an already involved constituent of the real. Consequently, any analysis of the film experience must bring to light the relationship of the lifeworld (the world of experience) to the film world, which constitutes its unique ontology. The phenomenology of film consciousness would take into account film's relation to concrete reality as well as explore the spectator mindset. This is the equivalent of saying that it must use the core principle of intentionality to look at the way consciousness is always a consciousness *of* something, in the sense of being directed at an object. By describing the way the subject, or the spectator, consciously experiences the intended object, the filmed representation, we can clearly isolate the specific form of consciousness involved in the film experience. We are also free to analyze the structure of perception resulting from a unique rendering of the lifeworld through its filmed reproduction.

The experience of film imagery is complex. It comprises a unique mixture, a showplace where the act of vision is itself visualized and a showtime where filming's sense of time creates a unique temporality. By implication, any claim that filming imparts a unique spatio-temporal vision means that film consciousness involves not the mere understanding of an aesthetic experience but also an exemplary way of experiencing the world. Spectator fascination with film and film's fascinating power of vision comprise an enterprise of exchange, a buffer world between two similar sensibilities — film inscribed in the world and human agency inscribed in film. The exchange is worldly, yet intimate, intimately private yet publicly projected, all-encompassing yet artistically distancing, something that is at the same time singularly unique yet universally meaningful; an experience saturated with the familiar yet visited by the strange. At the instant film penetrates the world with its effluent sensibility, it simultaneously hides from view everything beyond its frame as off-screen space. The camera's probing eye discloses reality, it relays back to spectators who then become active co-participators in a visual-sound discourse. Whether the contact of images with filmed matter, as in a contact print, can truly demystify or merely reinforce an already ungraspable and evasive lifeworld remains to be explored.

The Spectrum of Film Consciousness

The raw materiality captured in filming is the first stage of dialectic, one comprising an impasse, or limit point, leading to the ineluctable need for restructuring through the deconstruction of space and time. In general, dialectic is ignored by film theorists who rather have an impassioned agenda for locking film into systems of ideology, psychoanalysis or semiotics.[2] This is not to underestimate these approaches, indeed, the semiotic system of signs, psychoanalytic identification and catharsis, and ideological appellation have all aided in the understanding of the film experience. However, each approach takes for granted what phenomenology insists must be thematized to formulate a genuine presuppositionless grounding, and what Deleuze will insist must be a unique form of making concepts. On the one hand, through the correlation of intentionality, the blinkers of preconceived value systems can be removed "now that ideology has disintegrated, material objects are divested of their wraps and veils so that we may appreciate them in their own right."[3] On the other, film is liberated from a system of representation to a singular brain-world comprising feelings, affect and passion.[4]

Film experience comprises an interfusion of consciousness and the understanding of this encapsulates both the work of phenomenologists such as Husserl and Merleau-Ponty, as well as the irrationalists, Bergson and Deleuze. Though the phenomenologist, Merleau-Ponty, is apparently in an opposing camp to Deleuze, his notion of non-individuated consciousness and subjectivity in terms of temporalization would resonate with Deleuze:

We are saying that time is someone, or that temporal dimensions, in so far as they perpetually overlap, bear each other out and ever confine themselves to making explicit what was implied in each, being collectively expressive of that one single explosion or thrust which is subjectivity itself. We must understand time as the subject and the subject as time.[5]

Using Merleau-Ponty to understand film consciousness is further encouraged by his treatment of the human cogito in terms of self-awareness, or its lack thereof. The registration of vision is usually taken as emanating from a particular site of consciousness but Merleau-Ponty's bodily vision combined with film's mechanical vision allows for a pre-personal perceptual consciousness through the camera eye (I). The fusion of consciousness implies a (return) journey comprising a kind of visitation to where Being appears and a completion that involves absence and displacement before any return to self: "Vision is not a certain mode of thought or presence to self; it is the means given me for being *absent from myself,* for being present at the fission of being from the inside — the fission at whose termination, and not before, I come back to myself."[6]

This departure and return must be seen as impersonal since it is in both human and film terms a vision and consciousness relating to the sensibility of dehiscence in Being. Film vision is not only at home here, it has no other place to go, and this may explain Merleau-Ponty's relevance to film philosophy. As with the primordial film condition of recording without reflexivity, we find with Merleau-Ponty an attack on the cogito that seeks to exclude the possibility of an act of reflection, where the subject would achieve complete self-transparency. With embodiment, self-presence finds expression not exclusively in the mind but in the prior bodily experience with concrete reality, a fundamental change of emphasis from the Cartesian position; prior giving of oneself to self via vision supersedes the transcendental vision of reflection on self. If there is a semblance of immanent subjectivity in Merleau-Ponty's tacit cogito, it is dissipated in his later work through the chiasmic intertwining with the world, "behind which there remains no subjective retreat of nonbeing."[7] Film consciousness makes brute being approachable, it allows silence to speak in a way unencumbered by subjective agenda.

We find that Merleau-Ponty's discussion of self-consciousness is particularly appropriate to film in its usage of images of reflections and mirrors. This is not reflection in the sense of the self objectified under the system of representation. Merleau-Ponty's theory of the pre-self in the form of preconscious or incarnate subjectivity is lived directly through the flesh in its adherence to the world. The body is a perceiving subject-object. By touching oneself, one expresses both objectivity and subjectivity and this is a form of reflection, as touched and touching is an active-reactive echo of parts, rather than pure reaction. Film consciousness suggests the same process by its exploration of changing perspectives, narrative and dysnarrative, "both film and

the spectator are engaged in the act of seeing a world as visible, and both
inhabit their vision from within it — as the intrapersonal relation between
'myself, my psyche' and 'my introceptive image.'"[8]

Film enters into flux as a capture of movement, at the point of emergence from non-visibility to visibility, from the undeveloped to the developed, from the intricate to the extricate, from impression to expression.
Moreover, when interaction takes place between imagery, formal deconstruction allows for a return to the hyle and sensation of unformed matter.
Through segmentation of formalized materiality we tap into the virtual and
contact the reality of what was always a past, what has prematurely been
perceived and fixed, to regenerate and rejuvenate inventive possibility. The
subjectivity that enables this capture is couched in the intentionality of
noesis to noema but becomes with Bergson and duration the subjectivity
that escapes us in pure past. And with Merleau-Ponty, consciousness is the
result of the dehiscence or opening up of being into the sensing-sensible chiasm, so that filming is a presence at that place where Being's interior lights
up. Being manifests its own meaning, one that is a configuration occurring
as being differentiates itself from itself. Filming does not make the presence
of the world, it finds it there as a process in action and by visioning it, it envisions itself as the visibility of seeing, both a catalyst and witness to Being's
upsurge.

Admittedly, with Bergson, we are forced to revise some of Merleau-
Ponty's perceptual norms and deviances and the taken-for-granted spatial
perception involved in embodiment. Most important, Merleau-Ponty looked
to the realization of possibilities, whereas Bergson held that "living beings and
the actions of living beings are not a matter of realizing one of several possibilities...."[9] Possibility for Bergson cannot precede its reality, whereas phenomenologically possibilities inherent in a situation as actionable precede
existence, they can *be* before coming to be. For Bergson the possible is not
"a less," an existence that is realized from a passed state of waiting, it is the
reverse. Once something is realized, we see the possible as real with "something added, since the possible is the combined effect of reality once it has
appeared and of a condition which throws it back in time."[10] In other words,
only when something is real does it retroactively become possible, its reality
must come first; the possible "remains the shadow of the real."[11] The intellect sees possibilities as pre-existing, divisive, anti-process and linked to the
sensory motor mechanism of representation. Reality is rather created "as
unforeseen and absolutely new such that one can never speak of the actualization of possibilities but only of the actualization through differentiation of
the virtual; the real but unactualized multiplicity."[12]

Even accepting this as a critique, Merleau-Ponty's position was still not reductive. Rather than advocating a subjective, logocentric ontology, for Merleau-Ponty consciousness emerged from the mediation of worlds where the subject was present to and knows itself through the body. Even more, Merleau-Ponty's argument for inherent ambiguity was directly relevant to Deleuze's ambiguity of the time-image. The perceiving subject exists in an ambiguous mode, neither exclusively a thing nor exclusively consciousness and as a result "calls into question the traditional distinction of subject and object ... and one of the central foundational principles of philosophy, the so-called law of excluded middle (a thing must be *either* this *or* that)."[13] Rather than artificially suppress the temporal flow,[14] Merleau-Ponty was firmly within a phenomenological tradition that emphasizes temporal flux and prefigures the emergence of fissures and the dissociate forces of the time-image dys-narrative.

As an art form, film has created a new reality and, its accompanying consciousness, a new way of thinking. There is dialectic at work that helps us understand the way film imagery speaks, contextualized within a frame or dialectic "boundary" always in the act of surpassing itself. The frame relates to the world as given or unfigured, and radiates out from ground zero in terms of sensuous matter. The dialectic tension of the process manifests as an antithesis that pressurizes enframing. Primal impression is tautly stretched to the limits of the frame, contents decompose and threaten to lose meaning. Fragmentation occurs and in this disruption a negated (or inverted) world emerges, comprising shadows and doubles.

Out of the tension and struggle to make meaningful markers, phenomenological positions are assessed and identity put in question through narrative structure. There are as many self-narratives in phenomenology as there are multiplicities in Deleuze. There is synthesis too, with a synthetic return to the lifeworld of imagery, but subsequently on a higher level of consciousness. That level is only attainable through specification, discussion, and self-knowledge, putting in relief imagery that transgresses the norms of sensory-motor activity. Predictably, film analysis tends to focus on isolated aspects of the dialectic and thereby misses the fluidity and elusiveness of film consciousness. If the journey to understand film consciousness is circular, it is an intended "loop," one to be acknowledged as both an enticing departure and a familiar return, an eternal return of difference.

Film's recording is a recording *of* something just as essentially phenomenological consciousness is a consciousness *of.* Lived experience implies a proof of the actual encountered world similar to photographic proof where the phenomenon of the appearing object is caught and attested to by a durational flux on a "plate" of consciousness. Here, phenomenological description helps map out components of the film experience and its relation to film ontology, especially film's existential body as a pregiven encounter in the lifeworld. Film's mechanical reproduction receives shock as an insistent reminder that the film experience is founded on the cusp of the human and mechanical, neither wholly one nor the other.

Film consciousness, like human consciousness, has both a passive and an active condition. Passive presence in its primordiality corresponds to a changing, passive ego. It carries through the laws of its consciousness as reflected in film's viewing-view and the mirror of human perspective. This gives the parameters for the structure of what turns out to be reproduced, enabling specifications for perceptual reading after editing. The transcendental presence, the totality produced, is the overall vision of automatic recording, the pictured world-view. At the same time, filtered through the transcendental viewpoint of film, there is an active "I," which is not passive subjectivity but a machinic, serialized consciousness emerging through intervals in imagery. In the phase of film reconfiguration, memory and virtuality are paramount in the intentional act that comprises the fusion of projected and spectator vision. The spectator acts as the catalyst for the embedded virtuality of film to crystallize as temporalized, split imagery. Film consciousness, through the show of time, comprises the spectator; it takes up a subject position that is constantly changing, or fracturing, under a reading generated by a productive "I." The filmwork's own transcendent position ensures the pure form of this constant change in time, as a resource of pure recollection. This is the return of Bergsonian memory, where ontological unconscious and film's spiritual automaton coincide to manifest indeterminate and noncausal situations. Here there is constant fluctuation; the brain is like a filter that lets emotions through to thoughts and the past collective into present instances.

With Merleau-Ponty, if there is a sense of agency it is not a causal one but one made up of a fluid and shifting force, not unlike that of Deleuze. The whole is made up of configurations sensitive to what happens in all the others, and "knows them dynamically."[15] Film consciousness may be without the reflection that attempts to dispel the opacity of the lifeworld but it retains the complex mindset of lived experience in a creatively reconfigured way. The film body mechanically records to produce imagery as formed consciousness. The artwork:

> Constitutes an organ of the mind having an analogy with every philosophical and political idea if the latter is productive; the work contains, even better than ideas, *matrices of ideas* furnishing symbols whose meaning we can never exhaust. It is precisely because it is installed and installs us in a world whose significance is foreign to us and gives food for thought as no analytical work can.[16]

Dialectic Misgivings

With the movement-image, Deleuze emphasizes the indirect projection of time, duration in movement that is a synthetic achievement, a product of image and mind, a Hegelian unity of a higher order. In this context, Eisenstein is philosophically closer to Hegel than Bergson is. Relating this to Hegel is to insist on intellectualizing montage, "thought-montage," since it is only with the dialectic of self-consciousness that the concept of the whole, film as consciousness, is thought. Yet, when Deleuze shows the crucial contribution of Eisenstein's sensuous thought relating mind to nature and emotion, it is enabled by similar shocks and disjuncture of thought Deleuze feels to be the kernel of the modern time-image. We find that though we are relating shock to Hegelian dialectic, its import carries over to the time-image. The interrelation of feeling and thought is an unbreakable bond. However, in being aligned to Hegel it carries with it all the critique Deleuze has mounted against the Hegelian system.

Both Phenomenology and Deleuze are needed to understand the evolution of film consciousness. However, Deleuze's analysis is inclusive only up to that point where the movement-image and time-image separate. This is a move by which Deleuze describes a natural qualitative difference, one that reflects an historical, evolutionary shift away from organic or Hegelian oneness into dispersed, Nietzschean multiplicity. Deleuze wants to oppose descriptions of the subject as a limited, reactive, manufactured construct generated by slave mentality, through a feat of envious transvaluation and self-denial, in favor of an autonomous, self-generating agency at home in the openness of matter. This is self-generation as opposed to the desire of negation that attempts to seek out the Other and incorporate all that is different.

We need the will to power and a non-dialectic multiplicity of impulses to burst out of Hegelian desire. We need to oppose assimilation into identity and enjoy alterity as an intensification of the play of forces. There is abundance rather than scarcity, joy rather than fear. For Deleuze, theories that insist repetition be seen in terms of a preconceived identity will only limit understanding by referring it to the form of identity in the concept. For Deleuze there cannot be such referencing, there can be no underlying realm of immutability. Deleuze is searching for change as causal negation, an intrinsic change that does not come from similar identity. Hegel is reproached for couching difference, and the extreme of contradiction, within the ground of identity:

> Hegelian contradiction does not deny identity or non-contradiction: on the contrary it consists in inscribing the double negation of non-contradiction within the existent in such a way that identity, under that condition or on

that basis, is sufficient to think the existent as such. Those formulae according to which "the object denies what it is not" ... are logical monsters ... difference is already placed on a path or along a thread laid out by identity.... Difference is the ground for ... the demonstration of the identical.[17]

This underscores that for Deleuze we have not yet reached difference-in-itself. Fundamentally, Deleuze's difference is non-dialectical; Hegel's vision is recuperative:

The dialectical negation is always directed toward the miracle of resurrection: It is a negation "which supersedes in such a way as to preserve and maintain what is superseded, and constantly survives its own supersession." (*Phenomenology of Spirit*, §188) Nondialectical negation is simpler and more absolute. With no faith in the beyond, in the eventual resurrection, negation becomes an extreme moment of nihilism.... Nondialectical negation is absolute not in the sense that everything present is negated but in that what is negated is attacked with full unrestrained force.[18]

There is no room in the dialectic for the out-of-control; any sign of excess comes under what Deleuze disparagingly describes as "the insipid monocentricity of the circles in the Hegelian dialectic."[19] The move here away from the negative inclusiveness of Hegel's dialectic seems decisive. Deleuze would resist Hegel's initial presentation of the opposition between being and nothingness in the *Science of Logic*. The essence of determinateness is its negation; its move away from inertia is sparked by contradiction, what it is-not. However, this is an external impulsion related to determinate being, whereas for Deleuze emphasis is on indeterminate becoming, closer to Bergson's notion of intuition. In the process, the being of being takes a back seat to the more fundamental being of difference:

For being to be necessary, the fundamental ontological cause must be internal to its effect. This internal cause is the efficient cause ... it is only the efficient cause, precisely because of its internal nature, that can sustain being as substance, "causa sui." In the Bergsonian context, then, we might say that efficient difference is the difference that is the internal motor of being.[20]

For Bergson the thing differs with itself immediately and first whereas in Hegel the thing differs with itself because it first differs with all that it is not. For Bergson, the combination of synthesis and antithesis are abstract and cannot be concrete and real. An effect cannot contain more reality or perfection than its cause, so the dialectical synthesis must remain contingent and abstract. In fact, Bergson's indeterminacy and virtuality has little to do with Hegel's immanence, it is inspired rather by the unforeseeable. Dialectic movement is considered false movement: "The concrete will never be attained by combining the inadequacy of one concept with the inadequacy of its opposite. The singular will never be attained by correcting a generality with another generality."[21]

In this way, film as referential, or as an unveiling of truth picked up mirror fashion from the recorded world, is anathema. Recovering the already preformed is not truth but rather a confirmation of the already known, "truth cannot be said to be the product of a prior disposition or schema, but is the result of a tremendous violence in thought.... One will never find truth, one will never philosophize, if one knows in advance what one is looking for."[22] Thinking only comes into play when it encounters the unthinkable. The simulacrum, for example, is contradictory; it jolts thought into action with novelty and originality. It is a part of becoming rather than the being of a state of affairs. The lack of substance in film, unlike a piece of sculpture, a painting or even a still photograph, lends itself to the transience of the simulacrum, film is invisible and has no being until projected. It is not on show until shown.

Intrinsically, film has no chronos of being. For Deleuze multiplicity is a task to be carried out, we must always make connections.[23] To connect is to work with other possibilities. The multitude of connecting possibilities in film makes it a prime example of this. The connection between modalities is made after the event in the film process through montage imagery. Yet this only supports, or reinforces, the already split nature of time we come to see in crystal imagery (thus not a mirror of, but a mirror within). The film work is ideal for showing time, showing time-in-action, and the inaction of time in the interval, as a mobile mirror.

At the same time, however, there is a lingering sense of unease in the rejection of organic representation that we find in the ultimate time-image. Film has its (dialectic) duplications, re-presentation and intentional framework between recording and recorded, reel and real, frame and beyond-the-frame, identity and difference, part and whole; all of which seem comfortable with Hegelian negation and organic movement. This is not to say that film should be so, only that there are elements intrinsic to film ontology that disincline it acceding completely to the way of thinking Deleuze argues for the time-image. From this it may well be that the circularity of Hegel, where Spirit's self-actualization is the process of its own becoming, is still applicable to the inclusiveness and unwrapping of a self-contained film work; a process that already carries with it its own becoming-other.

Deleuze's actuality, as expressed potential, is rather a step removed from the latent world of possibility so close to the sublation that both retains and negates the original lifeworld. Film is, on a basic level, if not a system of representation then a system of mediation. Involved in film's mediated system is an internal integration of the re-presented world as a natural force of immanence. The result of this is an entity containing multiplicity but also encouraging coherence and self-reference. Moreover, in terms of the sets and systems we find in film, the lifeworld itself has a dialectic need for film as a way to become other to itself, in order to know itself. Even though there is qualitative difference in the images of film based on concrete reality, it is a difference that strives for identity in difference rather than difference in difference. This may account for the various bottlenecks we find in the crucial transition from moving-image to time-image and possible need for a new form of technology rather than a new form of consciousness.

There is a sense in which both phenomenology and Deleuze have set the parameters for this self-knowledge, film's self-consciousness. Film consciousness pervades a spectrum, one end of which is a phenomenology tending towards spiritualized matter, the other end of which we find an insistence on materialized spirit. It is partly due to the breadth of this spectrum that shadings within film consciousness are so provocatively sustained. In a move that is anti–Deleuzean, the act of filming is a way by which the represented world comes outside itself to know itself and return to itself through a hermeneutic circle. The otherness that exists in the filmwork, even in those that are anti-narrative and radically disruptive of spatio-temporal reality, is an otherness that is inevitably co-opted by the organic structure of film, and the desire of the spectator to write in a comprehensive whole. The idea of telos, in whatever form it takes, is an inherent part of the film experience as an anticipated urge to realization. The notion of "concorde fictions" points out we can never provide solutions to life's mysteries and temporal aporia, but nonetheless we repeatedly show those aporia in art in different contexts:

> We create fictions because we do not know what happens after death. In short, we try to improve upon the fictions created by philosophy and religion which ascribe portentous meaning to life and assume for existence a significance which is entirely hypothetical.[24]

Conclusions will be justified and endings, no matter how unlikely, provided. Hegel's dialectic does not lead to stultification and closure but a certain satisfaction, which if "out-of-time" in a Deleuzean sense may be so because filming is out-of-time in a phenomenological sense. Accepting this leads us to a Deleuzean notion of film consciousness that may rather be laying the groundwork for future media, virtual reality and cyborg and digital consciousness with subjectivities that are fluid, larval and interactively negotiable to begin with. Here there is not a finished or completed artwork at all waiting for projection, or a power struggle for transcendence and assimilation, but rather a force expressing internal differentiation naturally and unencumbered through creative mappings of pathways that affirm the generation of life and possibilities for connective exploration.

As Deleuze claims, it may be that cinema had to go through a slow evolution before attaining self-consciousness. If this is true then it is a consciousness attained through the expression of both its movement and time-images. Ultimately, film consciousness is most characterized by its auratic attraction, sensuality at a distance, dazzling imagery and flashing in-sight. Its jagged peaks and troughs bear testament to its coursing lifeblood; resistance and force. The affront to human consciousness, with its own comfort zone, perpetrated by machinic consciousness, bereft of conscience, fixes it on a course for creative, invaginated pathways.

2

Phenomenological Grounding

Realist Theory

Film's verisimilitude attracts comparison to a naive, scientific imaging of the material world. There is an established scientific-realist theory that emphasizes the technical abilities of film to replicate concrete reality in a way that is objectively peerless. The high ascetic requirement to achieve genuinely realistic films practically becomes a self-conscious style of its own that tries not to tamper with events or definitively interpret their import. The role of the spectator is neutralized as are the influences of perspective and prevailing ideology, "any critical analysis of the ideological character of cinema meets the strongest resistance ... it is an insistent claim for the autonomy of technical processes."[1] It is argued that film technology allows for images that are outside ideology and in conveying the meaning of imagery it effaces itself as it communicates pure denotation. The focus of the initial act of recording is shifted from the original intentionality of the filmmaker to the sheer power of technology and the camera to enact reproduction:

> Film is clearly a scientific invention, not a product of ideology, since it is founded on a real body of knowledge and on the properties of the matter which it activates ... it is not the filmmaker, but the camera, a passive recording instrument, which reproduces the object or objects filmed in the form of an image reflection constructed according to the laws of the rectilinear propagation of light waves (which in fact define the effect known as perspective).[2]

Film's proclivity for reproduction is seen as the ideal tool for a scientific mirroring of the real and an assumption that the real is readily given to scientific understanding. What is found in the real world is carried over into the reel world, the only question being the manner of the transference rather than its eventuation. One advantage of the scientific-realist theory is that it makes us look at the mechanics of the process involved. The technology of film, captured through the film body, cashes out into human action making it a visible paradigm of our inherence in the world. Technology, and the increase in knowledge that accompanies it, inevitably transforms the natural world and our actions within it. As such, there are repercussions for human consciousness; "new modes of production constitute not only a 'new age' but also new modalities of consciousness and, most significantly, self-consciousness."[3] In other words, film meaning and its sense-giving perception would not be possible without first being grounded in technology, just as the human body "apparatus" makes perception possible and gives life its experience in the intersubjective and expressive lifeworld.

But the danger of a non-phenomenological approach such as this is that it categorizes film experience as a non-intentional medium, silencing film's voice, trivializing its aesthetic effect and effectively denying the aesthetic content of the technological artifact. This results in a division between the two bodies, one human and one instrumental, and hinders our understanding of the genuine fusion of consciousness that takes place in film consciousness. More helpful is to search out similarities. As non-human, film's material body comprises, "metal ... glass ... and electronic circuitry.... And yet, like the human body, the film's body is animated and lived with existential prospects and purpose."[4]

The naive, scientific-realist description of film experience positions film's significance entirely in its primary reproductive phase, ignoring what is processed in film, its secondary phase of reconfiguration and projection. More than this, it ignores phenomena-as-experienced by abstracting them from experience. The intricate bond between image and world or the relation of film to its referent will always be interlaced with the segmentation and fragmentation of constructed expression. This is an expression that is not only linguistic but also visual and carnal. We are led to believe that the truth of being is accessible through the objectively given, but for phenomenology this is anathema. Husserl's own scientific project revolved around dynamic construction, discovery, constitution and the efforts of intentionality to conceive consciousness in a sensually perceived world.

If the film work is to be considered in this context, while taking into account film's insistent verisimilitude, resemblance cannot be accredited with objective proof. Film recording and the experience of what is filmed must include an experience from the inside-out rather than the outside-in. In fact, even though film is apparently concerned with the outside, the surface appearance we find in phenomenology is always dealt with through the unveiling of surface by depth penetration.

Real to Reel

The reality-effect of film is powerful, vivid and encompassing, in large part due to verisimilitude, reproducing the same imagery and perceptions we experience in everyday life. Filming, however, directs and places the spectator within perceptual sites of its own making. These perceptual sites approximate real life to be convincing but they are fabrication. To acknowledge this, any film ontology needs to reflect on the represented world and the re-presentational, seeing them to be an aesthetic link based primarily not on equivalence but on sensuous force. That is to say, as artistic medium, film's reality-effect can only succeed if it relegates to the background what ordinary perception places in the foreground: "The aesthetic object carries the world which it reveals within itself. Rather than referring to the world outside itself as things do ... the aesthetic object refers to itself alone and is for itself its own light."[5] The aesthetic object never merely reproduces the real, if it did it would be redundant, the real can never be reproduced; it would be a failure as an impression or a copy. Rather, it *expresses* the real, giving it meaning in a way that goes beyond documentation or reproduction. Original events can be depicted in various ways. Each representation shows only what is necessary for intelligibility and by doing so rejects the need for preserving the original representation in its totality. From the initial reality an illusion of parts is substituted.

Husserl's general description of artistic representation helps us understand film ontology as an expression of real life, the focus of realist film theory, but includes understanding the film spectator not in terms of a scientifically objective onlooker but as an active constructor of the film text. The movement of film as moving imagery allows for the most thoroughgoing explorations of spatio-temporal reality as a lived experience in-depth where the intimate yet public projection of multifaceted visual perspectives rests in the real world while simultaneously transcending it. Filmed space is a lived space, which is both distantly viewed and bodily implicated, a vision that is temporally measured yet disjunctively fragmented. Film discovers and uncovers an aesthetic meaning rather than mechanical mirror, a meaning that resonates through unexpected visions and dislocated spaces. The infinitely open lived world and the internally cohesive filmed world come together in dynamic consciousness. Horizons expand, systems shift and the ungraspable totality of the real reverberates through subjective sensibility in aesthetic overdetermination. It is subjectivity in all its vital guises that draws upon the overflowing character of the lifeworld to make an endless series of significations. The intaglio of the real world is raised into a selected, discriminated number of worlds with recognizable, intentionally given significations. The expressive artwork is a realization of one possibility from the infinite possibilities experienced in brute reality, a possibility that comes to enlighten the real. The real world is a world that demands of us attention and action as we focus on the immediately given and concretize absent indeterminacies that constitute the existential world. The aesthetic world makes no such demands but it does penetrate this otherworldly reality casting fresh light on it, "art is true because it helps us to know the real."[6] The film work is a distillation of the real world through similar structures of experience:

> The aesthetic experience is not just one kind of experience among others, but represents the essence of experience itself.... In the experience of art there is present a fullness which belongs not only to this particular content or object but rather stands for the meaningful whole of life.[7]

Lifeworld Encounters

Where most aesthetic works are characterized by distance and the artifact of otherness, film ontology is noteworthy for reducing the gap between expression and the expressed, the signifier and the signified and establishing entry points in tandem with intentional experiences. To understand the import of filmed reality we must look closely at how phenomenology describes the perception of reality. For Husserl, we understand concrete reality directly through the image rather than through the distancing effect of semiotic codes. The example of Dürer's engraving of "The Knight, Death, and the Devil" is apposite:

> We distinguish ... the perceptive consciousness in which, within the black, colorless lines, there appear to us the figures of the "knight on his horse," "death" and the "devil." We do not turn our attention to these in aesthetic contemplation as objects. We rather turn our attention to the realities presented in the picture — more precisely stated, to the "depictured" realities, to the flesh and blood knight, etc.[8]

Reality here is both a product of human perception and a presentation of the represented world. The core component is apperception where we pass through various qualities of the image to depicted reality. We pass through sensa to

grasp what is represented.[9] Beyond this we will be able to apperceive and
interpret whatever is symbolically shown. For Husserl, the picture has a consciousness in the mode of a neutrality-modification of perception "[t]his
depicting picture-object stands before us neither as non-being, nor in any
other positional modality; or rather we are aware of it as having its being,
though only a quasi-being, in the neutrality-modification of Being."[10]

Husserl's position encompasses a broad spectrum of film theory. It
accommodates the initial phase of film recording as an embodiment in the
life flux as well as the transcendental position of artistic creation and omniscient expression. It allows for the exploration of noemata, the object side of
consciousness, to concrete reality, a reality that can be understood in its broadest interpretive capacity. This is pivotal for judging the contribution of spectator activity as participator in the construction of artistic meaning through
spectator time-awareness and phenomenology's inner time-consciousness.
The transcendent (material world) and the transcendental (consciousness and
life world activity) are not separate spheres but mutually dependent:

> Life-world and objective-scientific world ... are related to each other. The
> knowledge of the objective-scientific world is "grounded" in the self-evi-
> dence of the life-world. The latter is pre-given to the scientific worker (and)
> what is built is something new, something different. If we cease being
> immersed in our scientific thinking, we become aware that we scientists are,
> after all, human beings and as such are among the components of the life-
> world, which always exists for us, ever pregiven.[11]

Husserl rigorously pursued the recurring phenomenological concept of the
lifeworld (lebenswelt). The lifeworld has its own taken-for-granted spatial
and temporal coordinates that facilitate everyday experience, and in his later
work, Husserl looked at the larger horizon of the objective world such as previous subjective achievements of community, historical development and
world history. As the lifeworld is an anonymous, pre-theoretical horizon, film
recording within the real world naturally picks up on the horizon of world
history in an irresistible fashion, saturated by its imagery. This is not a transcendental search for universal adequation but a reflection of changing values, a doxa with practical orientation. When film documents the prepredicative
spontaneity in the lifeworld, it is as an experience that will only later be subjectivity thematized into knowledge. By envisioning the world through gen-
erative inception and spectator reception, film presents its images together
with horizons of the lifeworld. What Husserl called "preliminary presences"
are the constituent elements of all that enter into the background of our field
of consciousness. It is this background we equate with primary film recording, a presence which is part and parcel of a general environment making up

the world of all pregiven objects. We are presented with the raw materiality of life, a depiction of a presuppositionless condition. The immediacy of film, its instant registration, begins here where understanding is constituted. For film to attend to the pregiven means it exists in the natural attitude, in the purely affective confirmation of being, a duplication of the earliest murmurings of dynamic perception.

Engagement in the prepredicative lifeworld is characterized by its opacity to reflection. Phenomena are made present by the presence of consciousness in direct-grasp, in immediate evidence, rather than through representation. What this self-givenness amounts to is a total intuition, an instrumental, non-reflective presence, "*a passive belief in being,* in which there is nothing yet of cognitive achievement: the mere 'stimulus' which proceeds from an existent in the environing world."[12] This passive belief within preliminary presences can be seen as "encounter"; a meeting with the Other before conceptual sense deals with it. By not yet crystallizing concepts, we avoid abstraction and categorization. We remain with the particular: "*Original substrates are therefore individuals, individual objects,* and every thinkable judgment *ultimately* refers to individual objects, no matter how mediated in a variety of ways."[13] The constraint of presence, being (t)here, is absolute. A space in time is created and it is within this space that subjectivity comes to be as a disruption within undifferentiation. As a similar presence and encounter, filming bears witness to the place and time where the invisible subsumes the visible to record a complementary showing. Encounter, then, can be seen as the establishment of presence in direct intuition where stimuli are met in the flux of change without abstraction. If this experience is categorized as passive, or receptive, it is only in a special sense. Passivity as phenomenological experience is nascent, unexpressed thought: "Passivity is that very experience of the birth of thought before it has been crystallized in a word ... the very potentiality of thinking"[14] Passivity's openness and potentiality characterize its quality. It avoids coming under the tutelage of conceptual completion, "it is synonymous with a non-actuality that may be actualized at any moment."[15] The roots of film recording in the pregiven world are in accord with being situated as both a passive receiver and an active producer in a world of valid givenness. Equally, the film spectator's observer status is never passive but involves a heightened state of awareness and sensitivity, "being passive means being able to be completely open towards the other, to welcome him in full awareness ... the preeminent power of a non-activity which is ... a real activity engaged in observing itself at the very moment the act is being performed."[16]

Automated film consciousness, by its sheer presencing, registers the world as passively yet primordially active and alive, on the cusp of redirection, on the verge of diversion. There is something "automatically" meaningful about passive presence. It is a flux of entities that encounters presence, either human or mechanical, together "*with* their structures of association, affection, etc."[17] Processes of appearance passively combine into unities in an endless stream of formations: "[T]he processes of appearance passively combine into unities in just the same way whether or not the ego turns toward what appears in them in receptive apprehension."[18] Encounter lies at the origin of sense. The capture of the unreflective bedrock contributes to film's reality-effect because it is a dimension we believe undoubtedly to exist. Film recording informs this worldly environment and grasps it for us without yet relating similarities containing associations. Inherent in recording is an awaiting-for-completion, an element of openness, a lack of closure resisting totality in a temporal flux without end, a quality of filming that survives through to modernism and the Avant-Garde.

Some classical theorists have incorporated Husserl's phenomenological insights into their own description of film experience, notably, the German theorist, Siegfried Kracauer. Kracauer spoke of humanity in the flow of material life coming under threat, the same threat Husserl described in, "The Crisis of European Sciences." Phenomenological presence, focusing on the phenomena themselves, had to vie with scientific abstraction and the general way science rendered the lifeworld: "Due to the exaltation of theoretical thinking we have moved away from reality to a horrifying degree, a reality which is filled with incarnate things and people and therefore demands to be seen concretely."[19] Scientific dissection and artificial construction broke up spatio-temporal reality and its continuity. Once science got underway it applied abstract laws and reasoning to redefine the empirical world and structure it according to its own precepts. For Kracauer, film especially could serve as an indispensable aid in reclaiming humanized perception of the lifeworld: "were it not for the intervention of the film camera, it would cost us an enormous effort to surmount the barriers which separate ... (us) ... from our everyday surroundings."[20] The mechanical eye was praised for going beyond the human capacity for probing reality, microscopically delving into the amorphous, palpitating life force and uncovering the minutiae of the everyday. Filming could penetrate the particularity and elusiveness of surface reality and be a gateway leading to the fleeting nature of the lifeworld, "the ripple of leaves stirred by the wind," nature "caught in the act."[21] Film images could encapsulate raw materiality and, more importantly, intend it in a fresh way. Only the film eye rose high enough to embrace a vista that exceeded human vision or contracted small enough to pick up on the minute movements of natural phenomena in action. Science, and to a degree the traditional arts of painting and sculpture, worked from distance and abstraction moving downwards from a broad sweep to the concrete. Film worked in the opposite direction, beginning with concrete imaging and keeping us literally in touch with the world. This rawness conveyed both purity and unrefined expression mirroring the randomness of material life. As with Fellini, "a good picture should not aim at the autonomy of a work of art but have mistakes in it like life, like people."[22]

In emphasizing the lifeworld Kracauer claimed the self-effacing camera could latch onto transient impressions, seemingly in tune with a quantum physical world where the substantiality of particles submit to the insubstantiality of waves. Film ontology reflected things-in-themselves, infinite nuances, shifts of direction, overdetermination, randomness and ineluctable openness, "everyday experience as materially constituted by the incalculable accumulation of events and situations precipitated by human praxis."[23] The lifeworld, as its history "is full of intrinsic contingencies which obstruct its calculability ... historical reality is virtually endless, issuing from a dark which is increasingly receding and extending into an open-ended future ... it is indeterminate as to meaning."[24] If the lifeworld is incapable of being contained and resists universal, macro ideologies, filmic expression should reflect this. Nonetheless, structure and order still survive in the rendering of the lifeworld through narrative and artistic construction; sense and order are conveyed through mimetic relation, "this relation is not one of unmediated expressivity. Rather history and photography render the *Lebenswelt* intelligible through their structural correspondences or affinities with it."[25] Film recording relates to fleeting moments as they are ensconced within natural laws, and they are capable of being colligated and described:

> [S]ociety is full of events which defy control because they happen to occur in the dimly lit region where mental intensity is reduced to zero ... (yet) the social universe ... would seem to fall under the rule of nature ... it is possible and legitimate, to break down the phenomena that make up this universe into repeatable elements and analyze their interrelationships and interactions for regularities.[26]

The images mirrored in film can be correlated to those captured by history as both relate to phenomena within nature that have a shared resistance to closure. To compare film imagery with history Kracauer employed the notion of the anteroom:

> One may define the area of historical reality, like that of photographic reality, as an *anteroom* area. Both realities are of a kind that does not lend itself to being dealt with in a definite way. The peculiar material in these areas *eludes the grasp of a systematic thought:* nor can it be shaped in the form of a work of art.... I consider it my task to do for history what I have done for the photographic media ... to bring out ... the peculiar nature of an intermediary area which has not yet been fully recognized and valued as such.[27]

The anteroom corresponded to the mediated status of film as it wavered and alternated between givenness in primordiality and expressivity in configuration. One could appreciate the tensions exhibited by the work of art as a tug of war between the particularized manifestation of the work and its reference to universality and meaning, between being enclosed in spatio-temporal presence while at the same time effecting an aspiration to a world of transcendence. Kracauer saw manipulation of pregiven nature unnecessary for creating drama because drama already existed, "manipulative techniques would have worked against the form of the film whose purpose was to make visible a drama created by nature, not by filmmakers."[28] The preference to leave the tacit in tact implied a confidence that when voice became audible it would necessarily contain the ingredients for drama and narrative. This cannot mean a completed story in the conventional sense since such symmetry would be artistic device, not the stuff of everyday realism. The "found story" Kracauer repeatedly referred to is more in keeping with the mesh-like notion of a "slice of life," described by Jean Epstein in film's formative years:

> On the screen, conventions are despicable. Stage effects are absurd.... Presentation of the characters is pointless; life is extraordinary.... The drama is as continuous as life.... Life is not systemized like those nests of Chinese tea tables each begetting the next. There are no stories. There never have been stories. There are only situations, having neither head nor tail; without beginning, middle, or end, no right side or wrong side; they can be looked at from all directions.[29]

For Kracauer, there were stories but they were to be assimilated into the richness and multilayered levels of meaning of the lifeworld and thus retain their intrinsic ambiguity. Kracauer's found stories were to be discovered rather than constructed or, rather, constructed in and through acts of discovery, emerging from the raw material of physical reality as they inscribed the documentary impulses of filming. Documentary impulses were not necessarily documentary films but were rather a range of documentation and potential paradigmatic space where certain kinds of films could flourish. What is significant is that Kracauer's notion of the everyday world incorporated the filmmaker's intention of being neutral or non-interfering and the corresponding prepredicative state of being pre-judgemental. Kracauer emphasized the documentary potential of film medium to express and disclose the unbounded and latent sensibility in the flux of the lifeworld's quotidian time. The direct connection of film to material reality by virtue of its dynamic movement brought with it a material train of indelibly fixed associations where the spectator was encouraged to absorb manifold connotations over and above denotated narrative meaning, so that shots appealed to unstaged reality within the staged story, what Kracauer called "suggestive indeterminacy." Shots alluded to contexts unrelated to the events they were intended to depict enabling them to yield a slew of psychological correspondences. As for the artist, Kracauer was reluctant to elevate the role of the individual filmmaker over and above film's own natural propensity for revealing reality, even though the artist's formative role was acknowledged. On an unconscious level, spontaneous structuring brought about "the inflowing impressions; the simultaneous perceptions of ... other senses, certain perceptual form categories inherent in (the) nervous system, and not least ... organize(d) the visual raw material in the act of seeing."[30] Yet there was also conscious input as nature "is unlikely to give itself up ... if the (filmmaker) does not absorb it with all his senses strained."[31]

Kracauer was one of the first to give a distinct and perspicuous description of film consciousness, opening as it does to the fullness of life and its flowing indeterminacy. For Kracauer, film consciousness is not an indicative sign of something else. It is direct, manifold, and fully expressive. The meaning-intention that Husserl prescribed to language as direct expression adheres to the film image as the directness of an inner presence:

> Film renders visible what we did not, or perhaps even could not, see before its advent. It effectively assists us in discovering the material world with its psycho-physical correspondences. We literally redeem this world from its dormant state, its state of virtual non-existence, by endeavoring to experience it through the camera.... The cinema can be defined as a medium particularly equipped to promote the redemption of physical reality.[32]

Kracauer's description of the transition from the immediacy of the prepredicative to deliberation in the predicative took the form of a *surrender*, "[a] minimum requirement for the aesthetic success of a photo image is ... its reflecting the photographer's surrender to the experience ... of a natural-cultural world that is both elusive and accessible."[33] In that filming penetrates the world around us to form the visible, as witnessed by a community of observers, it enters into the flow of what is represented not to disturb or unhinge it but to surrender to its integrity, so that film leaves its raw material intact. Thus, even in the act of creating narrative and with a mind to re-creating the given, the force and hold of being immersed in the lifeworld has an innate pull Kracauer respectfully recognized as overwhelming in its palpability.

The process of making sense of reality begins with Husserl's constitutionality, always exceeding the individual at any one moment. But this ultimately took a different turn with Kracauer. For Husserl, the task was one of completion, where the reception of the matter of perception was a stage in the perception of identity through categorical structures. The sensuous

intuition of the perspectival act is united with categorical intuition and there
is a making-visible and making-present through a series of perspectival adum-
brations leading to essential insight. For Kracauer, any formalistic completion was to be taken more as a task in progress. In keeping with his predilection
for anti-systemization and the randomness of materiality, specific concrete-
ness must be allowed the freedom to be self-explicit if the film image is to be
allowed to redeem the world of things.

What we find with Kracauer is not a reproduction of the perception of
nature or the experience of history as subjectively interpreted but a highly
powerful consciousness where the remnants of nature are presented through
reproduced images, where the presence of humanity is realized by film materiality. It is not surprising, then, that we find a fractured subject, recognition
that subjectivity is not ready-formed but carried along as a mobile self within
film consciousness. This mobilizing framework shocks the spectator out of
attempts to form an "integrated self."[34] Film's materialist capability:

> [N]ot only undercuts the sovereign subject of bourgeois ideology but with
> it a large anthropocentric worldview that presumes to impose meaning and
> control upon a world that increasingly defies traditional distinctions
> between the human and the nonhuman, the living and the mechanical, the
> unique (integrated, inner-directed) individual and the mass subject, civiliza-
> tion and barbarism.[35]

In his later work, Kracauer's insistence on physical reality was an expression
of his reaction to the events of the 1940's. Kracauer emphasized film was
uniquely placed to mirror a world that had experienced unthinkable horror.
Film's plasticity, its visualizing facility, was compared to the Head of Medusa
myth with Athena's advice to Perseus not to look at the destructiveness of the
Medusa face directly but only at its reflection in the polished shield. Kracauer
astutely used this analogy to make such horror reflectively viewable as a way
to overcome our associated fears:

> Now of all the existing media the cinema alone holds up a mirror to nature.
> Hence our dependence on it for the reflection of happenings which would
> petrify us were we to encounter them in real life ... in the films made of the
> concentration camps, we redeem horror from its invisibility behind the veils
> of panic and imagination. And this experience is liberating in as much as it
> removes a most powerful taboo.[36]

This is an inverted return of the gaze, a way of holding and sustaining a veiled
truth that can only be disclosed indirectly. Liberation came about through the
deep affinity film technology has with material reality. Kracauer was insistent
that film was the "alienating intervention" of an apparatus that allowed the
gaze to explore psychophysical correspondences and the wholly unbearable.

Intentionality

For Husserl, the analysis of the way mental states were structured in relation to objects centered on intentionality. The meaning of an object as distinguished from the object as such, the perceived as such from the thing perceived, the object as intended from the object that is intended. With intentionality we analyze the experience of objects and situations on both a carnal and reflective level where intentionality is a motor to thought thinking itself. In the film experience, intentionality is complicated by its layered character, with the original intentionality of the filmmaker siphoned through camera instrumentality vying with spectator intentionality enabled by the instrumentality of projection. Perceptual understanding as described by phenomenological intentionality is a complex process centering around a precise correlation between the mode of consciousness, noesis, and the object as intended, noema (its ideal meaning). This cannot be taken as a simple correlation in a reductive manner. As Husserl and other phenomenologists worked through the notion of intentionality we find a series of imbrications that stretch the margins of the intentional act by introducing an extended sense of the present. As described by Husserl and elaborated by Merleau-Ponty, intentionality describes phenomena as experienced directly as a givenness through various modes of consciousness, each of which constitute reality as experienced. Following from this, film intentionality can be considered as duplication through an experience that recaptures primal impression and then offers it up in a derived aesthetic experience with its own form of consciousness. Of the several interpretations of noema, most useful in the present context is Gurwitsch's focus on the gestalt structure of perception, where perceptual noema is directly given in sense experience and where sensuous aspects constantly refer to others as hidden aspects.[37] Noema belong in an abstract way to the sphere of meaning but in order to ground Husserl's phenomenology of perception Gurwitsch looked to the internal organization of what is perceived, the perceptual gestalt. The perceptual gestalt effectuates self-presentation, equivalent to its intuitive sense. This sensuous givenness contradicts readings of Husserl as overly idealistic. The spectator is rather benchmarked by hyletic data, "the sensa, lines, patterns, size and shape relationships, the camera movement, camera placement, editing forms, sound textures."[38] These sensa are apprehended, or passed through (apperceived) to realize what is meant by intuitional directness. Understanding is still in the end an intentional act of meaning but one that is initially dependent on a gestalt arrangement of part and whole, foreground and background, aspect and totality.

In that film is both a visceral experience as well as a motor to thought thinking itself, intentionality will reflect the possibility for logical reflection.

We experience and we reflect on experience in the same way as film is a constant show of experience and a metacritique of that experience. In a realist account, the intended object coincides with the actual object in reality: "It need only be said to be acknowledged that the intentional object of a presentation is the same as its actual object ... and that it is absurd to distinguish between them.... If the intentional object exists, the intention, the reference, does not exist alone, but the thing referred to exists also."[39] Though not an argument for objective proof, this does allow the possibility for repeated perspectival views, not unlike the re-running of a film. Husserl's account of intentionality engendered a mental state that avoids a juggling act of comparison and reference between film representation and the represented world, thus avoiding Cartesian dualism. We also sidestep linguistic objections to intentionality where believing, hoping and fearing are objects as-intended rather than the object as-is. Through the show of film, intentionality removes experience from these solely mental contents to deal with those aspects directly concerned with seeing and perceiving. It also removes discussions of the objective existence of objects or their illusory status, since in film all images are seen as real but illusory presentations.

In sum, in all cases of intentionality there is an other to consciousness, and that other can be fictive or real, of the real world or of the reel world. Here Bergson would agree with Husserl that there is no re-creation of objects into images that are then perceived through representation, but only the direct givenness of transcendent objects to different modes of consciousness, or for Bergson, direct image objects. With Bergson and Husserl there is no duality between the perception and the perceived, or the images of the lifeworld flow, they are part and parcel of the one consciousness, though not within consciousness. This is what makes the film world open to intentionality as a regional ontology that also carries with it ways of experiencing not only the aesthetic object but the world in general. Film's quasi world finds expression through intentionality since intentionality is not based on the metaphysically independent existence of objects. This allows us to speak meaningfully of film consciousness as one based on a particular kind of perspectival experience that is engineered through a mechanical-human composite. The object correlation of the composite — film imagery — is just as mind dependent (noesis) and mind independent as everyday non aesthetic praxis that come to encompass all experience. In a transcendent sense images are there to be shared, for all to see, as a communal expression, but intentionality also emphasizes that the experience is characterized by its immanent content where each viewer will bear a relationship to each other through the eidetic in combination with the particular concretizations. These two facets of intentionality always go hand in hand and, in the case of film, make for a communal experience as filtered through the particular, something Benjamin saw in his appreciation of film's mass appeal. We will also see in our examination of the hermeneutic that Husserl left no doubt that phenomenology must be rounded off not merely through the givenness of appearance but through the acts of interpretation that go towards fulfilling perceptual sensations.

On one level, it is true that intentionality establishes noema as an unchanging, ideal meaning, an identical nucleus that can withstand numerous perspectival variations, "in transcendence, the objects reached out to (in their existence) are indifferent to mental acts involved in their apprehension; accordingly, they exist, in an important way, in-themselves."[40] But because our experience is always constrained by prenoetic (already-present) factors of history, body, language and tradition, intentionality is never simply consciousness of something but always consciousness of something as it is becoming — as well as having an identical nucleus that comprises meaning, noema is always part of an expanding interpretive act, "the intentional object for Husserl is always something interpreted."[41]

Intentionality, meaning and language cannot be taken in isolation. They must be combined with intuition, the other side of the intentional coin. On the one hand, we have the intentional, woven by the self-enclosed language system, on the other, the various perspectives by which we directly and intimately come into contact with the world. These spheres of consciousness are the unresolved tension of the two major motifs in phenomenology: the purity of formalism and the radicalism of intuitionism. Meaning intention is not dependent on the givenness of objects, it is the result of the differential basis of language systems. Intuition, however, *is* based on sensuousness and for Husserl it carried a direct revealing of categorical essence. If the categorical essence was revealed then nothing for Husserl could any longer remain hidden: "Nothing will remain invisible from now on, since a mode of intuition tracks and hunts down each of these objects as so many modes of presence."[42]

With fullness of intuition, perception permits us to speak of the categorical and in particular of universal intuition. This broader notion of intuition is what carries over film from its embedded situation in the lifeworld into the "as-if" reel world and the universal. For Husserl, the universal is appearance in the singular not outside it, the categories as they are intuitively given. This is to say that as film reproduces so-called objectivity by capturing appearance, it encompasses states of affairs and properties with real forms and dependent categoricals. These ideas comprise "objectity," the broadest notion of reality. It is objectity rather than objectivity that is reproduced in film, just as intuition is broadened beyond the sensible. Both objectity and broadened intuition lead to the same, the categorical horizon as directly given, so that broad objectity includes categorical forms. The universal is given in person — all houses, all impossible or possible houses as well as this particular house here. We have two intuitions from the one intentionality.[43] Thus, we are directly apprehending ideal objects as they truly exist as evidently certain categorical truths relating to ideal objects.

For the film experience this means the consciousness of a mechanical eye, that is both the show of vision and the vision of show, is intuition in an extended way, containing both invariable meaning and particular variability. The appropriateness of achieving this through vision is discussed by Merleau-Ponty in his analysis of the invisible-visible correlation. Just as we need the universal to recognize the particular so we need the real world of concrete reality to recognize the reel world of film. The categorical requires the givenness in person of phenomena just as film intuition requires the contact and knowledge that is acquired through worldly phenomena.

Film plays upon intuition and intentional invariance, self-consciously moving bodily placement to allow for diverse points of view and reflexivity of bodily situation. Bodily position is always a consideration in intentionality so that whatever comes to be seen implicates a reflexive relationship to actual body. This means that the film camera interposes between the intuited object as it reflects back the position of the intending noesis. Its surrogate emplacement repeats the intentional correlation with regards to reflexivity, in the case of viewed objects, as a visual technics. So the intuited experience speaks back as a movement from what is experienced towards the position from which the experience is had. As we will see, this analysis can be carried over and extended from spatial embodiment to visual reflexivity in the return of the gaze.

Understanding meaning needs intentional analysis as those structures of meaning which are "neutrally" recorded are not pre-stabilized but must be the result of a sense-making activity enabling the registration of being on multi-dimensional levels. Film technology becomes part of a dynamic force that intermingles with the flux of vibrant nature to match it in movement. Merleau-Ponty's movement of consciousness between sentient being and worldly materiality as the sensibility of Being, directly relates to film presence:

> The subject of sensation is neither a thinker who takes note of a quality, nor an inert setting which is affected or changed by it, it is a *power* which is born into, and simultaneously with, a certain existential environment or is *synchronized* with it.[44]

Ultimately, film fluctuates within the parameters of opaque and transparent instrumentality to take on a visible life of its own, a transcendent, intentional world for the spectator.

Phenomenological Hermeneutics

By strictly adhering to its presuppositionless stance and search for essence, it has been said that phenomenology reaches its limit in a negative way. It stops short of dealing with the ontological condition of understanding. In this respect, phenomenological hermeneutics completes the task. It looks to understanding in terms of primordial belonging in the world:

> The first declaration of hermeneutics is to say that the problematic of objectivity presupposes a prior relation of inclusion which encompasses the allegedly autonomous subject and allegedly adverse object. This inclusive or encompassing relation is what I call *belonging*.[45]

Here there is no pretext of being able to escape from being-in-the-world. The hermeneutic shift that takes place broadens the phenomenological project without abandoning it. Indeed, both phenomenology and hermeneutics are mutually dependent, "*phenomenology remains the unsurpassable presupposition of hermeneutics.* On the other hand, phenomenology cannot constitute itself without a hermeneutical presupposition."[46] It is important to remember that as phenomenological theory progresses there is a recasting of emphasis in description away from the inherently static to the more open hermeneutic and genetic phenomenology of the lifeworld. Many worlds are conveyed and opened up by the film world, worlds that the spectator appropriates and inhabits, where meaning is generated and self-understanding increased. We recognize in intentional horizons the existence of indeterminations that in the lifeworld take the form of historical horizons.

Within the objective real world lie readily given structures that become narrative worlds we live by. They enchant and seduce us, evoke memories and invite exploration. Through this bank of potential situations and ready-made stories, "we feel at one with the real, and it seems as if the real seeks to find in us all its amplitude and its resonance ... the real *needs us....*"[47] These natural interactions with the regions of concrete reality which include us as part of an ongoing narrative are reproduced in the affectivity of film's aesthetic attitude — creatively designed stories concomitant to spontaneously artless ones. It is apparent that the use of fiction, whatever its basis in truth, gives greater narrative scope than where events can be verified in objective time, "the fictionalizing act outstrips the determinacy of the real"[48] and adventurous, affective journeys can begin: "expression is like a step taken in the fog — no one can say where, if anywhere, it will lead."[49]

Consciousness engendered by the film work can be a springboard into the unknown and the uncontrolled: "the meaning of the work ... cannot be stated except by the work itself: neither the thought which created it nor the thought which receives it is completely its own master."[50] The object is always incomplete; it can never include all horizons since this would be to constitute its completed sense. Rather, the interpretive process as it takes place on primitive levels of perception and higher levels of acts of judgment remains open-ended. It is a process in constant search of a meaning that can never be finalized. Whatever artistic signifier is used there will always be excess in meaning and rightly so, since it is in excess that the work's life continues to thrive, embracing a wider configuration of the real and the possible than the immediately intended.

As hermeneutic horizons open they transform not only the aesthetic work but also self-identity. In film, images can be questioned and probed and avenues of concretization extensively explored in terms of an anticipated future and self-temporalization, no matter how ambiguous or dense the images may be. According to Husserl: "[W]e also have, and know that we have, the capacity of complete freedom to transform, in thought and fantasy, our human historical existence and what is there exposed as its lifeworld."[51] This urge involves not only temporalization, the constant breaking up of the present into what it is not yet, but also the decomposition of the ego. The ego ceases to be a completed state, instead becoming an identity in formation. Contrary to reading Husserl as locked into a fixed notion of subjectivity, we have a displacement of subjectivity that questions radical origin and allows for refiguration of the self through greater self-understanding. The process of re-appropriating subjectivity is carried out through personal and interpersonal projection. In placing the meaning of a text in the lifeworld, we displace the notion of an anchored subjectivity but do not disperse it to the extent we find with later postmodern thinkers. Emphasis is no longer on radical origin but on a detoured refiguration of the self which offers potential for self-understanding and ethical questioning.

The film spectator, too, has the capacity and freedom to transform experiences and create personae in an activity of free variation that involves the exploration of diverse expressions. The breaking up of the ego takes place in keeping with unfolding film flux. There is give and take that is part of the creative discoveries that make phenomenology not static and predictable but dynamic and experimental. Film consciousness starts taking shape here through the fusion of the mechanical and human mind as boundaries are broken down through the uncovering of strata, "the significance of the work ... does not lie in the meaning sealed within the text, but in the fact that meaning brings out what had *previously been sealed within us*."[52] There is always excess, an overabundance of meaning that outstrips attempts to be reductive. Every dialogue is incomplete and within this excess the critical moment becomes a distancing of self from self. The process is writ large in film by its divergent subjective placements and interactions with a mobile camera eye. There can be no locked down predictability when film interrogates the spectator by posing its own questions through complex states of subjective displacements.

Phenomenological hermeneutics would acknowledge that spectator participation in the film experience brings about diverse changes of attitude and states of mind. This ranges from distraction to alienation and from jouissance to shock. Hermeneutic moments, where cultural horizons are described, unraveled and questioned, arise in those gaps where identity is dislodged. In the hiatus, the aesthetic world becomes inhabitable, a proposed world where potentiality can be explored through imaginative variations. In this activity subjectivity is re-appropriated, "to understand is not to project oneself into the text; it is to receive an enlarged self from the apprehension of proposed worlds...."[53] Surrendering is a prelude to thought.

For the meaning of a film text to open up within film consciousness something of the self must first be given up, boundaries between the inner and outer lowered and the sense of temporality transformed. The importance of narration lies not with a completed act of storytelling but its dynamic process, implicating the spectator into a narrative act of understanding and re-telling of the self. Projected worlds and alien regions encourage the potential for genuine insight, personal growth and indulgence. They do this by virtue of being non real, resisting real life manipulability and instead demanding leaps of faith within a space designed for exploration and the destruction of boundaries.

Those films that offer such challenges potentially allow us to explore the very limits of life's aporias and imponderables. *Jacob's Ladder* (1991) is a case in point. Though overtly concerned with the tragedy and treachery of the Vietnam War, on a deeper level the main character, Jacob Singer, is on a philosophical quest to understand and accept death. To show this struggle, temporal experience is refigured through a reliving and re-telling of a cataclysmic Vietnam battle attack resulting in mass slaughter. This is the cosmological marker by which phenomenological time is set in motion. The temporal aporia is to accept the finitude of death within the infinite. To this end the film weaves parallel time dimensions that include objectively setting time within the moment of battle and Singer's fatal wounds, compressing phenomenological time as a projection towards accepting death in life, and the ultimate retrieval of the past and future inheritance to the present. The hermeneutic search to make sense and the concomitant performance of establishing self-identity into a fragmented life are the key to Singer's authentic becoming. To find identity and authenticity, the future-past in the present are shaped around contradictory circuits that include the events of Singer's wife, Sarah, the remorse and guilt felt for the death of his son and the events leading up to Vietnam. This past, drawn into the future, serves as a catalyst for a future past that is expressed through the affair he has had with Jessica, a fellow worker. We hear about Jessica in the parallel past where Singer wakes up from a dream to "confess" to Sarah that he has had a sexual fantasy about Jessica. The reality of this dream is played out in a temporal zone that could not have happened in cosmological time. Jessica acts as a temptress preventing Singer from finally accepting the past and moving on to his destiny.

The time zone that becomes the space in which Singer tries to solve the mystery of the battle of war and his own life is a nether region of time. *Jacob's Ladder* works within what Aquinas termed the aevum — a temporal zone somewhere between eternity and infinity, between nunc movens with its beginning and end, and nunc stans, endless life. Various figures, situations and dilemmas play around this intermediary order of what was the "absolute distinction between time and eternity in Christian thought ... a peculiar betwixt-and-between position of angels."[54] This intermediary position is personified by Singer's angelic chiropractor, Louis, who manipulates Singer's back to manipulate his psyche and advise him how to achieve salvation. The aevum figure of Louis gives the opportunity to reflectively explore Singer's movement forward and the temptation of Jessica holding him back. Tormented by guilt and remorse over his son and the war, Singer is told by Louis, "if you've made your peace then devils are really angels freeing you from the Earth." Only by rejecting fear, accepting life and its injustices, and coming to terms with the reality of death can Singer move on, with the "ladder" the linking symbol for rising above base instinct (Jacob's fraternal rivalry with Esau) to a higher level of consciousness (stairway to the divine). The overall struggle is a fitting symbol of the hierarchy of temporalities Heidegger fashions from being-in-the-world and the need to assimilate them before authentic life can be achieved. As a unique duration, belonging neither to the finite or the eternal, the aevum also allows us to consider the origin of the act of narration itself and the combined metaphysical and fictional roles the characters play. As a double reconciliation between God and matter, time and eternity, the aevum reconciles the irreconcilable present with the future that never was, or only might have been. Jacob's quest has been to discover his own fate but in doing so his fate is not exclusively individual. He has inherited a communal problem, a controversial war that touched many physically and a whole nation spiritually. Without reconciliation inertia ensues, without disclosure there can be no closure and it is the role of the artwork to explore these dilemmas: "We create fictions because we do not know what happens after death. In short, we try to improve upon the fictions created by philosophy and religion which ascribe portentous meaning to life and assume for existence a significance which is entirely hypothetical."[55]

Kermode's notion of concord-fictions establishes links between the given and the unfathomable. Once placed within narrative contexts aporias become concord-fictions, conceivable and manageable. Concord-fictions do not provide solutions but appear and reappear in different contexts and under different guises, amalgamating apocalyptic visions with renewal, offsetting being with becoming, lining decay with hope. Ultimately, the hermeneutic quest for knowledge takes place through a poetics of narration, as an area for exploring imponderables and unlikely time junctures.

Gadamer's Play

The procedure of retaining self while conjoining with another world and other selves along a shifting spectrum, alternatively relinquishes and retains the "sense" of self. In phenomenological terms, we can express the experience of the appresented world of narrative through notions of empathy or contrastive pairing. In hermeneutic terms we speak of gaining meaning through appropriation. Film viewing is a way of living in the film's universe and appropriating a world unfolding the world horizon implicit in it. Gadamer's phenomenological hermeneutics clarifies this through notions of mimesis and the performative. Gadamer's use of "mimetic imitation" plays on the fact that the work is not designed to be believed but to be understood as imitation.[56] This makes the film work not a false showing but a genuine show. Imitation is not to be seen representatively as a copy of an original but as a showing-in-appearance, something which supersedes reality: "What is shown is, so to speak, elicited from the flux of manifold reality. Only what is shown is intended and nothing else."[57] The activity is one relating to film's intuitive experience not a critique searching for objective explanations.

Spectators transport themselves into a distant life experience through the film work. The more open the text is the more it will correspond to what is already an ungraspable and mysterious lifeworld, "instead of an intelligible world there are radiant nebulae separated by expanses of darkness. The world of culture is as discontinuous as the other world, and it too has its secret mutations."[58] On this basis, the film experience cannot be taken as a substitute dream world, a convenient escape, or a catharsis. On the contrary, the play of art is a mirror that through the centuries constantly arises anew and through which we catch sight of ourselves askew, in ways unexpected and unfamiliar. Gadamer claimed authentic understanding can be reached only if insistence on method in traditional hermeneutics is dropped. He thus tended to reject the principle that says text must be understood in its own context and thereby diminishes standards of confirmation and falsification for finding methodological truth. His concern was rather with process and a gestalt part-whole relationship consistently emphasizing the prenoetic approach to Husserl's intentionality within historical horizons:

For there is such a thing as givenness that is not itself the object of intentional acts. Every experience has implicit horizons of before and after, and finally merges with the continuum of the experiences present in the before and after to form the one flow of experience.[59]

The flow of experience has the character of a universal horizon consciousness, out of which only particulars are truly given as experiences.[60] Intentionality of meaning becomes transitional within the continuity of the whole. Horizons are non-stable, not rigid frontiers but the absent-present unity of the flow of experience. Above all, to experience a work mimetically is to live with and through the work as if in a "spiel," the element of play: "What is immediately clear is that the turn to Spiel as a basic ontological concept breaks the imitative universe of mirrors, and it does so by accenting, not the static correspondence of artifact or world to 'idea,' but the self-disclosure of the world."[61] Here we can see the self-disclosure of the film world achieved not by an imitative or reflected image of a given state of affairs, a representation of an objective reality, but by the same involved immediacy of a play of movement we find with Bergson and Deleuze, "the movement of play as such has, as it were, no substrate ... the play *is* the performance of the movement as such."[62] We say "something is playing somewhere" in film, so that the spectator will join "in media res" and become a part of the on-going process. Here direction and control only make sense through the activities of the Spiel not through the authority of personal subjectivity. Spiel is tantalizingly easy to conjoin; in fact it invites such activity. Though effort may be required for understanding, there is still an ease of participation especially in the all encompassing film experience, "the ease of play which naturally does not mean that there is any real absence of effort, but phenomenologically refers only to the absence of strain ... structure of play absorbs the player into itself."[63]

This is not to say that the Spiel is indifferent to the spectator, on the contrary. When film "becomes" the game, rather than say a ritual, it becomes "open to the side of the spectator, in whom it achieves its whole significance ... it is experienced properly by ... one who is not acting in the play, but is watching. In him the game is raised, as it were, to its perfection."[64] Thus the presentative character of film would be realized through spectator contribution as she fulfills and transforms the work with a certain constraint of not being lost within it. Gadamer theorized about the transformation resulting from human play into the artwork designed to incorporate reception and saw it as permanence within transience:

There cannot here be any transition of gradual change ... the transformation into a structure means that what existed previously *no longer exists*. But also that what now exists, what represents itself in the play of art, is what is lasting and true.[65]

The artwork takes on a life of its own, in no way imitating or representing reality but gaining a truth-value. Spiel is self-realizing movement and brings from Being something into presentation, it is the mode of being of the artwork. Particularly important for film is the description of the way Spiel relates to the free movement of self-presentation. There is a force of movement here, an irrepressible dynamic that we also find with Bergson that speaks the very life force:

> This movement must have the form of self-movement. Self-movement is the basic character of living being.... What is living has the force of movement in itself; it is self-movement. Spiel appears only as self-movement which through its movement strives for neither purpose nor aim but rather movement as movement ... which means the self-presentation of the being of life.[66]

Presentation of the self is precisely in accord with film's temporal unfolding and depends on this dynamic of movement and time. The fragmentation of subject identity and position comprises film's narrative mode as we are paced, placed and shifted according to camera perspective and point-of-view through separate character identities and the omniscient voice of the implied author. With Gadamer, identity splits and re-emerges through the performative acts of mimesis. We have the to-and-fro movement of those involved in the Spiel as the exchange of positions, where the inter-reaction of spectator and film communes with, and negotiates for, various sites of understanding.

In comparing film to festival we find a similar experiential mode of a completed timelessness and a reconstituted freshness. Celebration in the festival involves an uneasy confrontation between celebration as repetitive essence and the need for it to always be performed differently as times change and perspectives naturally shift:

> For the essence of the festival its historical connections are secondary ... it is its own original essence always to be something different.... An entity that exists only by always being something different is temporal in a more radical sense than everything that belongs to history.[67]

Even though film is an entity that unfolds unerringly between start and end reel, film consciousness is constantly challenged by the singularity of its experience. Though fixed through the reel, the phenomenological experience of effective horizon will always ensure particularity and unique experiences. The play of Gadamer and expression in celebration exemplify the constant interaction of the act of filming and the world as film. There is an irresoluble tension engendered through the flux of personal and world horizons and the significance of a lifeworld mechanically reproduced.

3

Body and Transcendence

Merleau-Ponty's Embodiment

Merleau-Ponty's work on body as foundation for experience particularly suits a way of looking at the film experience as one founded on the mechanical body-camera-eye. It is to insist that the body is not to be taken as a mere container or even as a mark of presence. The body cannot be objectified, to do so would separate it from the mind, nor can it be pigeonholed as a mere encasement. The mind and body work as one; the mind expresses the body. The body-as-mind-expressed makes possible the world for us, it catalyses and acts as ground for all phenomenal objects in the world as a precondition for the way objects come to be objects.

The body is the unperceived given perspective that is the ground for all phenomenal objects in the world, allowing things to happen, initiating experience and manifesting phenomena. The camera eye and film body are equally the situated precondition for filming, an unperceived, perceptual presence bringing about a view of the world. Moreover, as part of the intentional experience within the aesthetic work, the camera eye serves to create images that subsequently become the spectator's temporary habitation as virtual body. By concentrating on the significance of the body as a unified sensibility of incarnate consciousness, Merleau-Ponty argued that mental experience, which seems to be internal and hermetically sealed, is always externally expressed in bodily behaviour and directed pathways. Inner perceptions immediately become outer expressions as an accomplishment of the body. The field of sense is a plane, a plateau in which anything within it that is dissimilar will come into prominence by drawing attention to itself. In a similar way to

56

Husserl's notion of encounter, Merleau-Ponty clarified the processes in the lifeworld in terms of the reciprocity of the enworlded body: "Neither body *nor existence* can be regarded as the original of the human being, since they presuppose each other, and because the body is solidified or generalised existence, and existence a perpetual incarnation."[1]

Merleau-Ponty's phenomenology envisions a synaesthetic modality of embodiment including time and spatial depth. Shifting the focus of perception, "by starting with the visible and vision one replaces intentionality and acquires a whole new idea of subjectivity,"[2] it opens up the consciousness of sensibility. For Merleau-Ponty, the traditional description of depth resulted in artificial abstraction. By making the sense of depth either a flat projection or a subjective act of synthesising multiplicities, thickness and dimensionality are turned into an elongated side-view or a foreshortened flatness. But things of the world involving corporeality should not be seen piece-meal or without dimension. They perdure in a state of co-existence giving rise to interconnectedness, mutual reliance and indissoluble relationships; spatial depth is the founding dimension of the lifeworld: "More directly than the other dimensions of space, depth forces us to reject the preconceived notion of the world and rediscover the primordial experience from which it springs: it is, so to speak, the most 'existential' of all dimensions."[3]

The description of space in terms of interconnectedness and depth is fundamental to lifeworld experience as the unseen founding presence that subtends everything. Film's unique transposition of concrete reality creates its own aesthetic style that includes the self-expressing sensation of depth through internal figure and ground. Through filmed movement the fundamental dimension of depth emerges from a constantly variable ground-figure structure. Figures change shape according to backdrops that are fluid force fields. Filming has an inbuilt fluidity through its inherent capacity to show movement. One could not describe the process of recording like a sense organ bombarded by a series of atomistic sensa, as the synthetic mechanism for decoding irreducible atoms is missing. Rather, film in movement explores the chimerical quality of the phenomenal field and shows a remodeling of the environment by establishing an interlocking system of matrices and contexts. Perceptual themes are indeterminate, part of the constantly reinvented moment where meaning only takes shape within an ever-renewed, disseminated context, "completion is made impossible by the very nature of the perspectives which have to be inter-related ... to other perspectives, and so on, indefinitely."[4] It is from within primordial depth that integrated vision emerges to comprise meaning. In the pregiven lifeworld, we are spatialized together in our environment and, in the film world, it is the power of self-projection within movement that gives that same sensation of inclusiveness, placing the viewer in the midst of things. Movement within space creates the feeling of real depth. Filming picks up on the primordiality of depth as an opening of meaning and in doing so brings with it a vast array of techniques to give three-dimensional impressions. The point is to always bear in mind that depth is a lived and total sensation not based on fixed standards. It is an expression of the way the overall phenomenal field opens up to consciousness. Being-of-the-world is not an imposed construction but a setting and a background field from which our perceptual phenomena emerge. Within the experience of depth we experience the world as embodied and dimensional in an operative way, without stepping back to consciously create a third dimension.

We cannot see dimensional depth but we inhabit it and it encompasses our ground zero spatiality. Each move of the film camera is likewise an adjustment of depth and the figure-ground correlation, a readjustment of the seen and the seeing, a simultaneous alteration of perspective creating openness to meaning. If realignments were experienced as fragments they would result in jarring experiences but with film mobility spatial shifts occur giving the same experience as real life, interlacing in the phenomenal field.

The relationship between theme and horizon and the way this forms meaning is the principle of autochthonous organization, a fluid auto-figuration dynamically unfolding in time. This dynamic means figures are not "a priori" but emerge from the body trajectory as it actively creates configurations in a lived field of activity. Before perception can be predicated or made an object of consciousness, it must itself provide the horizon and ground upon which predication is possible. As articulation emerges from indeterminate and unformed horizons, the figure-ground correlation is seen as reversible and irreducible. What at one time forms a background for figuration another time emerges to become a source point for what then fades. The perceptual body itself is indicative of this, both a source point and background as it emerges consciously in relief or fades in pre-reflection.

Depth subsists unintended by reflective consciousness, invisible because unintended. Film fixes this invisibility in its own sense of depth, which is viscerally communicated as a way of being-in-the-world. With film's ability to record movement by movement, to move by removal, we get not only a fresh objective "take" on reality but shifting relationships of figure and ground that originate new meaning. In filming this structure may be expressed as pulling-focus onto what is attended. The activity of pulling-focus is part of directing consciousness; it includes the forefronting of the immediately visual as well as directing awareness to subject position, a kind of thetic consciousness or existential awareness. In both cases the role of vision is twofold. It is passively reflective and actively inflective, relating both to doxa and theoria.

Merleau-Ponty's analysis of depth and spatial perception was part of a wide-ranging concern with the meaning of vision in all the arts. It was an approach that helps us make sense of film as an automated consciousness, a perceptive and receptive sensibility unselfconsciously participating in the flesh of the world, "the visibility of the world, is admittedly not self sensing as my flesh but it is sensible."[5] This is a sensibility that throws back an active picture of surface behaviour and picks up on the invisible and undisclosed as it becomes activated, not through self-awareness but by emplacement within the circuitry of flesh. Perception reaches its object because perception is the flesh touching and seeing itself. This means there is no representation at the level of perception, there is only flesh in touch with itself. The being of a tree is a quasi-perception of me, its being pays testament to the fact that I am visible from the standpoint of the tree as we are both flesh of the world as immediate visible experience.

From this perspective film consciousness, just as it is broadened intuition, is also broadened vision, including points-of-view and the invisible. It takes shape and takes place in the rough and tumble of visible exteriority, in the perceptual realm of textures and expression, "there is a circle of the visible and the seeing, the seeing is not without visible existence."[6] The film experience underscores what comes-into-view by conjugating different levels of subject positions in a circuitry of flesh. The subject viewing film that is viewing a represented scene where there are viewing subjects being visible subject-objects for each other.

The way the spectator is included in this filmic circuitry of vision is comparable to the immersion of sentient beings in the phenomenal field. The field in which understanding takes place is one of dissemination, discovery and linkage, all open for exploration in the work of art. Its base is one of opacity rather than transparency so that creative expressions are never totally graspable and only partially realisable. This means the film experience is characterized less by the fixity of an object given to vision than it is by the experience of what the process of vision entails. We exceed the specific incarnate frame of reference to include further perspectives in an ever-widening phenomenal field. The reception of visual data is determined within this phenomenal field by the interplay of horizons that comprise vying levels of presence and absence:

> The visible is itself a correlation, not a fixed object and this makes it a web, binding together the interior and exterior horizons. In turn, horizons do not remain fixed but are rather horizons of possibility so that each visible is prevented from being an object and from acquiring the self-identical positivity that defines the object. Intentionality is at work here but without founding consistent identity.[7]

When we view film we also bring latent horizons which are related to the depth of our body, a body density which is not removed simply because we appear immobile in a viewing situation. In the film experience, intentionality is linked to a notion of body that is visually flexible, pivoting as it does around the seen and unseen and the viewer and viewed.

Merleau-Ponty couches his observations on the invisible substrate in terms of a mystery, where objects attain presence not as invariable identity but through relative elusiveness:

> The ipseity is, of course, never *reached*; each aspect of the thing which falls to our perception is still only an invitation to perceive beyond it, still only a momentary halt in the perceptual process. If the thing itself were reached, it would be from that moment arrayed before us and stripped of its mystery.... What makes the "reality" of the thing is therefore precisely what snatches it from our grasp.[8]

Each film image is received in a motion that dislodges stable states and relates to a mobile corporeality based on successive perspectives. The invisible is transcendent in that it exceeds the visible but is not unapproachable or unattainable, rather a constant task to be realized. The visible has what is proper to it as a surface but a surface with an inexhaustible depth, opening up visions other than our own, "the *invisible* thus provides the grounds for the *visible* and is not only a *condition* but also a *content* of the act of seeing."[9] We capture the unthought and the unsaid, extrapolated from its lifeworld emplacement, brought into the light as if electrically charged. In this manner, film duplication becomes not reproduction but invisible induction, setting off an expression of the world through the unseen. It enacts a mechanical intentionality as it senses and makes sense of the world. From induction we get the possibility to realize potential that becomes manifest as a coming-to-visibility. As a revelation of its being, vision is film's ontological strength. Merleau-Ponty described the strong faith in vision as akin to an immediate, unquestioned condition of knowing in certainty. The experience of our perceptual presence obviates "the need to choose or even to distinguish between the assurance of seeing and the assurance of seeing the true, because in principle they are one and the same thing."[10]

Merleau-Ponty's phenomenology is a shift to an operative intentionality that is both experiential and non-reflective. It complements notions of vision, depth and the body within the pregiven dimension and helps us understand how filming reflectively shows the unreflective prepredicative condition and the body's material presence as concrete activity. As subjects in the world we all perceive and view, and as subjects for other subjects in the world we are seen by others to perceive and view. The body is not only the field in which perceptive powers are localised but also the field in which the powers are seen to be exercised and expressed by others. In the film body, emplacement is part of the circuitry of intersubjective perception and the look is registered by its mechanical sensa.

Film's powerful aesthetic mechanically embodies the whole array of perceptual schema as it is enfolded in the phenomenological field. It presents and re-presents, resembles and reassembles; it is both a vision of the world and the world visualizing. As a mechanically placed body amongst other materiality, the film eye presents the perspective on the perspectives of viewing as a viewing-in-action. But whereas humans use body communication as part of the primordial sense of being-in-the-world, an immediately perceptive-expressive signification with an affinity to like-minded beings, film has no such outer shell to direct intentionality as it maintains its body invisibility to create visualization.

Expression to Meaning

Merleau-Ponty made it clear that with embodied perception there is always already meaning, "because we are in the world, we are *condemned to meaning*, and we cannot do or say anything without it acquiring a name in history."[11] From its initial ground point, filming is bodily positioned in a world to view things and bring them to life, "*significance* is revealed only if we look at them from a certain point of view, from a certain distance and in a certain *direction (sens)* ... our collusion with the world."[12] Yet this is a view that, of necessity, becomes liberated in time and transcendence, "thus we are always brought back to a conception of the subject ek-stase, and to a relationship of active transcendence between the subject and the world."[13] In film terms this is naturally aided by the fact film communicates visually in an extremely direct manner. Though present, the spoken word in film is not needed to explain imagery. The act of filming responds to the commensurability of the film body and human corporeality sharing an incarnate engagement in the world that is immediately expressive:

> The moving picture, too, perceives and expresses itself wildly and pervasively *before* it articulates its meanings ... as a significant cinematic trope or figure, a specific set of generic configurations, a specific syntactical convention ... a film makes sense by virtue of its very *ontology*.[14]

The world pre-maturely means and film corporeality reflects this. Acts of perception and bodily expression work through and out of a signifying embodied existence. The lack of self-conscious deliberation allows an equivalence to be drawn between the primordial condition of human perception and the mechanically functional, unselfconscious root of filming. Filming is put on a comparable conscious pedestal by virtue of it having a comparable consciousness platform, the body-in-the-world as perceptive expression. This existential viewing platform has "the capacity to localize and unify (or centre) the invisible, intrasubjective commutation of perception and expression and make it visible and intersubjectively available to others."[15]

Originary commerce with the world, an already-presence, a natural being-in-the-world, has to be rediscovered. To understand behavior in the concrete world we look at the expressions of that behavior. In existential terms, a film work accommodates the expression of inner feelings and emotions precisely because they are behaviorally observable. For inner states to be realized, indeed to meaningfully exist, they must be expressed through behavioral and observable patterns through the body. Emotions and attitudes take shape as physical manifestations; they are not locked away in the psychic recesses of the mind but become significant when expressed in the lifeworld through intersubjective exchanges. Film's movement imagery picks up on the immediacy of expression through body action. The expression of emotion in manifest behavior and gesture is part of the overall structure defining individuals as a style of being-in-the-world.

This clearly emerges when Merleau-Ponty directly relates film to what he called the "new psychology," referring to the patterning role of gestalt perception.[16] Visual data is not seen as a mosaic of sensations needing subjective reasoning to make intelligibility. In gestalt, the relation of the organism to its surroundings is not explained by the causal action of external stimuli upon the organism because, in phenomenological terms, the subject is reacting in a milieu that has no purely objective existence outside consciousness. Gestalt directly relates to what is sensed. The meaning of the concrete world *is*, it is not a mediated creation but an involved proximity, "I do not think the world in the act of perception: it *organizes itself* in front of me."[17] This is where film differentiates itself by being an act of seeing that makes itself seen, an act of hearing that makes itself heard, and an act of physical movement that makes itself reflexively felt and understood.

Unlike individual human communication, the filmed artwork concretizes its perceptive-communicative facility by public projection. But it initiates significance in the same way as the human body by providing a fulcrum for subsequent sense-making. Its primordial presence is sufficient to extend expression in its encompassing gaze, an exploratory tracking view that accompanies motion. Where film and philosophy come together, Merleau-Ponty suggested, is in the spelling out of the process whereby perception becomes expression, where the activity of perception as intrinsic to activity in the lifeworld becomes visible in terms of what is perceived and in terms of how it is perceived to become meaning. The fact that film recognizably shows and expresses the same viewed concrete reality as human perception, as well as the intentional process bringing meaning to that view, allows for the aesthetic film work to function as a unique space for the spectator. Perception is part of a work-in-progress, where body and senses already have a natural, primeval familiarity with the world, born of habit and cognizable through sedimented knowledge. Film plays on and explores this implicit knowledge and familiarity of experience. Even though it is consciously set in motion by the filmmaker, filming automatically sets in motion its own active-receptive perceptions both as a conduit for, and as a purveyor of, meaning. The mechanized sensibility the film body has for automatically and unselfconsciously picking up on the lifeworld is little different from the same automatic human one:

> If I wanted to render precisely the perceptual experience, I ought to say that *one* perceives in me, and not that I perceive.... It is true that knowledge teaches me that sensation would not occur unless my body were in some way adapted to it, for example, that there would be no specific contact unless I moved my hand. But this activity takes place on the periphery of my being. I am no more aware of being the true subject of my sensation than of my birth or my death.[18]

It is this direct, operative level of perception realist film theorists are referring to when they claim that reality in its brute existence can be filmed without manipulation to make it meaningful. The assumption is that the viewer understands the natural language of film as a pre-linguistic tacit structure founded on the lifeworld structures of experience. But these structures of experience are hardly simplistic, they are complicated, fluctuating areas, at all times reaching out to exceed themselves; unfixable and uncontainable, they still come to be framed. The ontology of film is as dynamic and vibrant as the lifeworld in which it originates, as a living embodiment it is significant because it is simultaneously a sense receiving and sense performing subject with feelers infiltrating the vital realm of indeterminacy.

Filming reflects back the excess significance of objects and situations belonging to the expansive, phenomenal force field of life. This is the world of phenomena taken as both a field and a force overflowing with potential meaning. Film recording is synchronized mechanically at a rate to be in tact with this force field, like the power to synchronize the processes of phenomenal life itself. This force field as process is hidden; withheld but nonetheless the condition for the givenness of phenomena. Thus, it would be a mistake to describe the process of filming in a similar way to a neutral sense organ bombarded from the outside by a series of atomistic sensa. It would be equally wrong to see it having an immanent function of making sense of the world. Both positions were rejected by Merleau-Ponty when he described the human condition. There is no process to register messages from determinate or irre-ducible elements in an objective world. Nor is there any mechanism for a sub-sequent synthesis that could decode or process irreducible atoms as they are originally found. Both human perception and filming through movement imagery explore the chimerical quality of the phenomenal field, visually and aurally remodeling the environment by establishing an interlocking system of matrices and contexts. All perceptual themes are indeterminate, part of the constantly reinvented moment. Meaning only takes shape within an ever renewed and disseminated context, undermining claims for closure in the objective world:

> Thus it seems we are led to a contradiction: belief in the thing and the world must entail the presumption of a completed synthesis — and yet this completion is made impossible by the very nature of the perspectives which have to be inter-related ... to other perspectives, and so on, indefinitely.[19]

This openness of meaning was embraced by Merleau-Ponty's notion of "wild meaning," where expression makes sense before the use of discrete symbolic systems. Wild meaning is the undifferentiated significance of existence as it is lived rather than reflected upon, where body, action and language come together as direct expression, an area directly reflecting film ontology as it relates to raw materiality, "we have a meeting of the human and the non-human and, as it were, a piece of the world's behavior."[20] Filming, as mechan-ical embodiment, functioning as an emplaced recording of modulation, is language in this wild, undifferentiated sense because film's directness and automated duplication reflects back the existential significance of behavior:

> With symbolic forms, a conduct appears, which expresses the stimulus for itself, which is open to truth and to the proper value of things, which tends to the adequation of the signifying and the signified, of the intention and that which it intends. Here behavior no longer has only one signification, *it is itself signification....*[21]

For Merleau-Ponty, in the phenomenal field everything already speaks to everything else. The sign is understandable contextually and in terms of other signs, "the sign is always a sign in use, if you will the sign is a gesture."[22] As such, meaning as present in signs is not a referential phenomenon but meaning *is* the signs, "signs are the perceived-perceiving, the speech-speak-ing, the thought-thinking, in short, the phenomenal existence which is man."[23] With Merleau-Ponty, the sign is the synoptic result of immanence and transcendence. The move from perception to expression occurs through the fusion of intentionality and the operative world in constant flux, modification and constitution. We intercede or break into this prepredicative ferment as it surfaces into embedded dialogue among things. It is at this surface level where speech is underpinned by speaking, where invisibility tips over into the visible, where the phenomenal field gives birth to vision, and filming takes its place.

When speaking-as-expression occurs there is no solidifying of moments, no abstractions, no turning back into the self but a primeval surfacing of the what-is and the who-is. This coming-into-expression is a spontaneous act of perception that takes shape as it lays the ground for communication's interconnectedness. With filming the "image is there before words, even as words strain to create new images."[24] This is a "milieu of communication," an "intersubjective diacritical system"[25] that is communally shared, though uniquely experienced from individual perspectives. Film expressions are received in this perceptual way, immediately reacted to and drawn from the sedimented pool of cultural meaning by which the psyche of others, as well as the perception of film's psyche, is read. Here, through film consciousness, a perceiving process speaks through materially externalized signs in a direct form of thinking with its own signification, without the means of reflection as an act of retrieval.

Speech comes out of the silence of the primordial, essentially the mute sense of the perceptual world. Filming relates to the mute sense of the perceptual world, reflecting it as brute being, silent yet expressive, it lets muteness speak by directly contacting it in shared corporeality and concrete setting. It brings expression to the world from the depth of silence by delicately opening the inherently pre-linguistic to its own visual semiotic. Filming is the imaging of the world already expressed within it, an opening into the world and a catalyst for the upsurge of worldly Being.

Unlike the transmutation of the original that takes place in painting (more "an appropriation" or "exercise of power")[26] film is a "submission," a total effacement before the world as it negates itself "to coincide with objectivity."[27] Film visually speaks the language of the world because it carries through the specificity of the phenomenal world and the web-like, intercommunications that are opened up. This is film's primordial condition, indifferent to the autonomy of the world, other than the world, yet by its instrumentality interpenetrated by it. The utterance of the film image "makes possible the paradox that the world unveils itself as it is in itself, pro-nounces itself ... prior to all human language."[28] This submission to the lifeworld allows the world itself to become language in the same mute sense of perception described by Merleau-Ponty as an uttered silence:

> All this leads towards silence where the only word pronounced would be that of the world, mute, unprecedented inaudible ... the tree expresses itself only with treelike means. The street recounts the street, but no one knows exactly what it says or how it says it. This "hitherness" does not yield itself

precisely because it irreducibly remains a "hitherness" for us.... The real bespeaks no more than itself. For us, no word is spoken.[29]

This is what Munier refers to as the "fascinating image," a world from which we are apparently excluded yet in which we are nonetheless magically engulfed in the midst of things. We are trans-fixed and enthralled by a complex of the imaginary and real. In these terms, the film image is presentation without mediation, an immediate logos and direct language. The imaginary, the realm of the human spirit as pure logos, becomes that of the "alogos," without man.[30] This is the sheer presence of nature indefinitely captured by filming in an act shown to repeat that capture. The specific film experience accompanying this can be compared to a pursuit of knowledge that is "foreign to language," one that calls for another way of conceptualizing, "demanding a development of the optical mind."[31]

The bond between perception and expression, like the alternating and mutually dependent schema of gestalt's figure and ground, has a characteristic detected throughout phenomenology. This is "Fundierung," the relation of the founded to the founding, both ambiguous and reciprocal: "The relation of reason to fact, or eternity to time, like that of reflection to the unreflective, of thought to language or of thought to perception is this two-way relationship that phenomenology has called Fundierung."[32] This is a way of looking at the priority of the perceptual over the conceptual while acknowledging a being that must have self-knowledge. It is equally applicable to the indivisible relation of kinesthetic corporeality to material nature, as well as the dependency of film's reel world to the real. Expressive perception and perceptive expression co-exist in this mutual way as a chiasmus or reversibility, the notion that encapsulates Merleau-Ponty's thinking on expression and experience, sense and sensing, existential speaking and sedimented speech.

Bazin's Ontology

In his film theory, André Bazin was directly indebted to phenomenology in his exploration of expression and its physical link to the lived world. Bazin began with the same pregiven world described by Husserl and Merleau-Ponty and insisted that filming concretizes facts through events and situations within the housing of originary primordial flux. It was a deep lying respect for the primordial reality of the represented world and a belief that it could be penetrated through existential connection that led Bazin to put forward a phenomenological film theory encased within a spiritual sensibility. For Bazin, luminous impressions of light formed a mould on film that created something more than mere resemblance. We have, rather, an identity card necessarily and mechanically linked to the reality that is reproduced. Bazin's predilection for a certain kind of film making utilising spatial continuity and deep focus, was meant to extract from the lifeworld, and particularly nature, an embedded truth. This was to be pursued by a phenomenological realism which never adjusts reality to meet the needs imposed by psychology or drama.[33] The documentary style in fiction film using long-takes, authentic locations, minimal montage and naturalistic acting sets out to convey the irrevocable bond between image and reality. For Bazin, Neorealism met this ideal:

> The Neorealist film has a meaning, but it is a posteriori, to the extent that it permits our awareness to move from one fact to another, from one fragment of reality to the next, whereas in the classical artistic composition the meaning is established a priori, the house is already there in the brick.[34]

Dramatic realism retains a visual, ongoing reciprocity and density between actor and environment and foreground and background. Psychologically, this brings the spectator more authentically to the real conditions of perception, a perception never completely determined a priori. Thus, in Fellini's *La Strada*: "It is not a film that is called *La Strada*; it is *La Strada* that is called a film.... I am not saying that the camera has photographed the caravan in a very plain manner ... but rather that the camera has simply *shown* the caravan to us, or even better, has *enabled* us to see it."[35] Fellini, for all his flamboyant reflexivity, is faithful to a conviction that action must be allowed to speak for itself, "nothing Fellini shows us owes any supplementary meaning to the manner in which it is shown ... the cinema achieves fruition as the art of the real, Fellini is a great director ... who does not cheat on reality."[36] Emphasis is placed on the lifeworld experience of the spectator to introduce a personal positioning. This allows for variability and the spectator's creative scope, an empowerment unleashing potential for diverse interpretations. The spectator perceives the ontological ambivalence of reality directly, in the very structure of its appearances, without artistic intervention coming to our assistance. Bazin's view of this was similar to Husserl's description of the move from passive receptivity, with its structure of association, to deliberate, productive spontaneity: "A fragment of concrete reality in itself multiple and full of ambiguity, whose meaning emerges only after the fact, thanks to other imposed facts between which the mind establishes certain relationships."[37]

The re-ordering that takes place comes afterwards through spectator construction but the ground is laid by a montage of discrimination taking place on-screen rather than in postproduction. This accounts for Bazin's deep focus preference, the use of wide-angle lenses to reproduce images of depth without the need for elaborate editing. There is a "decoupage in depth" that

uses mise-en-scene to convey segmentation in action. Realism is sustained by
restoring to object and environment their existential density and weight of
presence. This is a return to the Quattrocento, two-dimensional illusion of
third dimension brought about by the "gradation in size of the objects represented (diminishing as they are presumed to be further away)"[38] and aided
by on-screen lighting effects to enhance relief. Bazin wanted to minimize ideological bias inherent in the cinematic apparatus, insisting on the need to be
free to explore and extrapolate meaning from within phenomenological intentionality. The importance of deep focus and depth of field was "not just a
stock-in-trade of the cameraman ... it is a capital gain in the field of direction, a dialectical step forward in the history of film language."[39] No mere formalistic tool, it "affects the relationships of the minds of the spectators to the
image, and in consequence it influences the interpretation of the spectacle."[40]

Deep focus restores conditions of perception in the lifeworld and retains,
what Bazin insisted was most important, ambiguity. Bazin's insistence on
ambiguity demonstrates his debt to the French phenomenological school, in
particular, Gabriel Marcel, who similarly reflected the tensions of nature and
the mystery of the transcendent. Being is a mysterious encounter and ambiguous realm:

> To postulate the meta-problematical is to postulate the primacy of being over
> knowledge ... it is to recognize that knowledge is, as it were, environed by
> being, that it is interior to it in a certain sense ... there exists well and truly a
> mystery of cognition; knowledge is contingent on a participation in being for
> which no epistemology can account because it continually presupposes it.[41]

Experience in the real world comprises continuous movement, where the mystery of reality seeps through the pores of surface manifestations. Film imagery
as movement can reflect this condition. Long takes and continuity are the
figurative manifestations of a Marcelian desire to remain in the "presence" of
being as its mystery and spiritual influence take effect. This presence is crucial if egocentric preoccupation is to be broken and the soul allowed to open
out into a compassion for others on a higher spiritual level. Bazin wanted this
sense of presence and its concomitant sensibility to be retained in film. We
come closest to understanding this with Marcel's notion of "influx," the breakdown of Cartesianism into a closer intentional relation with the other:

> I am unable to treat him as if he were merely placed in front of me ... he is
> not only before me, he is also within me ... influx conveys ... the kind of
> interior accretion from within, which comes into being as soon as presence
> is effective.[42]

Bazin saw the substance of reality somehow hatching out through surface
appearance and in glutinous fashion adhering to manifest content. The link

between filming and reality assumed as if by a physical cord set up an amal-
gam of sensuous and cognitive experience, fusing aesthetic sensibility with
revelatory epiphany. There is a commitment to subjective experience implicated in phenomenological consciousness that is likened by Marcel to the
openness and receptivity of "creative fidelity." Creative fidelity "consists in
maintaining ourselves actively in a permeable state ... there is a mysterious
interchange between this free act and the gift granted in response to it."[43] With
Bazin, the transcendent, if not the transcendental, was clearly spelt out in
nature: "Photography affects us like a phenomenon in nature, like a flower
or a snowflake whose vegetable or earthly origins are an inseparable part of
their beauty."[44] This transcendent tendency is expressed through nature where
photography possessed a power to transfer not only reproduced physical traces
but also the spiritual and transcendent inheritance in the fabric of nature. For
a thinker such as Sartre, manipulation and the creative hand of genius are
indispensable for the communication of spiritual significance but for Bazin
the film apparatus was sufficient, the creative hand of the genius works with
this fact in order to nurture it.

Film consciousness attains an attunement to the ambiguity we call the
world. A great artist would listen to the world and disclose it. For Bazin, the
sense of intensity and focus derived from filming a situation was sufficient in
itself for transcendent revelation. This is far more than the duplication of surface phenomenon or the gloss of appearance. As Marcel argued, to exist is to
manifest oneself, or equally, to be manifested, it is really irrelevant whether
we say, "I experience (Ich erleben) or it lives in me (Es erlebt in mir)."[45] Both
express humanity's fundamental presence in the world, a presence without
which the fact of existing would not have the density it has for me. Man is
by nature expressive but objects and things also express through him and it
is this Bazin believed film could reflect. As with Merleau-Ponty, it is the primacy of being that must hold sway, "knowledge is *environed* by being."[46] It
is only by being involved within being that one begins to genuinely live with
its mystery and ambiguity. For Bazin, the world interpreted itself, inspired
by the sense of God to speak itself. To relate to reality we must reveal it and
art relates to the deeper realities that occasionally flash into our marginal consciousness. Mystification does not center on the unknown but emerges from
the uneasy alliance between the stark materiality of social convention and the
transcendent; a union of communal experience in a communal setting with
universal truths. For Marcel, mystery is not something to be overcome but is
a permanent state of the world to be enjoyed and continuously explored.

Marcel specifically turned to film, finding it could be a significant
reminder within life's routine not to become blind to our surroundings, to
our relation to earth, to our "habitat." He saw film ensconced within the life-

world yet at the same time transcending its link: "The best means we have
at our disposal today in order to bring man into the presence of a certain image
of himself, an image which ought to surpass the limits of purely anecdotal
realism."[47] Marcel described primordiality as a mix of Husserlian encounter
and Merleau-Pontian ambiguity, retaining body as the ground of knowledge:

> Here I am in the presence of a mystery.... I who inquire into the meaning
> and the possibility of this meeting. I cannot place myself outside it or
> before it; I am engaged in this *encounter*, I depend on it, I am inside it in a
> certain sense, *it envelops me and it comprehends me* —even if it is not com-
> prehended by me.[48]

And for Bazin film was the best testament to the miracle of creation where "a
spiritual sensitivity and its enablememt through film" showed how we are
"obligated to God, to honor God's universe by using film to render the reality of the universe and, through its reality, its mystery-cum-musicality."[49]
Bazin's reluctance to artificially fragment the perceptions of life through unnecessary montage now appears not as a mere stylistic preference to uphold a
reality-effect but as a way of striving to maintain flux in the mysterious natural order. This reluctance to leave the natural context behind has the same
excess, promise and revelatory implications for Marcel:

> But I would point out that no revelation is, after all, conceivable unless it is
> addressed to a being who is involved.... Supernatural life must ... find a hold
> in the natural ... there is in the depth of Nature, as of reason which is gov-
> erned by it, a fundamental principle of inadequacy to itself which is, as it
> were, a restless anticipation of a different order.[50]

With filming as documentation and preservation, the possibility for rec-
ollective function is not the photographic effigy of a frozen moment of time
but a capture through dynamic movement and contextuality of humankind
within a changing environment. Only in this way can Bazin's insistence on
organic movement and integrated action make any sense. The presence established by the particularity of the reel image and the real world ekes out life's
mystery without a prior agenda or conscious theoretical stance. On the one
hand, Bazin wanted to ensure film reflected the continuity of the spatio-temporal continuum and convey the authenticity of lived experience, the multi-
farious plenitude of daily problems and the mystery of spiritual presence. On
the other, Bazin saw film had a unique ability to embalm events and thereby
extract them from this integrated flux for re-view. By doing this, not only the
events but also the transcendent mystery associated with them could be preserved, reproduced and explored. There results, therefore, interplay between
contextual incorporation and segmented detachment, with film's automated
facility adding dimensional distance to an otherwise implicated proximity.

The Negating Self

Merleau-Ponty helps us focus on the various sources of meaning and expression in the lifeworld. His description best fits a journey that moves from the silently implicit to the manifestly explicit. Merleau-Ponty's analysis of the tacit cogito allows us to explore perceptual meaning as an unfolding process by way of an impersonal instrumentality. The tacit cogito is a first stage concept that predates the individually fixed concrete ego of the lifeworld and the impersonal and abstracted life force of the transcendental ego. As film consciousness takes shape through vision it introduces a non-individuated consciousness, not unlike the tacit cogito as it forges the transpersonal status of human consciousness:

> In so far as I am a consciousness, that is, in so far as something has meaning for me, I am neither here nor there, neither Peter nor Paul; I am in no way distinguishable from an "other" consciousness, since we are immediately in touch with the world and since the world is, by definition, unique, being the system in which all truths cohere.[51]

The registration of vision is usually taken as emanating from a particular site of consciousness and this applies to both the human and film body. But this is not an inert posture physically fixed; rather it implies a journey comprising a visitation to where Being appears and a completion through transcendental displacement. This is to figure departure and return as impersonal since they are the benchmarks for a way of thinking that takes one out of the self, "vision is not a certain mode of thought or presence to self; it is the means given me for being *absent from myself.*"[52] Film vision and the way it envelops the spectator through identification and projection is ideally suited for experiencing this journey. Merleau-Ponty attacks the self-awareness we are familiar with in the Cartesian cogito seeking "to exclude the possibility of an act of reflection in which the subject would achieve complete self-transparency."[53] With embodiment, self-presence finds itself in the prior bodily experience in concrete reality, a fundamental change of emphasis from Cartesianism. We have a prior giving of oneself to self via a visual circuitry that supersedes transcendental reflection on the self. As described by Merleau-Ponty, the tacit cogito, non-conscious reflection, is a disabled ego, a lacuna in pure immanence, a movement of transcendence through a chiasmic intertwining with the world "behind which there remains no subjective retreat of non-being."[54] The tacit cogito is not cogito as thought, but as sensation awareness. Film also has a trajectory of veering away from implicit, introceptive subjectivity to one which is able to make brute being approachable and allow silence and the visceral to manifest. Filming's affinity with images of reflections and mirrors parallels an active-reactive echo of parts, where the touching is the touched and the body is both subject and object.

We find this debate deepened in Merleau-Ponty's reaction to Sartre. For Sartre, the subject-object correlation was cast in terms of dependent negativity, the nothingness of the "pour soi" and the plenitude being of the "en soi." The very fullness of the "en soi" is dependent on the self-abnegating dynamic of the "pour soi." Consciousness is the relationship of consciousness to that which it is not. When accessed through reflection the prereflective cogito is seen to contain no "I," it is egoless:

All the nonreflective memories of unreflected consciousness (the past) show me a consciousness *without a me*, and since, on the other hand, theoretical considerations concerning consciousness which are based on intuition have constrained us to recognize that the "*I*" cannot be a part of the internal structure of *Erlebnisse*, we must conclude there is no "*I*" on the unreflected level.[55]

Sartre defined the "pour soi" as a nothingness, in terms of a tacit ego whose reflexivity is based on the fact that it realizes it is not the "en soi" and is "constituted" by a nothingness against the fullness of the "en soi," which it is not. Were the camera eye to have a tacit cogito that became self-conscious it might reflect on its status as a recording instrument and acknowledge that its reason for being is to be totally open to recording the "en soi." Sartre's radical ontological dualism can be seen to pick up on filming's primal self-effacement. Its originary duplication is where the oneness of signifier and signification can be couched in terms of an unreflective negation in pure visibility.

For Sartre, there is being not because consciousness gives rise to being but because it supplies the "there is." Sartre's "pour soi" is a being such that in its being, its being is in question, "what is present to me is what is not me."[56] Nothingness into being is not an indeterminate unfolding but a determinate reliance marked and delimited by what is other than self. This reliance is total and dependent so that being nothing in the world in order for the world to be is part of the way the human condition inhabits the world. Insofar as this being is essentially a certain way of not-being-a-being, there must be a founding negation given first as an a priori foundation of all experience.

The concrete reality film duplicates is other than its corporeality. It is offered up as the total result of its visual capacity because its own being is apparently effaced whenever it picks up on objectivities or sentient beings. The source of vision, in this case the camera eye, is not self-apprehensible but owes its viewing-view to what brings that view about. In return, what has been visually reproduced owes its existence to the acts of film without which it would have remained undisclosed. Primordial film consciousness based on recording something, which it is not, and making its viewing-view available to others can be couched in similar terms to Sartre's definition of the human:

> The being which I am not represents the absolute plenitude of the in-itself. And I, on the contrary, am the nothingness, the absence which determines itself in existence from the standpoint of this fullness.... The knower ... is nothing other than that which brings it about that there is a *being-there* on the part of the known, a presence ... this presence of the known is presence to nothing, since the knower is the pure reflection of a non-being.[57]

The presence of the film eye as emanating from a pure reflection of a non-being is perhaps easier to accept in terms of mechanical "non-being" than it is from the presence of the human ego, "the visible has to be described as something that is realized through man, but which is nowise anthropology."[58] To a degree, filming carries out and enables the visual coming-to-presence of the "en soi" without intrusion or interference. In the "total indistinction of being, there is nothing but a negation which does not even exist but which has to be.... Being in-itself *gives itself and raises itself* in relief on the ground of this nothing."[59] This is one version of the gestalt Merleau-Ponty examines as figures becoming determinate, but now based on a founding and negated "pour soi." Film consciousness is possible here because it does not rely on a substantial ego for self-confirmation but rather on an absolute presence, the otherly condition of plenitude that formalizes figures out of undifferentiation. Sartre's presence of the materiality of being is immanent, though with transcendental repercussions. In the initial phase of film recording it is this total immanence that counts as the object appearing to consciousness and materiality appearing to film reproduction.

As a rejoinder to Sartre, Merleau-Ponty's critique comes at the point at which being and nothingness are set up as mutual exclusivity. If the "pour soi" is to be, it is as nothingness totally envisioned within the "en soi," where the possibility for a phenomenological coming to vision is founded on the emptiness of a non-being. The inherent separation between the non-being that sees in order for the seen to be seen and the plenitude of the "en soi" that feeds off of this separation is put into question. What Merleau-Ponty found lacking in Sartre's account was the acknowledgment of shifting perspectives that come with embodiment and the phenomenological acceptance that the hidden and invisible add to the depth of being, something which was elided in Sartre's philosophy of negation. There are gaps and in film terms, an outside-of-the-frame, that must be acknowledged and ultimately entwined within pathways that include the incarnate. Sartre's work helps describe the pure non-being and pure vision as it pertains to the initial mode of film recording. But Merleau-Ponty initiated an understanding of film in terms of perspectival horizons and the acknowledgment of the other through the exchange of looks. Unlike Sartre, the look of the other does not threaten my annihilation but rather, with the film eye as part of the same Being of materiality that Merleau-Ponty insists is shared by all, a relay of looks and vision is instituted that runs through the depth and hidden dimensionality of Being.

If there is hypostasis here it is as a prereflective cogito reliant on exteriority, only at one with self through incarnate, lifeworld emplacement, "the subject of sensation ... need not be a pure nothingness" but is rather a part of individual history with sedimented natural powers not, "in Hegel's phrase, a 'hole in being,' but a hollow, a fold which has been made and can be unmade."[60] Film is not conscious of itself being conscious as something other than the noemata of consciousness, as it would be for Sartre. Crucially, unlike the "pour soi," filming does not realize its-self being the obverse to materiality, as mechanical embodiment, it is itself materiality as an "en soi," even as it is a consciousness realizing the "en soi." There is no self-deceptive belief within film consciousness that it has an essence. More precisely, filming can be seen as a return to Merleau-Ponty's notion of perception as prepersonal power where perception of worldly things is not viewed as the action of my body in response to the demands of a separate world but as the moment of revelation of the flesh of the world. The direct contact of light with that which is filmed forms the indexical link and subject-object materialistic mirror. As a fold in being whose being touches itself through me "one can say that we perceive things in themselves, that we are the world that thinks itself."[61]

Transcendental Survival

In phenomenological reflection, the transcendental ego is the unity maintaining itself throughout all of its constitutive acts as a constitutive identity, universal and available to any existence. The transcendental ego never goes away in phenomenology, it is always co-present, though it is anonymous before the epoché and transcendental reduction. Its omni-presence is apparent through a change in attitude. For Husserl, to understand the "place" of the transcendental it is necessary to enact the epoché and the reduction as a "universal depriving of acceptance ... of all existential positions."[62] With epoché we put into brackets the real world of objects and people by laying them aside and by doing so philosophize in a state of abstention. The epoché allows one to reach being as such, as absolutely given to the pure intuition of the transcendental gaze. This is a radical move, which signifies the putting-out-of-operation of the belief in Being, ontology as the being of the world out-there, in favor of givenness as experience. But this is also the same ontological questioning that Merleau-Ponty is searching for as a way of looking at the experience and movement of life as qualitative plurality. What is important is that though the natural attitude is suspended in order to experience transcendental subjectivity, it is then reinstated and reconstituted through consciousness in the reduction. Thus, where epoché is a negative rejection in order to focus upon a pure realm of conscious experience, the reduction must be seen as a *positive* honing in upon the experience itself. The reduction is disclosure, an engaged performance of consciousness in and through which the world is both lost and regained. Regarding this recovery as a return is crucial in applying phenomenology to the film experience as it perfectly describes the circuit the film experience maps out. By introducing epoché and reduction, neither the significance of the lived immediacy of experience or its reflected meaning is lost, rather both are deepened. In the absence of the one, the presence of the other is always felt. The notion of a phenomenological residuum suggests the same conclusion:

> It is this which remains over as the "phenomenological residuum" we were in quest of: remains over, we say, although we have "Suspended" the whole world.... We have literally lost nothing, but we have won the whole Absolute Being, which, properly understood, conceals in itself, all transcendencies....[63]

To believe in the film world, a suspension of disbelief is needed and this corresponds to the suspension of belief in the naive and natural attitude of the lifeworld enacted by the epoché. A change of attitude is the core characteristic of both suspensions in which reality is nonetheless taken as foundational, where the natural attitude is encapsulated by the transcendental ego, not divorced from it. The transcendental subject as pure ego is the field including the natural attitude and natural experience but now accessible through meditation and other forms of consciousness, including film consciousness.

Clearly, no understanding of the phenomenology of film consciousness can ignore the inclusion of the transcendental. The phenomenal field is nonreflectively lived and envisioned and doubts creep into certainty only when reflection comes on the scene, when we abstract from direct and immediate involvement in the lifeworld and realize, relativity; our perspectivalism. But according to Merleau-Ponty, we have no need for a removed notion of the transcendental. Within the intuited profile we already have the essence as given, and this would apply equally to the film image:

> The thing is inseparable from a person perceiving it, and can never be actually *in itself* because its articulations are those of our very existence, and because it stands at the other end of our gaze or at the terminus of a sensory exploration which invests it with humanity.[64]

The film experience mitigates the aporia of the seemingly solipsist condition of an intimately enclosed perception. Within phenomenology we find that reflection does not bring about transparency but rather creates a mindset that acknowledges the world to be strange and paradoxical. Film consciousness allows for reflection on self-consciousness as a reflection-in-action, even though it is not itself its own reflection. Through reflection upon the pre-reflective activity of vision and pre-egological immediacy, film's reflection on non-reflection takes manifest shape.

Reflection takes many distancing forms as it turns back on consciousness through suggestive penumbra, mirror reflections and repetition. In all cases they "transcend the immanence of their immediate bodily experience ... using their lived-bodies and concrete situation in the world to imaginatively prospect the horizon for future projects and possible situations."[65] This "address of the eye," is a visual address housed in a situated personalized body experience, always able to extend itself to where that body is not, be it human or mechanized. In reflection, the body connects with its own future and past situations, as well as the body situations of others. Visual address is a spatio-temporal redirection, transcendence from the immanently actual to the actively possible. The transcendental is expressed as a form of control over self-projection, a freedom for self-creation by means of conscious manipulation. This power of redirection and visual refocusing transcends as it extends the lived-body's existential experience, beyond material boundaries to a vision that is "no longer bounded by the material existence of the body that originates its address."[66]

Film theorists have tended to emphasize an overly idealist and a historical bracketing of phenomenology's natural standpoint "[t]he problem is that transcendental phenomenology describes only the irreducible ground ... the static 'sameness' of consciousness ... invariant relations"[67] when what we instead need to understand is the dynamic and change involved in the *act* of viewing. Merleau-Ponty contributed to this distorted interpretation of Husserl in that in his critique of Husserl's early position, taken up in the preface to the *Phenomenology of Perception*, he appeared to reject the epoché on the basis that one cannot neutralize our cultural antecedents. In an over simplification, transcendental idealism is critiqued for simply signifying the non-empirical and the phenomenological reduction taken as a superfluous move from fact to essence. This is understandable since apodicity and transparency conflict with Merleau-Ponty's reversibility, ambiguity, and later anti-foundationalism. Even the very notion of the transcendental subject has been seen as redundant:

> The whole correlation is the noema for the transcendental ego ("I").... But if the correlation is itself the ultimate structural feature of human experience, then this transcendental move is questionable ... the transcendental ego is actually only a modification of the ordinary ego("I").[68]

Contrary to this, Jean-Louis Baudry, described the film experience as one that constituted the transcendental subject in a seemingly unmediated grasp of reality.[69] Baudry was one of the first to couch the film experience in terms of Husserl's transcendental phenomenology. Unfortunately, by failing to clarify precisely the differences between the concrete and transcendental ego and by adding the influence of ideology on subject formation, his text was distorting. Baudry's "reading of Husserl is ... mistaken with ramifications for the fruitfulness of his conceptualizations of the nature of cinematic representation."[70] Baudry's overly idealist reading of phenomenology misses out on the materialistic antecedents of film representation and ignores the prepredicative "it will not do for Baudry to try to make it look as if Husserl can justify putting aside the referent in analyzing cinematic representation."[71] Baudry figures in the transcendental as constituting subjectivity but he depicted the spectator to be an entirely malleable, acquiescent receiver of ideological messages, reinforced by film form. A competing battle of egos arises because the transcendental is somehow described as disassociating itself entirely from the concretized ego, both in the lifeworld and in the viewing situation. What should otherwise turn out to be an all-perceiving and absolutely constituting "I" becomes a distorted or only half-formed concretized "I" unable to withstand the pressures of identification or uphold a sense of identity. Film thus becomes both insidious and doctrinaire.

When Baudry characterized the camera's position, it was in the form of an oppressive presence, "an alien and monstrous objectified apparatus ... the film's lived-body as it is visible from its alien and alienating form of materiality."[72] This is a bias and denies the dialogical structure of the film experience, "[i]f we reflect upon our own experience as spectators and listeners engaged in viewing and hearing films, we can hardly describe moviegoers as 'motionless,' 'vacant,' and 'silent.'"[73] For Baudry, the only way to overcome this tyranny was by the well-worn tactic of making film self-reflexive, drawing attention to its production and narrative strategies by inscribing its own modes of expression. Even though Baudry's phenomenological position had an ideological agenda, it was nevertheless suggestive for bringing out the implications of phenomenological reduction for the film experience:

> The world offers up an object implied by and implying the action of the "subject" which sights it. At the same time, the world's transfer as image seems to accomplish this phenomenological reduction, this putting into parenthesis of its real existence (a suspension necessary ... to the formation of the impression of reality).[74]

"Transfer" is an appropriate term here, both in the sense of a spatio-temporal imprint through one surface pressing through to another surface and in the sense of a shift from one "framework" to another. Film objectively makes available its images to any existence, not an exclusively particular one. Images can be re-run to any viewer who troubles to watch, so film "Sinn" will be invariant and universal, notwithstanding the multiplicity of meanings and interpretations offered up. Film consciousness emerges as fluid and multiperspectival, a zone where the eye of the camera and the human "I" build a relationship within a transcendental stream of consciousness:

> And if the eye which moves is no longer fettered by a body, by the laws of matter and time, if there are no more assignable limits to its displacement — conditions assigned by the possibilities of shooting and film — the world will not only be constituted by this eye but for it.[75]

The camera picks up movement through time and "fulfills the most favourable conditions for the manifestation of the transcendental subject."[76] For Baudry, what the spectator becomes a part of is the world as imaged through a transcendental eye. Just as Husserl's transcendental reduction looks to the universality of an experience, so the filmed version of concrete reality becomes a corresponding transcendental image of this very pro-ject. Experience loses the specificity it had in the real, embodied world and is treated by film to become an other-than (or more than) it was in the lifeworld. Baudry, however, seemed to assume this is all that film is and this makes for only a partial and inadequate ontology, a deficiency that becomes apparent when we factor in temporality.

Husserl made it clear that real objects are directly amenable to perception, where physical things themselves are reached, gainsaying interpretations of Husserl as an idealist, "[t]he lifeworld is a realm of original self-evidences. That which is self-evidently given is, in perception, experienced as 'the thing itself.'..."[77] This directness and intended immediacy still applies to a transcendental consciousness "in general" and is experienced in a transparent and unmediated way.

Yet film consciousness cannot remain in the immediacy of its unreflective mechanized duplication. There must be a condition of the transcendental both within the originary phase, as awareness through the camera and filmmakers "I," as well as in the aesthetically reduced (purified) viewing condition. Aspects of the transcendental are not only necessary to film experience, they are themselves reinforced within the film aesthetic. For Husserl, the transcendental attitude in artistic expression has always recognized embodiment and the lifeworld:

> In Husserlian terms, traditional aesthetics has been carried on in the natural attitude.... Husserl does not hold this realm to be inferior to the realm of the transcendental attitude. On the contrary, the transcendental attitude, reflective in the phenomenological sense, exists solely to make possible the understanding of the subjectivity that functions anonymously in the natural attitude, presenting a world.[78]

There must be an acknowledgment that film consciousness begins with the natural attitude but becomes transitionally amenable to the transcendental. This is not to exclusively connect with the creative artist and constitute a communion of minds between creator and receiver, abnegating material significance. What is meant by the transcendental position in the film work is the ability to freely examine *how* the work means and subsequently the full spectrum of that meaning. The work does not disappear in a mental fusion but becomes an experienced world where understanding slides along a Mobius strip of one moment's opacity to another moment's transparency.

In film consciousness the transcendental attitude incorporates both Husserl's position, as one which demands the introduction of the epoché, as well as Merleau-Ponty's position that places the transcendental within the immanent. Even though film cannot enact its own reduction, the process still takes place circuitously. Film consciousness cannot think its own change of attitude or shift in imagination yet in film recording such reduction has taken place, inbuilt, so to speak. In other words, filming is a non self-conscious reduction of the empirical world at the moment it records the world. By bringing the world to expression through recording, it is transformed into a sign thereby introducing the transcendental reduction as the arena where meaning takes-its-place in-place-of concealed meaning. The already completed reduction only becomes apparent as the process of film ontology unfolds through the dialectic of particularized situation to universalized meaning, from the reality of recorded raw materiality to the hermeneutic of configured narration. By virtue of its mechanical consciousness, film enshrouds and preserves particularity and surfaces through its aesthetic contours to end in the inclusiveness of the eidetic. Just as the root of pure consciousness has to somewhere find its ground in the empirical ego, so the light of contingent natural attitude must somehow infiltrate and enlighten the world of the transcendental artwork with all its essential formalism.

What film consciousness accomplishes is not the erasure, or exclusion, of one domain for another but an accentuation of the movement *between* those domains, a reverberating echo-effect manifested as a chiasmic exchange, or reciprocal presupposition. The mark of the epoché is there, the ground has been laid, but it has not been consummated within the lifeworld. Intentionality inheres to an experience that intends the categorical but ends up with the particular. The transcendental experience is an originary presence (one which in film is given a presentable face). Its reduced modality of experience takes place in a field that is a "pure fiction," which is everything but life as it is led in the lifeworld.[79] From film's perspective, the repeatability of the film reel and its own non-human testimony comprise this same "unworldly" ideal. Its neutral, even in-different "presence," though originating in primordiality is the reduction which leads from the enworlded to a sense of transcendence, not solipsistic and isolated but part of the mutuality of shared experience. Here we are presented with a singular mental glance, a displaced yet encased, realized yet aestheticized, worldview available for exploration.

This is film's conceit — an impersonated impersonality, a false verisimilitude, a tantalizing deception yet persuasion of truth. The implications of epoché are significant in that the understanding of film world is constituted against a backdrop of the unthought and invisibly conditioned real world. The essential meanings arrived at intentionally in the real world become the horizon of possibility for understanding events in the film world. Film visualizes the facticity pertaining to the transcendental by figures, characterizations and actions in a film dialectic that engenders metaphysical insight. In Husserl's later genetic constitution of the world, transcendental subjectivity dwells in the unconscious, the hidden recesses behind all empirically given conscious performances.

To synopsize transcendental and existential subjectivity would mean to eliminate the tension and interplay of both perspectives. It would hinder the spectator from directly negotiating the path between concrete embodiment and direct eidetic intuition. Film is extricated from the lifeworld in order to maximize all the playfulness and experimentation of exploring the boundaries between the lifeworld and the aesthetic world. The transcendental shift from the spontaneity of the prepredicative to judgments of the predicative is a finely tuned act of experience inherent in film consciousness. Without such tension the dynamic of film consciousness, built upon resistance and friction, would be lost.

4

Reel Time

At the still point of the turning world. Neither flesh nor fleshless;
Neither from nor towards; at the still point, there the dance is,
But neither arrest nor movement. And do not call it fixity,
Where past and future are gathered. Neither movement from nor towards,
Neither ascent nor decline. Except for the point, the still point,
There would be no dance, and there is only the dance.

— T.S. Eliot, *Burnt Norton*

Temporal Objectivities

Consciousness is characterized by time, it is a temporal experience. To fully appreciate phenomenology's contribution to the understanding of film consciousness and the consequences of theories of duration, we must grasp how time makes sense in film terms. As a temporal art form, the film work both expresses time and is expressed by time. It shows time, but not as such. Phenomenologically, time is not substantially showable as a self-standing, self-manifesting dimension. It is indirectly expressed through action and in film by the movement of changing imagery: "The inner flow of consciousness is always accompanied by something it is an awareness of. We never have the naked form of time; inner time-consciousness is inner experiencing."[1] Any investigation into film as a phenomenological experience holds time as a priority for the way we understand imagery and the way time constitutes us as the totality of our awareness. The stream of time comprising temporal phases of the past, present and future is not an empty structure, or a skeletal facade. Time is felt, without having to be objectified, just as it is unnecessary to objectify self to

81

retain a sense of identity. Our sense of immanence and consciousness is intrinsically bound up with the continuity of objects, in the continuum of experience, "the constitution of immanent objects and experience of these objects
is the same process."[2]

As a presentational form, the film work avoids literature's descriptive
techniques in favor of images that speak themselves. In its prepredicative
mode, film recording as temporal reproduction is immanent to temporal
objects. When located in the real world, film imagery reflects the same temporal, perceptual maneuvers needed for normal functioning. We live through
film imagery and instantaneously react to that imagery as it unfolds in a recognizable spatio-temporal continuum. As will become apparent, the correspondence between the temporal unfolding of film imagery in its derived,
predicative phase and the temporal unfolding of internal time-consciousness
by which we understand imagery form an intricate dialectic, so much so that
it could be claimed that the film experience serves as a prime example of phenomenological time consciousness.

The comparison of film experience to phenomenological time-consciousness takes place not via content analysis but in keeping with the experience
of time's basic structural features and the structural relation of film to temporal reality. The transfer of concrete materiality through film imagery is a
transformation rather than a reproduction and the vehicle for this transformation is the temporal markers of film expression through diverse styles of
film narrative. The experience of film imagery is generally taken to be in the
present tense, the spectator apparently experiences action as it happens. However, isolating the instant of the now is an elusive task. The moment is experienced only as part of a complex, streaming process, or a "running-off."
Nonetheless, the nature of the present is still determinable. It has position
within temporal flux as extension and, though elusive, can be described, even
in absence, as an absent-present dialectic.

The present is incessantly on the verge of being replaced by the immediately future oncoming image — protention. It is also the intuited present
before becoming the just-having-been — retention. Crucially, the actual status of self-presence to the longevity of the now-image is noteworthy for being
a unity of affective-understanding rather than a scientifically measurable,
chronological event. The understanding of the now-image shows an increasing resistance to chronology in favor of a labile, composite of time dimensions. Phenomenology is committed to time in its explanation of the
transcendental eye as origin. Here comparisons between film and human consciousness are striking. The unifying stream of time constituting the film
work is similar to Husserl's description of the absolute self-identical ego. It
is seen as a stream of consciousness drawing upon disparate time elements to

bind itself together into one stream of experience. Equally, it is a succession of acts, coalescing as phases that comprise a unified, self-manifestation.

Film and the identical ego are, as Merleau-Ponty put it, not a succession of psychic acts "but one single experience inseparable from itself, one single 'living cohesion,' one single *temporality* which is engaged, from birth, in making itself *progressively* explicit."[3] For Husserl, the pole of transcendental subjective ego was a primordial timelessness; a vantage point from which time unfolds through concrete actualizations expressed through the now points of intentionality. This is not unlike the camera eye in the prepredicative, also a "timeless" mechanical registration of effects that perdures as a fixed identity through primordial impressions in flux. In film, the registration of primal impression is permanent, antecedent to its unfolding flux and viewer intentionality. Just as the experience of self is first accessed through embodiment to reach the predicative, so film automatically records the flow before itself being the catalyst for a complex and unified viewing experience: "The process of temporality in the living present is prior to the developed personal self. Husserl sometimes calls it *anonymous, prepersonal and automatic*. As identities within the life of consciousness, we owe ourselves to it."[4]

As a presence to origin, film recording is a permanent source of time, a spatio-temporal activity. All appearances, whether real or illusory, are time-giving and film recording of objectivities in the prepredicative is also a record of time constituting the form of all intuition. But film can never show time outside of the relationship of phenomenological consciousness. The non-being of past and future becomes an influential presence in time-consciousness, forming a complex interplay between the recording of sedimented history and points of resistance—subjectivities. Time recorded by film has everything to do with the movement of subjectivity in the world because subjectivity is the visualization of time as self-production. Subjectivities make sense of and bring order to Being replete with potential but depleted of differentiation. The objective world is:

> [T]oo much of a plenum for there to be time.... If we separate the objective world from the finite perspectives which open up on it ... we find everywhere in it only so many instances of "now." These ... have no temporal character and could not occur in sequence.[5]

Being-in-itself is plenitude; it simply is what it is. There is no intended deviation in film's recording of this. To re-order there must first be flow, to configure there must be pre-configuration. At this primal level there are no filmic temporal changes because film captures the flow of flux, paralleling it in represented time. There is no discrepancy; an event that takes place prior to another event retains that chronological position, as does its speed of occurrence. The temporal flow of inner time-consciousness can only be what it is in opposition to this, as an incorporation of past, present and future phases, "the past ... is not past, nor the future future. It exists only when a subjectivity is there to disrupt the plenitude of being-in-itself."[6] As such, film's plenitude in its initial phase is disrupted when intended by the temporal non-being of past and future.

The experience of the film work, like subjectivity, is not the imposition of a synthesis onto an unfolding series of images but rather a dynamic opening into a phased temporality. This would see filming at a stage of involvement higher then mere reproduction of objective time in the plenitude of being-in-itself. On this level of reproduction, filming is already a recording of time in process, albeit on a primeval level. That is to say, the field of passive data is never pure chaos, as such. It is rather a "field of determinate structure, one of prominences and articulated particularities *field of sense*."[7] Sensuous data on the passive pregiven level are reflected in film as unities of identity. To live this field of passive data, for them to be registered at all, they must already be products of internal time-consciousness:

> [T]he sensuous data ... are ... already the product of a constitutive synthesis, which, at the lowest level, presupposes the operations of the synthesis in internal time-consciousness.... Time-consciousness is the original seat of the constitution of the unity of identity in general.[8]

This is purely formalistic and revolves around synthetic understanding, succession and co-existence. At root, this is radical recognition and associative genesis. If there is primordial chaos it never appears as such to the mechanical eye. What appears is a unity of identity emerging from objectivities as a force of matter. Filming's re-presented imagery picks up on pregiven associative genesis relating to the field of sense in concrete reality, making it prominent, discernible and meaningful. At this level, the film eye presents intimations of the all-embracing connectedness of phenomenal objectivities as they come to prominence for the embodied "I." The unity based on connecting temporal form forces us to acknowledge the symphystic role of objective time:

> The time by which objects are united is not the subjective time of perceptual lived experience but the *objective time* conjointly belonging to the objective sense of this experience ... the objectivities intended ... as actually being are also intended as objectively and simultaneously enduring.[9]

Husserl finds recognition of objective time necessary, seeing it inevitable for understanding shared experiences in the lifeworld. Like Bergson, it will be seen as inherently mobile. Such communal, intersubjective vision makes film vision readily assimilable:

Reference to objective time ... is unavoidable here ... (it) already leads beyond this domain of being-only-for-me. Objective time, objective being, and all determinations of existents as objective certainty designate a being not only for me but also for others.[10]

Every new datum presented or objectivity that comes into frame, bring their own duration, their own microcosmic system, their own time within ever-present worldly time. Not yet related as the subjective complex state of affairs, real objectivities cohere with their temporal horizons interlaced, part of the universal flow of time, a world time that can be filmically storable.

Self-Constituting Flux

At the same time, Husserl's analysis of primal apprehension cements time-consciousness as foundational. Time-consciousness is understood as *self-constituting,* an amorphous constitutive flux that cannot be pinpointed in the same way as constituted objects. Husserl described the experience of inner time-consciousness as an intentionality entailing the auto-constitution of ego and subsequent transcendental awareness. In constituting the temporal unity of immanent objects, primal flux simultaneously constitutes *its own unity* through an *oblique* awareness of itself. Absolute flux relates to consciousness just as immanent time relates to temporal objects expressed within it, including film. This is akin to the camera eye that has an unreflective but pervasive vision of the life force. Just as the a-temporal pure ego is neither created nor passes away but is closest to a process-in-action, so mechanical recording registers the origin of primal consciousness in embodied space "in medias res."

Film recording's capture of the living present and primal phenomena manages what is a problematic phenomenological procedure. It reflects the primal present in a way the human ego cannot. It maintains the reflected world as a subject because it mirrors that subject as anonymously present while still retaining itself as a temporal form in movement. It passes through the same concomitant temporal phases without itself being a part of those phases, unlike the ego's involvement in the lifeworld that embodies an active-passive hinge. Film's unique correlation avoids artificially objectifying the primal present because it can show time in action and mechanically epitomize the ideal of the transcendental subject, "transcendental subjectivity is not only there unnoticed, but it is non-thematic and absolutely anonymous to itself."[11] The transcendental reality of the film camera has the capacity to bear and express all temporalizations, all identities of being and all worlds. Thus, the timeless consciousness discovered by Husserl in deep intellectual intuition as the basis of the constitution of all that is temporal, must likewise be seen as the element of film recording which holds transcendence in immanence and expansively incorporates more than the present into the infinity of horizons:

> As it is with the world in its ordered being as a spatial present ... so likewise is it with the world in respect to its *ordered being in the succession of time.* This world now present to me, and in every waking now obviously so, has its temporal horizon, infinite in both direction, its known and unknown, its intimately alive and its unalive past and future.[12]

There must be non-thematic consciousness prior to thematic consciousness for the transcendental to act, as well as both primary impression and retentional consciousness for recollection to occur. This is what we mean when we say reflective consciousness can never thematize its own constituting life. It is by nature unreflective but also involved in a reflective thematizing act. The only access to the primal source is that opened up by the interplay of an originally anonymous and subsequently thematic consciousness. The flux underpinning the human condition also subsumes film's ontology. The source of film experience as an exposition of temporal unfolding and a showing of time relates to the primal flux of human condition, indeed, it resonates with it. The appearance of flux is self-generating, "the self-appearance of the flux does not require a second flux, but *qua* phenomenon it is constituted in itself"[13] and it becomes apparent in the awareness we have of being able to reflect on our act of constitution.

The transcendental film eye as related to primal flux is an absent presence in immanent time; an absence in touch with the timeless flux of transcendence and a presence in touch with the rhythms of daily life. The locus of transcendental viewing is neither within the world as a concretely emplaced camera nor outside it as omniscient vision. It rather accords to unique temporal interactions derived from immanent temporality. The transcendental film eye compares to "that unique but verifiable space provided by the reflective structure of consciousness. As the space for the presencing of all objects, it is not contained within the horizon of objective presence. Hence it cannot appear to an empirical point of view."[14] The oblique area of non thematizable, primal flux is the gateway to meaning and to film narrative comprehension. On the one hand, touched by passive synthesis it "safeguards against speculative excess"[15] on the other, touched by chaos, it opens up to reflective pathways for exploring the unexpected and wholly uncontainable. Though lacking in persistence, there is something about the flux that persists, "what is abiding, above all, is the formal structure of the flux, the form of the flux. That is, the flowing is not just flowing in general; rather each phase is one and the same form."[16] This "form of flux" becomes clearer in the way inner time-consciousness structures the present of film experience into constituent parts.

Internal Time-Consciousness

The relationship of the real and fictive world is a continuum of primal memory and impression, mirrored, duplicated and continually streaming off. Film is a recording of the past, not a live production, but "takes its place" in the present. Everything that happens within the frame of perceptive life takes place in an apparently enduring, persistent present. But this is only made possible by the structure of internal time-consciousness:

> It is certainly evident that the perception of a temporal object itself has temporality, that the *perception of duration itself presupposes the duration of perception*, that the perception of any temporal form itself has its temporal form.[17]

If we only experienced the momentary presents of film the essence of film as movement and temporal unfolding would elude us in a series of moments or a one dimensional present. As we bring consciousness to objective reality we perceive movement in objects and situations in a shared immediacy, "the present is the immanence of causes and effects, that is, the state of *existing* perpetuating itself by changing; it is time passing, unconscious that it is passing, but which *is*. And which is everything it could be at every moment of itself."[18] The starting point for film's temporal phenomenology is also the immediate existence of the present as access to the actual:

> This reality, whether or not it is perceived, whether or not it can be perceived, only exists in the here and now, since the fact of existing is only justified by and predicated on "present existence"—otherwise it does not exist or exists no longer.[19]

But human consciousness always brings to the immediacy of the present a sense of past and intimations of the future. The film work plays on the sense of certainty in the presence of the present by using a variety of disruptive techniques; strategies that differentiate spectator time from represented time. It could be no other way. If we merely moved in parallel fashion to film's presentational images, the power of their presence would overcome the perception of duration and we would live without perspective through images. But film vision allows for the visualization of time displacement within a recognizable time continuum. This adds to the experience of film imagery being images-in-movement. What we experience is the presentation of an active, seismic plate of time zones "in the process of taking place."[20]

Spectator consciousness experiences imagery through a present duration noetically structured. This can be clarified in terms of William James' specious present, an analysis that has obvious affinities to Husserl's internal time-consciousness: "[T]he practically cognized present is no knife-edge, but a saddle-back, with a certain breadth of its own on which we sit perched, and from which we look in two directions into time."[21] The "vaguely vanishing backward and forward fringes" of James' specious present resemble but are not identical to Husserl's retention and protention. For James, for two successive events to be experienced in the present they had to be simultaneously represented and this involves a paradox, "namely, that to be aware of *successive* objects consciousness needs to compare the earlier and later objects in an operation that makes the earlier and later *simultaneous*"[22] thereby conflating the past and present. James accepts the simultaneity of succession; moreover, the experience of now moments is taken to be a momentary one, or a "durationless act of consciousness."[23] James' overall position cannot fully capture film's temporal experience because it involves a "structureless immediate intuition of duration"[24] and it is precisely an account of such structure that is needed. Husserl's "backward fringe" is the structure of retentional consciousness making possible the understanding of primal impression throughout the intuited duration of process. Husserl's version of the specious present comprises not a retentional moment but a retentional consciousness, so that retention is always present in consciousness and the memory aspect of the past image in the present is not one of re-presentation. We need to understand immediate consciousness not as momentary but as a structured experience accounting for temporality as extended duration. The way Husserl included the past in the present was not through a direct simultaneity of succession, a grasping of the present and past in a total moment but as a continuum. In terms of a melody, for example:

> Since a new now is always presenting itself, each now is changed into a past, and thus the entire continuity of the running-off of the parts of the preceding points move uniformly "downward" into the depth of the past.[25]

As each note passes, and equally as each film sequence unfolds, the momentary experience of the present is united with a continuum of past phases so that "any subsequent moment will have the previous moment *with its attached continuum* as one of its own phases."[26] What was once a primal impression and apprehended as such becomes, with a retained identity, part of retentional consciousness, no longer immanent but an absent presence nonetheless. Both primal impression and retentional memory are directly and immediately experienced in the span of the durational present.

> [I]f we call perception *the act in which all "origination"* lies, which constitutes originarily, then *primary remembrance is perception*. For only in *primary remembrance do we see what is past*; only in it is the past constituted, i.e. *not in a representative but in a presentative way.*[27]

This is also film's presentational mode where the spectator is relating to the sensation of film as a duality of concrete reality and intuited image. Non-thematic retention immediately becomes a significant latency in the experience of new moments, not unlike film's latency in the prepredicative as it surfaces in the aesthetic experience of film.

As film unfolds, not only the retentional structure of comprehending new images comes into play but also the content structure which carries a familiar echo effect of lifeworld reality onto each new now-image. The effect of meaning-bestowal is made possible by the presence of the retentive fading of an elapsed presence and the present absence of a once recorded lifeworld. Meaning is paramount as an experience belonging, not to the lifeworld, but to a particularized aesthetic: "The retentional performance of consciousness allows it to carry within itself an intentional sense or meaning of the past but not a real sensation of it."[28] This is a direct meaning intentionality of the past rather than memory images of it. For Husserl "perception automatically retains the past without the need for a full-blown act of recollection."[29] The retentive function built into perception deals with primary presence but as the *significance* of previous immediacy not as a present in itself:

> The just-past tone as far as it falls into the present time ... is still intended, but not in the sense that it is actually being really and immanently "sensed," not in the sense that it is there in the manner of a now-tone ... what pertains ... is ... an echo of the sensation, a modification that is no longer a primary content in the sense of something actually present.[30]

In this way, retentional consciousness brings with it thematic, intentional status. Past experience does not have the status of a sensed sensation though it is intended meaning. The presence of retention is not a repeated apprehension of primal impression, apprehension as related to new now moments, but rather the fading echo as just-present, a primary memory as the past-of-present indivisibly connected. It is time that ensures flux as constant change, an assimilation of every renewable present aligned with ever-receding retentions.

Meaning is conserved and preserved through the running-off of the film series. It is this continuity, constancy and indivisibility that also figures in Bergsonian duration. However, we will find this play of phases and contribution to the continuum re-figured by montage and film narrative. In addition, the status of sensation as an intentionalized significance will be expanded and redirected, opening up possibilities for exploring film on prelinguistic and physiological levels.

The way the film work shows the past in the present is literally a "keeping" the past in mind. Ignoring the past is to deprive it of its present repercussions and its inherent fulfilled or unfulfilled protentions. As Casey points out, memory is derived from "memor" that means being mindful, more than mere recollection.[31] Casey's description of the keep is useful for film memory as a concrete showing of place. Being mindful allows the memory to linger, fill the present with its presence in a way more than mere just grasping. The past is a "kept" presence with the possibility of exhibition or projection. Film images visualize the past, bringing its "keep" with it as a temporal place, an active/passive dialectic of memory both "receptive and spontaneous."[32] The dialectic at work here is between the space of containment and the pressure of time on the past through inner time-consciousness. Time disperses subsistence but in "its dispersing movement ... place offers protection against this very dispersal."[33] Having claimed this, however, it is important not to "literalize" spatiality as a place, since memory needs no such conservation. Time has its own non-spatial procedures that may be equal or stronger:

> Is it not memory that preserves the place rather than the place memory?...
> Time exhibits structures of repetition, of rhythm, of ordering, of sequential intelligibility of many sorts that are essential to the preservation that memory requires ... in the structure of the repeated event, we have a paradigm of a temporal gathering on which place memory, often, but not always, depends.[34]

Future Expectation

The presence of the just-having-been in immediacy, however, is only one aspect of internal time-consciousness. The about-to-happen is a mirror reflection of the just-past. When we first experience a present image, its protention-image is inherent in it but is not yet primary. It is still not yet present. "Every act of memory contains intentions of expectation whose fulfillment leads to the present. Every primordial constitutive process is animated by protentions which voidly constitute and intercept what is coming, in order to bring it to fulfillment."[35] The expectation of the not yet present image is present in consciousness as we tend towards a certain fulfillment. Fulfillment may be completed or, equally, the anticipated course may be frustrated. Yet the once future image having passed through the present will then have a different status in recollection. It will have been that image which had fulfilled expectation or that image which frustrated original expectation. Either way, it will henceforth be seen differently to when it was "mere" protention and future possibility. The attitudes we associate with original protentions are not based on perception but potential, though their confirmation is perceptual. Protention is as much a part of the present as retention but with the major difference that the future is foremostly unfulfilled. Protention sets up future parameters, "protention is the name for the way the adventure of the future — its fundamental openness — is closed off by anticipation."[36] Clearly there can be no protentional continuum but there is protentional horizon, or "forward fringe." For Husserl, the protentional future is intentionally meaningful in the specious present and equally (pre)visional expectation is integral to the dynamic course of film, more so than in the spatial arts.

Forestructures lie within the context of film images themselves, the groundwork that is temporally laid by film's time structures and spectator's inner time-consciousness. Protention speaks to image traces through meaning, "intentionality is possible only to the extent that the object is adequately foreshadowed, traced in advance."[37] The process is one of completing horizons in accord with a "frame" of expectations. The basic mode of appearance of an object or situation has an outlying zone of apprehension consisting of marginal co-data, "a more or less vague *indeterminacy*. And the meaning of this indeterminacy is once again foreshadowed by the general meaning of the thing perceived as such."[38] This indeterminacy is the source for more complete meaning but as "indeterminate" suggests, it is an unclear meaning. There are rather motivated possibilities belonging to essential types within a prior understanding of being. In this context there are constant ongoing temporal revisions as former horizons are filled and new ones opened up. In film narration, the perception of events in terms of incomplete contexts and indeterminate horizonal structures provide telos and dynamic. There are possibilities for discovery and the spectator projects towards them. The flux organizes itself into patterns which build up expectations in us. Husserl suggests that we are required to question and explore in what way horizons are played out.

The time of the lifeworld and that of inner time-consciousness coalesce so that film time takes off between the threaded parameters of recorded time and projected time. Once within this technological compound, film begins to mean and gain in signification through narrative and the workings of temporal perspectives. This dynamic makes the film work contingent upon chimerical horizons and spectator reconfiguration, highlighting the flux and interaction of all the modalities at work. Merleau-Ponty, while fully utilizing Husserl's weave of temporal intentionalities relocated noetic, structural presence to preconscious, lived embodiment, warning against both totalization and abstraction brought about by reflection:

> It is of the essence of time to be in process of self-production, and *not to be*; never that is to be completely constituted.... Constituted time, the series of possible relations in terms of before and after, is not time itself, but the ultimate *recording* of time, the result of its passage.[39]

One could add that the recording of time by film is not only not time itself or its finalized constitution, but rather the vision of flux in movement. But whereas human subjectivity can never be outside time, it is always dimensionally a part of it, film's recording of time allows for greater flexibility for experimentally synthesizing time phases and exploring the momentary from the outside in.

Such flexibility comes to the fore, for example, in Tarkovsky's *Mirror*. It is this flexibility that allows *Mirror* (1974) to be a film about process; the process of understanding and the way truth or insight is reached. In the film, both horizontal and vertical leaps of time abound through disjunctions, allusions and momentary spatio-temporal nexus. The multiplicity of viewpoints, the variety of perspectives on given situations, creates immaculately configured set pieces of reality, time capsules that generate visions and affectivities. Only through such film consciousness can we experience multiplicity that results in events being both complicated and purified at the same time. The invocation of a God-like gaze constantly circulates through temporal canals and merging sensibilities. We view through the parallel childhoods of Ignat and Alexei, the difference of the same in the experience of mixed worlds.

Real, historical events act as markers throughout the film, blending with subjectivity, to become the historical juxtapositions and dialectic images Benjamin explores in his discussion of correspondences. These upsurges of history populate Tarkovsky's landscapes in terms of actual events and the memory and personal import of those events on the protagonists. These events become other as they are enriched and fulfilled through the vitality of concerned mindfulness. Film imagery underscores both the visible throb of spatial actualization with the hidden, invisible bias of temporal virtuality. The unseen and unthought are in constant interplay with the present to create a rich fabric of diverse significances. Interpretations and reinterpretations through different temporal dimensions dislodge complacency to create circles of desire. For Tarkovsky, what we see in the frame, just as the present moment, is only a marker for much wider physical and psychological distances, "What you see in the frame is not limited to its visual depiction, but a pointer to something stretching beyond the frame and to infinity; a pointer to life."[40] One could reverse this perspective with equal validity by describing the imagery in terms of centripetal movement, not pushing outwards beyond the frame but implosively sucking forces into a whirlpool of intense presence, fluid, anti-gravitational and horizontally resistant. As the outside comes within the frame the thickness of time is experienced through parallel childhoods, parallel motherhoods and elusive fathers. It is these visual collocations that bring sense to the dialectic imagery, the bouncing off of tenses, the past brushing up against the present and the intrusions of social movements, all of which "short circuit the passage of time"[41] and allow the present to be unraveled and decentered.

The exploration of the past is an obsessional pursuit in *Mirror*, one which acts as a binding thread for fractured identities and the visual and oral temporal shifts. For the son it is like "I have done this before," yet it is the repetition of the eternal return as difference. In every manner possible, the past is integrated for both catharsis and renewal:

> For Alexei, and perhaps for Tarkovsky himself, the sense of longing and loss associated with the past is transformed in the present into feelings of anger, guilt, and responsibility, which can be exorcised only by recreating the past through dreams, memories, and projections.[42]

This is not to say that answers lie in the past, only that they bear the seeds for the actualizations of the present, be it in the form of controlled introspection or flashes of insight. But the actualized present is itself indicative of the past that actualizes it, the present environment can easily slip into the past that it once was. Through this temporal revolving door greater depth of meaning and expressive pathways are revealed, indicative of both subjective displacement and objective constraint.[43]

One scene in *Mirror* is particularly striking. Ignat is alone in his apartment and has been told by his mother, Nathalie, to expect his grandmother, Maria. In a continuous shot we pan with Ignat's gaze to another spatio-temporal dimension. In a room behind him an older woman is being served by her maid. The woman beckons Ignat into this other-scene and asks him to read a socio-political text by Pushkin. After the reading Ignat opens the door to receive an elderly woman whom we presume is his grandmother, but neither the boy nor grandmother seem to recognize each other, their time dimensions have crossed but cannot meet. There is an inbuilt resistance between the two spatio-temporal circuits. In the matter-of-fact coincidence of the two worlds there is only alienation and distance, even though something has taken place. It is the intensity of this registration that leaves its mark, a past expressed as an environmental seed, an affective response locked in the mind of Ignat that has been prized open. Tarkovsky shows the haunting of the past that never could have been in the way it was depicted by a visual after-image of the event, a vestige of time. It takes the form of a heat mark on a table from a now absent cup. The camera lingers on the mark as it fades from sight like a half-formed memory returning to the unconscious.

This is an evolved film consciousness writ large, no longer a Bazanian trace or the fixing of time as frozen embodiment. In the presentation of the disappearing heat stain is the evanescence of film memory, more a Derridean trace that leaves only originary differance and lack, a hiatus that has disappeared from view, a fading mark that subsists the present, making it present by a masked absence. In *Mirror* there is a constant retroactive reverberation of almost every scene and tableaux. This is effectuated not as recollection, which would be to demand too much abstraction, but rather as the materialization of the past in terms of retentive consciousness, visible, substantial traces echoing the possible, so substantial that they are indiscernible from the present.

Bergson: Movement and Intermediate Imagery

Bergson's contribution to film, especially in terms of time, owes a great debt to Deleuze's interpretation of his work. In fact, Bergson was an unlikely cinematic ally. For Bergson, neither film consciousness nor natural perception could capture his preferred form of vitalism, or philosophic intuition. He argued that rather than uniting the artificiality of phases into an extended duration, or transcending immobile components into constant flux, both filming and natural perception were based on the abstracted snapshot:

> Instead of attaching ourselves to the inner becoming of things, we place ourselves outside them in order to recompose their becoming artificially. We take snapshots, as it were, of the passing reality, and, as these are characteristics of reality, we have only to string them on a becoming abstract, uniform and invisible, situated at the back of the apparatus of knowledge.... Perception, intellection, language so proceed in general ... we hardly do anything else than set going a kind of cinematographic inside of us ... the *mechanism of our ordinary knowledge is of a cinematographic kind.*[44]

As a reply to this, Deleuze uncharacteristically defended the phenomenological position against that of natural perception or the snap shot of reality. In doing so he gives us an insight into the development of film consciousness:

> Phenomenology instead saw the cinema as breaking with the condition of natural perception ... phenomenology is right in assuming that natural perception and cinematographic perception are qualitatively different. In short, cinema does not give us an image to which movement is added, it immediately gives us a movement-image.[45]

Admittedly, we now lay aside (without discarding) the important phenomenological notions of the transcendental and the epoché, in favor of the perception of the virtual and actual. We also find a challenge to the centrality of subjectivity with its identity and unity. But these terms, too, are open to phenomenological interpretation according to which period of Husserl we look at and to whether we hold Merleau-Ponty, Sartre or later thinkers to be spokesmen for phenomenological development. In terms of time, we find a similarity between Bergson's durational flow and Husserl's flux of inner time-consciousness. Likewise, we see Bergson's incorporation of the forces of matter with the forces of mind to be comparable to Husserlian intentionality and intuition if we remember that Husserl's position aimed at opposing the dualism of Cartesianism, just as Bergson.

Both Husserl and Bergson agreed that our experience of life is constituted through time to the extent that either an absolute flux or an incessant duration defines what we are. Both thinkers opposed the tendency to abstraction and systemization we find in non-humanistic science. Husserl's search for the eidetic, however, was not the same as Bergson. For Bergson, intellect has led to dissolution and fragmentation instead of the process of becoming. The intellect had artificially cut up progress into phases and moved away from a continuous whole into discontinuous parts. There was a fall where the mind fell away from the unity of action into a myopic inertia. Abstraction cannot represent movement in progress and "much of Bergson's writing is devoted to conveying a sense of the indivisible unity of movement."[46]

Bergsonian movement is distinct from space. The space that is covered is past and divisible, but movement itself is present and indivisible. To reproduce movement it is necessary to use movements, not differentiated, divisible units of space or time. This would mean opposing the film work as a description of images simply conjoined to tell a story and instead seeing it as a continuous flux, uniting the artificiality of phases into a whole, transcending immobile components. Similarly, tying film perspective down to a fixed point of observation with steadfast vantage points would also ignore the implication of movement that encourages shifting centers of perceptual positions.

Reflecting on the philosophical mindset based on intuitive insight, Bergson postulated an *intermediary* stage between the "simplicity of the concrete intuition and the complexity of the abstractions which translate it, a receding and vanishing image...."[47] These are the vanishing thoughts haunting the philosopher's mind, though elusive, they come closer in terms of images than any linguistic attempt to communicate insight. The essential insight of primary intuition is an image. This image is free from being locked within specific time and place; it elicits the same expansive potential and flexibility that emerges with the experimental juxtaposition of film montage. From its first moments, the intermediary image, as expressive of philosophic intuition, is negating. It does not accept the ready-given, or any representation of it. There is an acknowledgment that thought, just as the lifeworld itself, cannot be pinned down or compartmentalized as it relates to something in movement:

> [T]he meaning, which is less a thing thought than a movement of thought, less a movement than a direction. And just as the impulsion given to the embryonic life determines the division of an original cell ... so the characteristic movement of each act of thought leads to this thought, by an

increasing sub-division of itself to spread out more and more over the successive planes of the mind....[48]

The intermediary image emits a uniqueness of vision, demanding an appreciation of novelty so as to penetrate beyond ordered predictability. The originary image does not reside anywhere as such, but is itself process, formed as
idea, subsisting in matter and conjoined with the power of wills from emerging source points, or areas of indeterminacy. The difference between an intuitive insight of a philosopher and the visual trace of a film image lies merely
in the material accessibility of the latter, not its appropriation. The intermediary image, so crucial to film consciousness, haunts original intuition like a
shadow, allowing us to reach its soul. It is an "image which is almost matter
in that it still allows itself to be seen, and almost mind in that it no longer
allows itself to be touched — a phantom which haunts us."[49]

This is a phantom that also comes to haunt *itself*. From the originary
force of the idea, in film the self-imaging of the image, division and sub-divi-
sions ensue as a springing impulse[50] that comes to disseminate and reconfigure
the idea. There results a re-contraction to the origin of idea, or primordial film
impression, but now enriched and diversified. The discrimination and perspectival preferences carried out by the two orders of "automata," human perception and mechanical recording, can be seen to manifest both mechanical
consciousness and intuitive insight. We begin with a contraction and reduction
before arriving at qualitative changes that result in multiplicity and discovery.

Initially, filming has a reproductive role encapsulating temporal unfolding, a role that cannot dissolve the manifest or delve into the roots of atomic
centers and imperceptible vortices. At this stage, filming plays upon the luminosity and tangibility of surface phenomena. But whereas the human eye is
colored by its partiality and utilitarian needs, the camera eye exposes its
reflective duplicity off surface phenomena giving, at least, the illusion of neu-
trality. The potency of the intermediary image lies with this twofold status,
emerging from within the surface materiality of formulated content while still
hovering around a spiritual maelstrom or intuitive force field. Bergson chose
not to bring film consciousness into the equation, unlike Deleuze who begins
by delineating it in terms of open totality and goes on to develop it into paradoxical indiscernibility.

The intermediate image and concurrence of matter and mind become
clearer with Bergson's examination of the circuitry of the brain. As Bergson
sees it, the difference between reflex actions and voluntary actions is only a
question of degree:

[A]s soon as we compare the structure of the spinal cord with that of the
brain, we are bound to infer that there is merely a difference of complication,

and not a difference of kind, between the functions of the brain and the reflex activity of the medullary system.[51]

The brain receives external stimulation "first" and allows the stimulation received to reach *at will* this or that motor mechanism of the spinal cord, and so to choose its effect.[52] The result is a multitude of possible paths or choices that can be taken leading Bergson to describe the brain as a kind of central telephone exchange, like a sorting-house, directing excitations to their most appropriate motor mechanisms as a preparation for action. Bergson's description of human perception is immediate, functional and mechanical. As objects normally play off of each other, the interminable movement of change continues unimpeded. When spontaneous perception intercedes, however, something virtual is inevitably manifested, not a naked disclosure but a momentary break in the aleatory network. At the moment some thing comes to light, its inner impulsion to extend and continue itself by becoming more than its momentary surfacing means it has already lost what it was within the flux of time. It becomes other.

Perception is the immediate expression of body image among the aggregate of all images. It results in actions, setting up a series of connections in the world of immanent flux as an outgrowth of the will. When fixity occurs out of virtuality, it is as a reduction (only partly in the phenomenological sense), a honing down of matter as an incursion into its movement. To make the virtual an actual is not a question of expanding or releasing something, but rather a *curtailment*, a subtraction to obscure aspects, so that what is perceived becomes the picture of the extensive thing. Our representation of matter is the measure of our possible action upon bodies and depends on this contractual form of actualization. This is to remove things from their virtual flux state by separation, in a similar way to the positioning of the camera into the flow of the lifeworld. Filming in its initial recording mode is like the activity of subjectivity making perceptible, of actualizing the virtual flux into a momentary assemblage. The only way non-perceived memory images in the ontological unconscious can become actualized is via human sensory motor activities, just as the film body registers and brings phenomena to appearance. This is a rejection of the belief in sensation as a projected externalization of internal states. Bergson, precisely as Merleau-Ponty, saw the cut-off point for affection and perception to be the *externality* of the lived body. Affection is the return of the real within the body and perception the condition for action:

> Everything then will happen as if ... the external images were reflected
> by our body into surrounding space and the real actions attested by it
> within itself. And that is why its surface (the body) the common limit

of the external and the internal, is the only portion of space which is both perceived and felt.[53]

Perception and body lie outside subjectivity, with the body as an image among other images, among the totality of the aggregate of all images. For Bergson, everything is image. External images affect inner images, including body, by transmission and the bringing of movement; afferent nerves transmitting disturbances to nerve centers stimulated from outside, efferent nerves conducting disturbances from nerve centers to the periphery as the body in motion; images as body, images as mind. All function without ever producing a single representation of the material universe. The body image responds by bringing back movement effects to outside object-images. So materiality is recast in terms of images, matrices, meeting points of senses, actions and reactions.

The reaction to stimulation will always be less than the fullness of the virtuality of matter, so that consciousness loses its flux and totality in the cause of "self" interest. Out of virtuality we get actualizations in movement. Images of material objects are never in the world as isolated objects but always multilayered, part of a burgeoning, contextual schema of the before and after, of the actions and reactions of myriad objective forces. To fail to acknowledge this is to artificially conceptualize the stream of existing temporal duration, which would be tantamount to retaining "only its external crust, its superficial skin."[54]

Film's emplacement within an aggregate of images, one that interacts with the areas of indeterminacy coagulating into perceptual form, is as legitimate as is the human body image. Both are immersed and involved in the heart of the lifeworld as bodily situated. But whereas those primal film images resulting from the film body become available for artistic formulation and expression, human perceptual imagery becomes the yardstick upon which action is based in the world of things. What is crucial is that both film and human consciousness feed off the presence of (absent) virtuality, mirror imagery and the ontological unconscious (pure memory). Circuits are set up. Film consciousness becomes a circuit between the operative lifeworld and the disengaged but meaning-seeking aesthetic world. This is duration as an interactive circuit of perception and recollective-imagery. The circuit is one of immanent, mutual tension connected to its power source, "solidarity between the mind and its object" which "must always find its way back to the object from where it proceeds."[55]

Reelising Memory

Present perception relies on the interpretation of memory images selected by reflective attention. This is literally a projection "outside ourselves, of an actively created image."[56] Sensation is a circuit transmitted from objects to the perception of living beings and continues through consciousness memory back to the object, expanding duration. Perceptual sensation is accompanied by a concomitant (and filmic) "after-image" where memories follow "immediately upon the perception of which they are but the echo," so that "any memory-image that is capable of interpreting our actual perception inserts itself so thoroughly into it that we are no longer able to discern what is perception and what is memory."[57]

The defining characteristic of the relation between past and present is not one based on present existence as opposed to the past's non-existence but rather on the way in which perception draws on the past to contribute towards present action. The link to the past is never broken because the past is qualitatively distinct from the present, its quality is never effaced and when expressed in the present it is as part of the virtual-actual relationship cemented at origin. The reasons for this were clear as far as Bergson was concerned since there can be no associative disruption eventuated by piece-meal imagery. Connections to the past cannot be disembodied ideas or free-floating sensations but are inexorably linked to contextual and situational materiality, regions of duration. To experience the past we must place ourselves within it and follow its path to the present, always as process, not as representation.

Individuals tend to concentrate on present moments to fulfill actions under the weight of a material world that far surpasses the capability of their innate purview. Preference is given to visible divisibility over the unperceived. The present is taken to be the real and unexpected memory images are unwelcome apparitions in need of rational explanation. Yet, for Bergson, the past and memory images were as real as the worldly objects we take to exist, even though we may not actually perceive them. What happens is not that the past ceases to exist when the present has become past but rather it ceases to be useful in a utilitarian fashion. Thus, individuals tend to seek order and predictability as a reassurance of identity. When associated memory images spring up in an involuntary fashion out of the past, the chain of order is apparently broken and control is felt to slip. But this reaction is unnecessary as the individualized link of experience is a natural synthesis of all past states, one we are more familiar and intimate with than the only partly perceived, external world. It is this liberation of temporal dimension and the encouragement of affinity with the unprepared and unexpected that Bergson saw intrinsic to the creative spirit.

Though Bergson seemed to challenge the immediacy of Husserl's primal impressions, we are in fact encouraged to think of Husserl's example of the melody as being exactly what Bergson was suggesting. For Husserl, there was no stasis, no one-to-one correlation between specific notes and consciousness. Notes only make sense within the flux of melody, the retentional consciousness of holding the just-past still "in the present" and the sense-giving wholeness that the overall melody brings to the understanding of each note. Similarly, Bergson was concerned with movement and change, not a series of mobiles changing position in space. Movement is time as process. Bergson used Husserl's example to illustrate the flow:

> Let us listen to a melody, allowing ourselves to be lulled by it; do we not have the clear perception of a movement which is not attached to a mobile, of a change without anything changing? This change is enough, it is the thing itself ... indivisible.... There are changes, but there are underneath the change no things as such which change ... movement does not imply a mobile.[58]

Bergson's notion of perception was filmic in that it accounted for spectator experience as a process of incorporating the past in the present and the power of memory recollection. As a temporal art form, film is already a part of the temporal reality of the objective world. It essentially marks time and is marked by time, markers which are both in the armature of temporal being and in the structured activity expressed through the filmwork. When filming enters the perceptual maelstrom of the lifeworld, as a potentially sentient consciousness, it not only records time through modulating movement but also opens the possibility for relating the present and past in a sphere of recorded memory and spectator recollection. Film alone cannot do this by simple mechanical recording but as an artwork it is open to Bergsonian intuition, conducive to imagination and the exploration of the past. Spectator consciousness conjoins with the sphere of memory to explore sheets of the past as a way of understanding narrative and its impact on experience. Here, too, film narrative allows for the flux of time to be experienced as felt duration, as a way by which human beings can discover themselves in the depth of memory.

As a region, the being of memory is not within us, but rather we are within it. Film creates an analogous sense of ontological memory, one that similarly does not belong to any one individual but which the singular individual draws upon. In terms of Bergson's memory-consciousness, it is we who move in a being-memory:

> Recollections do not have to be preserved anywhere other than "in" duration. *Recollection therefore is preserved in itself* ... we have no interest in presupposing a preservation of the past elsewhere than *in itself*, for example, in the brain.[59]

It is the past that is being in-itself, whereas the present is a becoming-past into the future. Bergson insisted on the real contribution of memory in making sense of a world where there are no individual instants but continuous flow:

These two acts, perception and recollection, always interpenetrate each other, are always exchanging something of their substance as by a process of endosmosis ... in fact, there is for us nothing that is instantaneous. In all that goes by that name there is already some work of our memory, and consequently, of our consciousness, which prolongs into each other, so as to grasp them in one relatively simple intuition.[60]

For Bergson, the past is simultaneous to the present it has been, "then *all* of the past coexists with the new present in relation to which it is now past. The past is no more 'in' this second present than it is 'after' the first — whence the Bergsonian idea that each present present is only the entire past in its most contracted state."[61] It is this observation that explains the thorny subject of just how it is that the present passes. Memory is the condition of the passage of every particular present in the movement from temporal expansion to contraction in present duration. Ontological memory contracts and is actualized from virtuality to have psychological existence. Pure recollection is the inactive and unconscious in a non-psychological sense. By being non-psychological it can function as the catalyst for creativity, including film spectatorship: "Strictly speaking, the psychological is the present. Only the present is 'psychological'; but the past is pure ontology, pure recollection has only *ontological* signification."[62] The act of entering into the past in general, the exploratory field for potential creativity, is a "leap into ontology" that only later becomes psychological in the sense of being actualized from the virtual.[63]

Bergson defined the present instant as "present reality" in distinction to the ideal present or "mathematical instant" of science and chronology. But this is a present circulating around *experience*, incorporating the past but also acknowledging the future, "one foot in my past and another in my future ... could I fix this indivisible present, this infinitesimal element of the curve of time, it is the direction of the future that it would indicate."[64]

Protention and the future are already concerned with action, the expressive movement to futurity. The states are intricately bound and help form the definition of the moment as action in the "interval," later adopted by Deleuze to describe film's movement-image. The condition, however, is a complex one. In theoretical terms, we can argue for the extended co-existence between the past and present but, in terms of consciousness, Bergson argued that there is no present as such:

When we think this present as going to be, it exists not yet, and when we think it as existing, it is already past.... Your perception, however instantaneous, consists in an incalculable multitude of remembered elements; in truth, every perception is already memory. Practically, *we perceive only the past*, the pure present being the invisible progress of the past gnawing into the future.[65]

As Deleuze puts it, "the present is not; rather it is pure becoming, always outside itself. It *is* not, but it acts. Its proper element is not being, but the active or useful. But it has not ceased to be."[66] Significantly, and in keeping with Bergson's insistence on continuity, when we recollect from the past we do so phenomenologically as an *act* of consciousness, for Bergson an act "sui generis": "We detach ourselves from the present in order to replace ourselves, first in the past in general, then, in a certain region of the past — a work of adjustment, something like the *focusing of a camera*."[67]

In fact, Bergson's description of process as activity was replete with film imagery; "a work of adjustment, something like the focusing of the camera ... little by little it comes into view like a condensing cloud; from the virtual state it passes into the actual; and as its outlines become more distinct ... it tends to imitate perception."[68] Remainders detach themselves from virtuality "as a picture," "rays of light" pass from one medium to another, "reflecting" each other to erupt in concretization and practical demands frustrate the pulsating "rays of luminous refraction." But where film is inherently pure perception, human perception is limited to reacting to human needs, practical in its diligence at discarding the unfocused and unnecessary. Bergson saw the fragmentation of duration as tantamount to a scattering of the self, where personality "descends in the direction of space."[69] "Any self, any 'I,' *is* the flow of duration as well as of the past, wholly brought along in the infinite levels of *ontological memory*."[70] This is an interpenetration of all levels of consciousness and being, including the recording of concrete reality.

The implication of Bergsonian movement is that rather than favor any fixed site of observation, there is a contrary move to diverse centers, a vacillating balance of forces and shifting perception. Bergson's description of the emergence of personal subjectivity is as a centre of indetermination, the system by which perception in the form of contracting imagery takes place. There can be no abstraction from the perpetual interaction of atoms and centers of force comprising the material world, a world always already there as virtuality, as movement-imagery. For Bergson "the model would be rather a state of things which would constantly change, a flowing-matter in which no point of anchorage nor center of reference would be assignable."[71] This has repercussions for phenomenological intentionality based on natural perception, the sense of self in terms of thetic and prethetic consciousness and for film, in terms of the movement-image and identity through narrative construction. The sense of anchorage one may find in a transcendental position, or even the focus of a fixed point-of-view offered through a sequence of film shots, is toppled by indivisibility, qualitative heterogeneity and a fluidity that no sooner than collecting around a nexus moves on to another collecting point. Through movement and the primacy of difference, the circuit will always be decentered: "Difference is at the center and the Same is only on the periphery: it is a constantly decentered, continually tortuous circle which revolves only around the unequal."[72] In opposition to the abstraction and superficial solidity of representational imagery, we have moved to multiplicity and a multicentered vision of life:

> Representation fails to capture the affirmed world of difference. Representation has only a single centre, a unique and receding perspective, and in consequence a false depth. It ... mobilizes and moves nothing. Movement, for its part, implies a plurality of centers, a superposition of perspectives, a tangle of points of view, a coexistence of moments....[73]

The limitations of natural perception and the self-referential ego are superseded by the possibility within film consciousness to jump to aleatory, intuitive apprehension:

> [T]he cinema ... has a great advantage: just because it lacks a center of anchorage and of horizon, the sections which it makes would not prevent it from going back up the path that natural perception comes down. Instead of going from the acentered state of things to centered perception, it could go back up towards the acentered state of things, and get closer to it.[74]

Bridging Gaps

Bergson's theories are pivotal for the exposition of film consciousness. However, they are a supplement rather than replacement for phenomenology. Phenomenology is equally concerned with flux and change. For Husserl, the power of primeval flux always asserted itself: "The flux is at once the raw material of phenomenology and its constant opposite."[75] There will be moments of confusion when the subject is robbed of intentional thrust into the world and exposed to the flux. Even though passive synthesis cushions chaotic barrage, when there is seepage through the cracks of intentionality, inspiration is possible. Inspiration is an accompanying force to an intentional drive that co-opts difference:

> [A]n intentionality that produces what it intends ... a driving intentionality directed towards temporalization, one that has as its "goal" moments ... that do not yet exist. It is an intentionality that fulfills itself by bringing into existence and retaining in existence new moments ... the very *being* of the present moment is one with an intentional drive that propels it to appropriate the future moment and bring it to present existence.[76]

Faced with the rawness of the flux, subjectivity responds through various time perspectives as a way of structuring this shifting bed of sand. Here subjectivity is not couched in the self but rather as a perpetuation and "gen-esis of sense and meaning"[77] so that consciousness tries to keep one step ahead of the flux. This resistance against the flux, standing, so to speak, outside it, is examined by Merleau-Ponty who suggested the inclusion of a greater open-ness, playing elusiveness and self-difference off against the realization of pro-tentions: "One of the central theses of phenomenological interpretation ... is that the object of understanding ... is ever in the process of becoming and thus ... never fully is."[78]

Here we find the link needed to appropriate a more open, postmodern turn to phenomenological determinacy and the potentially creative roots embedded in phenomenology's origin. The film body is the "place" of com-bat, passively placed to record and actively dis-placed to be lost in the mael-strom:

> The cinematic apparatus responds ... to ... the demand for the affirmation of transience, for the "apotheosis" of that which is perishable. It opens the door to a "base materialism" defined as the direct interpretation, excluding all ide-alism, of raw phenomena.... Cinema invites me, or forces me, to stay with the orbit of senses. I am confronted and assaulted by a flux of sensations....[79]

For Merleau-Ponty, Bergson perfectly defined the metaphysical approach as an intercession at that point before science applies systems to reality, acknowl-edging an inseparable link, or spontaneous convergence, between science and philosophy. Bergson was the inspiration for the revision of the distinction between induction and reflection, a way of thinking that forces us to ponder whether there really are two ways of knowing or whether there is rather only "one single way of knowing, with different degrees of naiveté or explicit-ness."[80]

On the other hand, as a philosophy of immanence, Bergson's version of the body is not Merleau-Ponty's who saw it as too "objective" and the difference between sensation and movement insufficiently delineated.[81] Berg-son's approach to historical epochs was considered too general and without content: "For Bergson, the 'historical inscription' has no value peculiar to it.... There is only an heroic appeal from individual to individual"[82] some-thing Merleau-Ponty believed to be "too optimistic about the individual and his power to regain sources, and too pessimistic in respect to social life."[83] Nonetheless, Bergson's description of duration was close to Merleau-Ponty's notion of interlacing, a contact with myself that is only a partial coincidence, "absolute knowledge is not detachment; it is inherence ... to present as the basis of philosophy not an *I think* and its immanent thoughts but a Being-self whose self-cohesion is also a tearing away from self."[84] Ultimately, there is an admiration for a similar description of brute Being:

Never before had anyone established this circuit between being and myself which is such that being exists "for me," the spectator, but which is also such that the spectator exists "for being." Never had the brute being of the perceived world been so described.[85]

Merleau-Ponty described the temporal flow in a similar way to Bergson. One could argue that Merleau-Ponty's spatio-temporal description of the primacy of perception, and the chiasmus of the flesh, comprise the intermediate link between phenomenology and Deleuze. Merleau-Ponty's modification of Husserl put into relief the fluidity of subjectivity without supporting claims for "the death of man." And while inspired by Bergson, Merleau-Ponty's temporality went on to challenge the master's own work. This is "a temporality 'functioning according to the barbaric principle,' a question of finding in the present, the 'flesh of the world,' an 'ever new and an always the same'—a sort of time of sleep (which is Bergson's nascent duration, ever new and always the same)."[86]

Merleau-Ponty's temporality was a shift away from Husserl internal time-consciousness, or more precisely the inner time continuum and running off of phases. Rather, we have a temporality of reversibility, where "the past keeps becoming itself through unfoldings which transform it."[87] Time itself is characterized by chiasmic reversals and upsurges, away from Husserl's analysis of progressive time to a Bergsonian time lodged within the world in its brute being. Merleau-Ponty's description of time in terms of lateralizing flashes of reversals, jolting institutions of new meaning and chiasmic leaps, was an understanding of space, time and depth that is in accord with mature film consciousness. As a "bursting of the world in tufts outside the realm of intentionalities and acts"[88] the materiality of film consciousness attains potential for independence.

5

Walter Benjamin: The New Realm of Film Consciousness

Materialism and Allegory

Walter Benjamin was convinced that of all technical revolutions in art, film was the most "dramatic" and this made him one of the earliest theorists to recognize the existence of film consciousness: "We may truly say that with film a *new realm of consciousness* comes into being."[1] Benjamin vigilantly explored the connection between works of art and political tendencies. For Benjamin every artistic epoch was an "historical configuration of consciousness,"[2] with political tendencies imbedded within the aesthetic experience. But in order for them to be understood, there had to be openings, or fissures, to reveal the conditioning substratum producing them, "deeper rock strata emerge only where the rock is fissured."[3] Political tendencies could be detected during times when artistic movements underwent technical revolutions which marked the fracture points of artistic developments and through these points and their impact on the work of art, the shifting sands in politics and society more readily took shape.

Benjamin acknowledged that film penetrated all levels of experience and throughout his copious articles and essays he clearly showed a phenomenological understanding of film phases. For Benjamin, in its first stage, filming of the lifeworld depicted styles, fashion and behavior as a prismatic reflection of "the spaces in which people live"[4] pursuing their avocations and activities, both on an intellectual and passionate level. In its second stage, the edited film work penetrated the consciousness of exactly those in society Benjamin was most concerned with: the collective masses. It affected them not in a private and intimate fashion, as did the traditional work of art, but through the collective viewing of public exhibition. Concerned mostly with the phenomenon of film and its reproductive ability, Benjamin was less concerned with the quality of individual films and their narrative content than the implication of the revolution in technical media.

The spaces that Benjamin saw film consciousness exploring were wide and varied, an understanding he expressed through insisting that *all* was image, so that space became image-space, and body, image-body. The extension of space into image-space incorporated a wider notion of experience and indelibly marked materialism with the emblematic ligature of the psyche. Changes in society could be read off of cultural forms and collective behavior, and film accomplished this through its apparatus, its viewing conditions and, above all, through unique ways of thinking generated by film consciousness.

The relationship between the social, political and cultural was underpinned by Benjamin's far-reaching probes into the status of the artwork and with it film and technology, or art as reproduction. Several themes and motifs permeated his ideas, from the earlier analyses on the traditional work of art, to Surrealism and film. For example, Benjamin's writings on the emblem and Baroque allegory, which figure in "The Concept of Criticism in German Romanticism" and *The Origin of the German Tragic Drama*, carry over to the "Arcades Project."[5] Here, preoccupations reflect the antinomy between the eternal and the transitory, the universal and the particular, and transcendence and immanence, themes we also find debated in Phenomenology and filming. The aesthetic antinomy honed in on the difference between symbol and allegory, with symbols carrying the "idealist sense of a transcendent, absolute and timeless value"; something that gave the work its "beauty and totality."[6] The idealist symbol was said to project a seamless continuity between the aesthetic and ethical realms, a harmonious and well-balanced worldview. The symbol's appearance was tied to its meaning. "In the symbol there is a necessary, if conventional, link between what an object, image, or speech says, and what it means."[7] Benjamin, however, was most interested in allegory, or, at least, his interpretation of it. Allegory, the counterpart to symbol, had suffered a German neoclassicist critique, but it exactly conveyed the discontinuity, fracture and elusiveness of meaning that Benjamin was seeking to isolate in contemporary society. By the very act of creating tension between the arbitrariness of signs and the corresponding futile attempt at grasping absolute meaning, allegory conveyed similar tensions and polarities we find in Benjamin's definition of the dialectical image and the temporality it was associated with. Benjamin used Baroque allegory together with the teachings of Kabbalah which were closer to his own views. The Kabbalists saw that divine knowledge "was revealed in nature pluralistically," and existed in "disconnected registers, presenting itself in metaphors, riddles and mysteries."[8] In a highly intertextual fashion, allegory begins as a network of meanings, in which everything can become a representation of something else. In the first instance, the allegorical sign has an immanent, meaningful context. It then, however, loses its meaning and becomes the "vehicle of something else ... what appears in the allegory, in short, is the infinity of meaning which attaches to every representation."[9] The stability and material embodiment of timelessness and perfection conveyed by the symbolic image, as it exuded spiritual essence, was to be contrasted with this allegorical form, which was earthly, replete with suffering and fragmented. Where the symbol connected to the greater idea beyond and was inexorably bound to it, the allegory "reveals the fragility of the symbol, its always provisional and momentary victory over the arbitrariness of the sign."[10]

Allegory and symbol resemble each other but allegory lacks the stability of the symbol, indeed it stands for transience, and has a particular dependence on the perception of the interpreter, making it socially and culturally sensitive. The profound link between the symbol's sense impressions and thoughts is disturbed by allegory, so that the symbol is "put in motion." This occurs through "distortion" and foregrounds the way changes "in sociocultural factors alter perception, which then alter the symbols that give rise to thought."[11]

This had clear implications for the way Benjamin read the impact of new technology on the functioning of the human sensorium. Where the symbol's material aspect loses significance once meaning is grasped, the allegory is intractably tied to its physicality and grounded in the moment. As in most of Benjamin's antinomies there is dependence and reciprocity, in this case a series of disturbances and subversions, a challenge to a symbol's unified meaning from the allegory's dispersion and multiplicity. The significance of the symbol was not to be underestimated but its relevance could only be sustained for Benjamin in a way that did not obfuscate the "radical transience of nature and human history."[12] Even though the symbol rejected the proliferation of meaning of the allegorical network, it made transparent "what is beyond expression," by presenting a "momentary totality" one that was "perceived intuitively in a mystical now — the dimension of time proper to the symbol."[13] This exploration of the depth of now, and what constitutes the now, is closely linked by Benjamin to his insights into dialectical imagery and auratic flashes derivative of messianic, or fulfilled time. As a result, even though the symbol is rejected for its false promise of happiness, reconciliation and freedom, it still has temporal implications for the "now" of time, the presence of now. (Jetztzeit)

Benjamin attached paramount importance to the form of the artwork and the concomitant role of criticism, which in his artwork essay is also placed in the hands of the collective. In doing this he re-examined where subjectivity and objectivity lie in the critical process, and by implication in the epistemology of the image. Both in the fragment associated with allegory, and time at a standstill associated with dialectical imagery, there is a corresponding reappraisal of accepted norms associated with the space of the image, and the time of knowledge. The work of art is conspicuous for its formal binding but also for the limitation this implicates, even as it germinates its ephemeral identity. New centers of reflection constantly form within a consciousness that marks the interfusion of objects and subjects "according to their spiritual seed,"[14] a seed that Deleuze will relate to the crystalline and the environment. The essence of a work as expressed in its reflection works through form, but each reflection, and thus form, is short-lived, comprising a relative unity "burdened" with contingency. In a lofty ideal, the seeds, or germ cells, will lead, in a critical way, to universal, formal moments but, in its more pragmatic enterprise, criticism has to acknowledge inherent limitations in the work. It is clear at this stage in his theorizing Benjamin was already pursuing arguments in favor of art as a dynamic, even unstable entity, decomposing and reassembling according to changing social and cultural conditions. At the same time, perception itself was to be seen in the wider context of a mutating experience, reacting to the particularities of history and actively creating its own world picture.

Reflection was fundamental here to an experience that is self-generating, one that grows from the experience not from the subject. In this way, though autonomous in its own right, the work is never absolute, but always contingent on the continuum of forms and the idea of art. Through reflection, the work becomes what it is, and what it will not be. It asserts its independence but simultaneously its frailty. Without form the artwork cannot enchant the chaos of the world, but it is a formalized chaos that dices with intransigence. With centers of reflection constantly pulsating around the artwork, emerging and retracting, folding and unfolding, limit-values can only denote relativity. Criticism, it is true, mortifies the work, but in doing so it gives renewed life to the work by replacing what is beautiful with the true. This makes reflection not self-reflection but object reflection, as the emergence of the true is a passage of the coming-into-presence. This can be likened to a polarized spiral that embraces the idea of art through an infinite regress of reflection that expands the space of life into ever widening circles while reducing it within ever narrowing frames.[15] The process of limitation and expansion, or construction and destruction, work together because in order to expand there must first be a cleaning of the deck to make "space" for the new. This can be expressed through the use of irony in, for example, Aristophanes'

comedies, which no matter how extreme could never destroy dramatic illusion, or through the deconstructive acts of film, which, no matter how con-
trived, still maintain their own reality-effect.

The paradoxical notion that just as the work is a formed unity it simultaneously exposes it frailty, and ultimately its own dissolution, has implications for its ontology and status as an independent, substantial entity. It is
indelibly marked by the possibility of being otherwise. Being other than it
is, or appears to be, is also the characteristic of allegory — "etymologically,
speaking otherwise than one seems to speak ... saying one thing and meaning something else."[16] Benjamin was concerned with exactly the point that
things are not what they seem, and that significance needs to be pried out of
all manner of cultural and psychological experiences, which are interwoven
with each other as in a layered garment. There is disharmony, and the work
of art is created, or comes into being, from this disharmony, hence it should
persist as "a thing of shards" or a fragment of the true world. In this context,
as a presage to what Benjamin will uncover in Surrealism and film, the objects
in everyday life that come to form the material of art reveal fundamental anti-
monies. On the one hand, the endless proliferation of meaning we find in
objects through allegory renders them merely exploitable, part of an endless
manipulation and excoriation. On the other hand, as the Kabbalists argued,
in that objects also contain the microcosm to hidden wisdom, they have an
unshakable integrity as they serve as the key to transcendence, a key that the
work of art struggles to protect.

At stake here is a subtle argument about the accessibility of the absolute,
one that impacts on closure, totality and truth.[17] The aporia that Benjamin
presented was that while positing the existence of absolute standards, they
were at the same time made unattainable. On the one hand, truth is beyond
knowledge; it is not intentional and has a different character from any sort
of objectivity. Therefore, it is not known in the same way as objects. Likewise, the same rift applies to the distinction between ideas and phenomena.
Ideas cannot be known in the same way as phenomena. "Ideas are not simply given in the phenomenal world, and phenomena are neither incorporated
nor contained in ideas."[18] Benjamin did believe ideas could be evoked through
material objects, and this belief amounted to an attempt to soften the edges
between formal idealism and material empiricism. The way to represent ideas
was through processes that involved shattering the pretense of unities and letting the prismatic face of experience shine through.

It was not essentially the idea of transcendence through the Kabbalist
texts that came most to fire Benjamin's imagination, but the prominent
Surrealist texts of the time, such as Aragon's *Le Paysan de Paris* (1926), or
Breton's *Nadja* (1928). These texts and their corresponding imagery were

more in alignment with the theological symbols of Kabbalah, than the harmonious, eternal world of the Romantic idealists. But they had the added advantage of relating to the very cultural artifacts and materiality Benjamin was so keen to dissect and penetrate. Benjamin would agree with Aragon: "An object transfigured itself before my eyes, taking on neither the allure of allegory nor the character of the (aesthetic) symbol; it was less the manifestation of an idea than the idea itself. It extended deep into *earthly matter.*"[19] Insight through aesthetic experience was determined by the relationship of the work as phenomenon to its truth-value. But the path to be traveled was a critical one, not a reconstruction but an evocation. Here, criticism and critical representation could not be neutral, but were an active intervention that changed the object. For Benjamin, the idea or appearance of the ideal "lies buried in a manifold of works, and its excavation is the business of critique."[20] The method for excavating the works philosophical truth content was by dissociating its elements, dismantling the pretense of unity and creating new centers or complexes out of these deconstructed elements. Only in this way could the ideal of the problem of philosophy be evoked.

Throughout Benjamin's projects this same deconstructive and reassembling antinomy is at work. Indeed, the very essence of time itself will be seen to have no inherent teleological dynamic. There is no natural unfolding, either in a phenomenological or historical sense. Nature, itself, was not considered to have a natural origin, it was neither "pristine nor lapsarian," origin (ursprung) is always found to be lacking, "already infected by natural decay and transience."[21] Origin is a "whirlpool in the stream of becoming, and in its current it swallows the material involved in the process of genesis."[22] Origin, then, describes something that emerges from becoming, and disappearance, to synthesize into something else. It always results in the impermanent, deriving from a prehistory and reliant upon a post history that is an incentive to its fuller unfolding. The fact that origin is already derivative and already infected by natural decay and transience lends it to the allegorical pursuit of ruin and fragmentation. This is a pursuit that centers on collecting, accumulating and finally arranging but in a way that minimizes direction and transfiguration. The process of destruction and then constructive representation through new complexes will take on its full relevance for film consciousness in the dialectical image and the Surrealist movement.

Dialectical Images

When Benjamin wrote in the context of Europe in the 1920s and 30s, he was concerned with ways of coming to terms with, and altering the vision of, the lifestyle that Capitalism generated. His speculation regarding imagery, which has wide-reaching implications for film consciousness, emerged as a key motif against the background of Modernism and high Capitalism in the nineteenth century. *The Arcades Project*, in particular, was "a Marxist-inspired, work of cultural critique."[23] For Benjamin, capitalism induced a dream-filled sleep: "Capitalism was a natural phenomenon with which a new dream-filled sleep came over Europe, and, through it, a reactivation of mythic forces."[24] But Benjamin did not consider what he saw to be the blatant promulgation of the endless pursuit of novelty and progress, to the detriment of personal development and creativity, an irreversible process. He believed that the particular kind of sleep induced by capitalist ideology could be disturbed in a positive way by the critical approach he coined "materialist histiography" and by the decoding certain art forms could undertake:

> It is not only that the forms of appearance taken by the dream collective in the nineteenth century cannot be thought away; and not only that these forms characterize this collective much more decisively than any other — they are also, rightly interpreted, of the highest practical import, for they allow us to recognize the sea on which we navigate and the shore from which we push off.[25]

Benjamin's complex notion of dialectical images directly spoke to this dream-filled sleep and could serve as the moments of awakening from the collective dream of humankind. They could offset the conscious bourgeois attempt at glorifying capitalist modernity by capturing "unconscious reactions" to the "hellish consequences" expressed, "in a thousand inadvertent, overlooked, or otherwise worthless cultural forms."[26]

In his study of cultural forms, Benjamin applied many of the classical tenets of Marxism, including the reversal of roles between commodities and producers. As Marx pointed out, the fetishism of the commodity is a reintroduction of pre-modern religious consciousness into the modern, and serves to alienate mankind from its nature as "free producers." Such alienation plays havoc with control over subjective identity to a degree that the role of object and subject is reversed: the commodity "assumes human qualities.... Subjects become transformed into objects through alienated industrial labor; objects, through the same process, are transformed into subjective beings."[27] As commodities are the intersection of both nature and culture they become ideal sites for the disclosure of a kind of historical truth about modern capitalism, and Benjamin was painstaking to analyze this transformation. In terms of the new means of production, their influence brought about images and wishes in the collective consciousness. Dream wishes of the collective were characterized by hopes for the future, hopes Benjamin saw as both "wedded to elements of primal history" and to "elements of a classless society."[28] According to Benjamin, "elements of utopia are left as traces in a thousand configurations of life, from enduring edifices to passing fashion."[29] Marxist insight into the materialist dimension of history was retained, but combined with a heightened graphicness to make the wish images of the collective amenable to Benjamin's dialectical images. Already here we find the method of analysis to be one that is familiar from the intent of the reassembled film experience: "In what way is it possible to conjoin a heightened graphicness to the realization of the Marxist method? The first stage in this undertaking will be to carry over the principle of montage into history ... to discover in the analysis of the small individual moment the crystal of the total event."[30]

As they were connected to the expression of collective wish projections, commodities integrated into cultural artifacts and artistic expression in the 1920s and 30s were so rich in significance they served as endless material for Benjamin's wide-ranging cultural and philosophic criticism. The question became how to transform the collective expression of commodities and cultural forms into a "politically shocking force."[31] Presumably this could only be achieved after commodity fetishism was shown to be "the delusional expression of collective utopian fantasies and longings."[32] For Benjamin, modern dream wishes were always colored by what had passed, archaic symbols and the influence of the ur-past persisted and insisted on a classless society. But wish images and utopian images need to be grounded on material objects rather than rest in the world of imagination, and modern developments in the form of media and technology reflected this:

> Even as wish image, utopian imagination needed to be interpreted through the material objects in which it found expression ... it was upon the transforming mediation of matter that the hope of utopia ultimately depended: technology's capacity to create the not-yet known.[33]

Under the auspices of an historical materialist who must be sensitive and responsive to both material struggles and spiritual fortitude, historical events and contemporary mores become significant no matter how small. The process is not one of singling out events or objects and looking for some inherent truth embedded in their infrastructure. Rather, it is the delicate reaction to an event that itself makes itself known in a time of danger, above all, in a time where conformity to ruling ideology threatens to crush insurgence and grind it into the ground. The superimposition of fleeting images, based on their actuality in the past and the present, offers revolutionary significance. Images that tune into the collective unconscious and materiality, especially those created by innovative technology, could, Benjamin believed, galvanize the masses and actualize their collective dreams. Throughout Benjamin's theorizing on the significance of cultural artifacts and political developments relating to class-consciousness, we find a drive to present "living images." In the Arcades Project, in particular, there is an emblematic exercise in picking out what characterized the age of the masses and contemporary society:

> The gambler and the flâneur in the first Arcades Project personify the empty time of modernity; the whore is an image of the commodity form; decorative mirrors and bourgeois interiors are emblematic of bourgeois subjectivism; dust and wax figures are signs of history's motionless; mechanical dolls are emblematic of worker's existence under industrialism; the store cashier is perceived "as living image, as allegory of the cashbox."[34]

All these are images in which thought has become embodied directly in relation to social materiality. Once materialized, wish symbols are to be decoded and unraveled as a wake up call to consciousness to come to its "senses."

For Benjamin, as for Bergson, images are real and expansive — all is image: "The primary mode and the primary material of thought and ideas are images."[35] What Benjamin calls image-space becomes body-space as a particularly pertinent Surrealist activity of translating Freud's model of the psyche from the individual to society. This image-space is not "contemplative," but a space "where the distance and boundary between subject and object image no longer obtain."[36] For Benjamin, the subject enters into the space by an initial act of dissolution where the body, in a liminal act, is first torn asunder before it embraces its area of reconstruction in the arms of an abeyant image-space: "no limb remains untorn ... precisely after such dialectical annihilation — this will still be an image space and, more concretely, a body space."[37] For Benjamin this extended space is one which embraces "political materialism and physical creatureliness" in order to experience a "dialectical justice" that is only achievable by materialistic reformulation. The same process of the work of art's destruction and reconstruction comes into play but now in a political and factual reality. What takes place, what is present to the image, is similar to the non-heteropathic experience of film where spectators fully identify with film images and are, so-to-speak, fully absorbed by them: "where an action puts forth its own image, and exists, absorbing and consuming it, where nearness looks with its own eyes, the long-sought image space is opened...."[38] Where political materialism coalesces with humanity in both its personal and social guise, a body-image space opens. Here, the body of the body space is the same collective Benjamin will address as a mass-in-movement, a space that is now molded by technology as political reality. Here the collective must find its rightful place.

The interpenetration of creatureliness with the individual and collective psyche, in an image-space that is the arena for material expression, becomes a two-way screen for reciprocal imagery. In an almost incestuous way, the same images that tune into the collective unconscious become those images that are the collective itself, made manifest in image-space through technology. The outside world and the dream world carry direct correspondence; the opposition of inner and outer is sublated in a dialectical constellation. With the development of image-space, Benjamin was determined to ground "perceptions of both psychoanalysis and materialism for the purposes of analyzing modernity."³⁹ Through Surrealism there is a "materialization of the image" in what Benjamin called corporeal innervation, or "an enfleshment of expressive matter." Here the body literally becomes the material of imagery. In the dialectical image, however, there is a "materialization of the language of the unconscious ... the materialization of the imaginary in the organic and inorganic external world, or body social."⁴⁰ If the landscape of the arcades can become the topographical paradigm for Benjamin's investigations, imagery as such will reflect back its own effulgent space. The act of filming here, in its first phase of material reproducibility, will clearly have a role to play by dint of its mechanical abilities to re-see, and replace human oversight by technical in-sight. It will be able to pick up on the projected materiality of the collective dream wishes that becomes the body image of the city. It is this materialization of the language of the unconscious that will be deciphered through dialectal images. Benjamin is in no doubt about the perceptual conversions set in motion:

> With the close-up, space expands; with slow motion, movement is extended. And just as enlargement ... brings to light entirely new structures of matter, slow motion not only reveals familiar aspects of movements, but discloses quite unknown aspects within them.... Clearly, it is another nature which speaks to the camera as compared to the eye.... "Other" above all in the sense that a space informed by human consciousness gives way to a space informed by the unconscious.⁴¹

Where in Deleuze we are encouraged to think the unthought of thought, in Benjamin we are encouraged to make the unconscious conscious, and through the power of reason overcome mythic forces. Imagination can take up the gauntlet thrown down by new technological forms and, shedding the skins of aestheticism and cultism, go about transforming collective social life. Here it would be a mistake to separate, or bifurcate, the two seemingly antinomic strands in Benjamin's work: the theological and the political. But equally it would be a mistake to separate the transcendent from the immanent since Benjamin is concerned with reaching ideas through the arrangement of concrete elements in the concept, not in spite of them. The formative elements as expressed through constellations are carried out by rational decisions but the intent is to let the results burst through rationality in much the same way as Bergson opposed any mechanistic approach to thought.

The fusion, or eruption, of past imagery in the context of the present, Benjamin's constellation, makes more sense if we understand Benjamin's notion of time as one in which there is an inherent split. The experience of the present is a complex process marked by temporal verticality and separate dimensions. In the dialectical image, the present is seen as a junction box, a place of intersection, or a collection point: "The dialectical image is a way of seeing that crystallizes antithetical elements by providing the axes for their alignment."[42] Philosophical ideas mature in a visual, labile field, one in which oppositions "can best be pictured in terms of coordinates of contradictory terms, the 'synthesis' of which is not a movement towards resolution, but the point at which their axes intersect."[43] This form of remembrance is "dialectics at a standstill," which questions conventional notions of progress and historical resolution. In Benjamin's observations in *On the Concept of History* we find both the phenomenological roots of filming as a letting-come-to-appearance within self-constitution and the constructive effort of montage and creation of shock as an act of the materialist histiographer. The historical object is constituted by being "blasted" out of the historical continuum in the form of a flashing image, into the now of recognition, at the null point. It is apparent throughout that the past resists becoming subject to the interpretive initiatives of the present as a manipulated field. The past is not a site to be explored, unearthed and then deracinated in order to meet prefixed notions, or to satisfy the demands of a complex interplay where it is negotiated through material struggles. Priorities are reversed. It is rather the present that is to be shocked to its foundation, without the imprint of a theorizing subject. In the process "time becomes an other for itself in order to be synthesized into a new form."[44] In his discussion on the images of Proust, Benjamin describes the oscillation between the past events and their remembrance, chronological memory and psychological memory, or objective time and phenomenological time:

> It is true that within Proust we find rudiments of an enduring idealism, but ... [t]he eternity which Proust opens to view is intertwined time, not boundless time... To follow the counterpoint of aging and remembering means to penetrate to the heart of Proust's world, to the universe of intertwining.[45]

This is Benjamin's temporal differential, a way of looking at time askew, edgewise, of recognizing its deviation, a way of seeing truth as intrinsically bound to a nucleus of time: "Resolute refusal of the concept of 'timeless truth' is in order. Nevertheless truth is not — as Marxism would have it — a merely contingent function of knowing, but is bound to a nucleus of time lying hidden within the knower and the known alike."[46] The substance to this thought is unerringly redolent of Deleuzean insistence on seeing the fundamental operations of time as an expression of the actual and virtual, as a crystal image which comes to light as a split, "time has to split itself in two at each moment as present and past which differ from each other in nature, or, what amounts to the same thing, it has to split the present in two heterogeneous directions...."[47] There is something within time which functions as a motor to ensure time moves on, while simultaneously preserving the past. Time consists of this splitting function. Similarly, the Deleuzean series, formulated as a sequence of images, does not progress anywhere but gives birth to other series of images that hold within the power to deflate the false or the cliché. It does so as an act of storytelling, one Benjamin has personalized into a genuine experience. For Benjamin, contrary to journalism's disjointed collection of data and facts that atrophy genuine experience, the traditional activity of storytelling opens us up to all facets of memory, recollection, remembrance and *mémoire involuntaire*.[48]

Time is split, and Benjamin's concept of time, opposed to empty or homogeneous time, is admittedly out of time: "What for others are deviations are, for me, the data which determine my course. — On the differentials of time (which for others disturb the main lines of the inquiry), I base my reckoning."[49] For Benjamin, phenomenological intentionality takes place within an inbuilt, blinkered sphere releasing perceptual activity but locked within the presence of the running-off of the time continuum. Benjamin wanted to break this continuum through a web of simultaneous time phases that dislocate comparison and even disavow association. Time differentials propose a dialectic experience which is known through language and imagery. This is an experience of life enriched by breaking the annals of history into one that redeems the past through remembrance. The training that is needed here will come from different sources including the introduction of technology in the arts, such as film. There is a pedagogical requirement: "To educate the image-making medium within us, raising it to a stereoscopic and dimensional seeing into the depths of historical shadows."[50] Images will then be understood as they flash into the now in a constellation with the present. The historical index, or the what-has-been that images bring with them, are to be read for what they are; portals into a space of truth: "Only dialectical images are genuinely historical.... The image that is read — which is to say, the image in the now of its recognizability — bears to the highest degree the imprint of the perilous critical moment on which all reading is founded."[51]

Proust, for example, who conjured up through his imagery the lifestyles and mores of social classes, did this not by reflection but by "actualization."[52] Rather than allowing experiences of the minutiae of life, or the ephemeral, to fade away they had to be rejuvenated, consumed in a flash, in order to infuse "an entire lifetime with utmost mental awareness."[53] Benjamin described the real or genuine passage of time conveyed by Proust as one that reflected personal aging; aging without, together with memories, or remembrance, within. This is the dialectic of intertwined time. The potential to be gained from image reading is like a fecund seed that will grow to enfold individuals within the collective: "Where there is experience (Erfahrung) in the strict sense of the word, certain contents of the individual past combine in the memory (Gedachtnis) with material from the collective past."[54] Ritual and festivals were a major contribution towards this intertwining of individual and collective memory.

Potential images from what has been in history contain the seeds of time as embedded and dense: "The nourishing fruit of what is historically understood contains time in its *interior* as a precious but tasteless seed."[55] The intertwining of forms of memory is mirrored in the appropriation of thought externalized in the historical object as image. Thinking is arrested and within the constellation it is fraught with tensions. An opportunity for political change comes from the shock that results, thinking becomes the crystallized monad, and with it "a revolutionary chance in the fight for the oppressed past."[56]

The crystallization and "dynamic" stasis of thought recalls Deleuze's crystalline monad, the same multifaceted reversibility and consolidation between the virtual and actual, the same chance and potential without guarantees, "we do not know in advance if the virtual seed ... will be actualized, because we do not know in advance if the actual environment enjoys the corresponding virtuality."[57] Thus, for Deleuze the material environment will determine just what and whether there is actualization, and for Benjamin there is a similar reliance on the constitution of contemporary society as to whether the dialectical image will be sustained and bear fruit. Breaking out of the historical flow was also to be dependent on where in history the images surface: "What distinguishes images from the 'essences' of phenomenology is their historical index.... For the historical index of the images not only says that they belong to a certain time; it says, above all, that they can attain legibility only at a particular time."[58] This time will be characterized by disturbances, since the images defy systemization and resist closure. There is no progression or synthesis but a peculiar confrontation of temporal sets and figures. Differentials have the majestic sweep of epochal import but nonetheless may comprise infinitesimal changes. Deleuze's ideal events come to mind here, though they are more pre-personal than Benjamin's. Ideal events, or singularities, are indifferent to the individual or the collective. Yet like Benjamin's differentials they are turning points: "inflection; bottlenecks, knots, foyers, and centers;

points of fusion, condensation, and boiling, points of tears and joy, sickness and health, hope and anxiety, 'sensitive' points."[59] There is also the same sense of dynamic stasis, excess and surfeit which crystallize and evaporate: "If the singularities are veritable events, they communicate in one and the same Event, which endlessly redistributes them, while their transformations form a *history*."[60] Each singularity is a shining point that internalizes condensed history and externalizes material imagery.

Benjamin's truth is legitimized as truth, not by being a contingent function of knowing, as in Marxism, or as a transcendental, timeless truth, but one that is bound to a nucleus of time. Each nuance and condition of the temporal nucleus will determine what emerges as the relativism of what *can* emerge from time. Each now is the now of a particular image made manifest, visual rather than logical, real rather than virtual. In it, truth is charged to the bursting point with time, a point of explosion. Benjamin describes the parallel process of thought and history and their intrinsic interfusion as a continuum that must be arrested. Then it can indulge in the explosive resonance of dialectical imagery. This is essential because each epoch in the stream of history is conditioned by what preceded it, and the coming to the fore or prominence of the past in the present involves the coming of new repetition. To understand this, each age must have its own method, its way of thinking and its own form of understanding. We thus find in an age of film consciousness there must be a corresponding method for understanding the dialectic of temporal spheres and time differentials within the constellation. We will see that, for Benjamin, one such method for realizing correspondences in dialectical images was the construction of montage.

Mechanical Reproduction and Aura

With Benjamin's "The Work of Art in the Age of Its Reproducibility," the ground is laid for a more precise definition of film consciousness. To understand this essay we must continually bear in mind Benjamin's analysis and reworking of experience and criticism in terms of traditional works of art, cultism and dialectical imagery. The advent of technology and its influence on artistic expression became a defining moment in the shift away from the classical notion of the beautiful form in artistic objects, as well as an innovative and far-reaching appraisal of individual subjectivity in terms of the collective. By dropping allegiance to classical aesthetic tenets and evaluating film in terms of its own consciousness, the film experience became indelibly political. Benjamin carried over the historical notion of dialectical imagery to the reality-effect of cinema and its montage transfiguration. In the essay,

Benjamin also developed the notion of aura. What is interesting in this regard is that even though Benjamin considered film praiseworthy for its contribution to breaking down the aura associated with traditional works of art, it can be argued that aura still survives in the film work, albeit in a transformed way. Though Benjamin welcomed the disappearance of aura associated with ritual art in mythic times, as well as art associated with the bourgeoisie, he also intimated what form the transformed aura would take.

At the root of aura was an archaic notion, something like the resonance and echo from an original birth. This echo effect accompanies all difference and otherness that has emanated from undifferentiation. Where once there was undifferentiation and a sense of the oceanic there became difference and the fall. Traditional artworks, combining immanence and transcendence through the work's cult value, relate at various periods to magic, religion and ritual. And aura connected to traditional artworks was always linked to its ritualistic function and this never disappears, "this ritualistic basis, however mediated it may be, is still recognizable as secularized ritual in even the most profane forms of the cult of beauty."[61] Aura underscored the work of art's basic values: authenticity, singularity and uniqueness, all ostensive desirable properties. Aura was defined as:

> [T]he unique apparition of a distance, however near it may be. To follow with the eye — while resting on a summer afternoon — a mountain range on the horizon or a branch that castes a shadow on the beholder is to breathe the aura of those mountains, of that branch.[62]

Distance, or the gap between the subject object experience, is retained but within the context of an authentic relation of being-in-the-presence of something. Even the shadow of a branch physically leaves it mark or is felt like warm breath. The shadow that falls over the contemplator has physical resonance; it touches the beholder and physically relates to a tree of origin at a specific time and place. The pastoral scene is characterized by the same ambiguity of closeness and distance Benjamin related to the inapproachability of the artwork. Both the work of art and nature have aura in common, what differs is their relationship to tradition and culture. For the work of art, the unique apparition of distance is a "formulation of the cult value ... in categories of spatio-temporal perception.... The essentially distant is the inapproachable. Inapproachability is, indeed, a primary quality of cult image; true to its nature, the cult image remains 'distant, however near it may be.'"[63] Traditional works of art are seeped in tradition; they establish continuity in tradition and act like an historical magnet. This is their authenticity.

The distance that can never be eliminated is best not to be considered as distance-as-absence but distance manifested as *appearance* because "auratic objects are appearances ... that is, manifestations according to the forms ... of space and time ... of something that transcends the phenomenal."[64] This makes the object unique, "a unique singular appearance of the distance in question."[65] As Benjamin put it, "the essentially distant is the inapproachable," manifested by "the unique apparition of a distance."[66] Distance constitutes the foundation of the auratic object. What "appears" in the unique distance of the auratic object is something that has transcended the foundational substratum.

It is not difficult to equate the authority of the work of art, its cult value combined with elusiveness and inapproachability, to Benjamin's comments on Romantic art in general. There is a similar interplay of distance and authenticity. In the aesthetic realm, "everything essentially beautiful is always, and in its essence bound up ... with semblance."[67] But semblance never comprises the essence of beauty: "Rather, the latter points down more deeply to what in the work of art in contrast to the semblance may be characterized as the expressionless."[68] This is not to say that semblance, or appearance, disappears from beauty, rather that there is a relationship or interdependence between appearing and the beautiful that Benjamin characterized in "veiled" terms, "semblance belongs to the essentially beautiful as the veil ... beauty appears as such only in what is veiled."[69] Beauty is the object in its veil and cannot be otherwise, for if it could be revealed it would lose its status as essence. In a similar way to the dialectical image that becomes known at a standstill, the expressionless brings order, or at least deters chaos, and has the opposite effect to animating the work:

> The life undulating in the artwork must appear petrified ... as if spellbound in a single moment ... what arrests this semblance, spellbinds the movement, and interrupts the harmony is the expressionless.[70]

The role of the critic and the understanding of the artwork no more involve a lifting of the veil than it does definitive interpretations, on the contrary, it must involve the holding back of pure beauty and the recognition of an intrinsic, effacing expressionless. The beautiful is not the veil, nor the object, "but rather the object in its veil." There is here an auratic shell that resists being prised open. Within the shell, the gaze of the beholder is transfixed in contemplation, trapped in the web-like intrigue between semblance and beauty.

Benjamin clarifies further the work of art and its aura as belonging to a unique time and place, something mechanically reproduced art lacks: "In even the most perfect reproduction, one thing is lacking: the here and now of the work of art — its unique existence in a particular place.... The here and now of the original underlies the concept of its authenticity."[71] Authenticity is the core of a work, it is all that is transmissible in it from its physical origin, throughout the history it touches and that informs it. In fact, history itself is a major determining factor in the way anything is perceived:

> Just as the entire mode of existence of human collectives changes over long historical periods, so too does their mode of perception.... The way in which human perception is organized ... the medium in which it occurs — is conditioned not only by nature but by history.[72]

That is to say, the use of technology and other innovation within cultural activity will be a conditioning determinant as to how the populace perceives. Changes in the medium of perception occur regularly gainsaying its categorical permanence and arguing for conditioning through culture and education. If aura is linked to the medium of perception, then the decay of aura that Benjamin discussed can be explained as part and parcel of social and material conditions.

On one level, filming involves auratic loss as it loosens continuity and mythical interconnectedness, facilitated by film speed, immediacy, reproducibility and montage. However, Benjamin always opened the way for considering aura in the modern age not in terms of dislodgement but rather transformation. There was always an assumption that the esoteric promise stored in the aura "will be redeemed *exoterically* by mechanically reproduced art — that there is a continuity between the two species of art" so that film's transformation of aura can make good the "utopian claims of auratic art."[73] We see an example of the tension in versions of aura emerging in Benjamin's "Little History of Photography" (1931), where preliminary comments on the photographic image have a Bazanian resonance. Early technology of photographic reproduction was slow enough for the passing on of aura in portraiture, effectuating an unbroken continuity. Subjects in early photographs had "an aura about them (through) a medium that lent fullness and security to their gaze even as it penetrated that medium."[74] Benjamin maintained that through visualization the significance of a rising social class could be fixed by virtue of the slow film speed and unobtrusiveness of the production. It was only when manipulative artifice was imposed by an indulgent bourgeois ideology that aura linked to authenticity and tradition faded. This was the same class Benjamin described as "impotent" in the face of technical progress.[75] Benjamin was quick to notice that many critics and theorists alike failed to acknowledge the momentous implications of the new media, either due to ignorance or intransigence. For them, the artist should "reproduce man's God-given features without the help of any machine." Such critics, Benjamin believed, only had a "philistine notion of art" and were "stranger(s) to all technical considerations" in what was a "fundamentally anti-technological concept of art."[76] Benjamin, on the contrary, concluded that with the possibilities technology offered for reproduction and reconfiguration, the individualized aura linked to aesthetic contemplation could justly be rejected along with the "degenerate" imperialist bourgeoisie and its intelligentsia.

Benjamin went on to analyze in more detail the extent to which the decay of aura related to film consciousness in the areas of subjectivity, perception and thought. An example he gave was the differentiation between the film and stage actor. The stage actor, performing live, retains aura, as he is directly presented to the public, in person.[77] This is communicated by the actor's bodily presence. Again aura is "bound to his presence in the here and now."[78] But the film actor is without aura, without any "phenomenalizing power"[79] of the here and now, all that matters is "performing for a piece of equipment."[80] This fact alone changes the spatio-temporal matrix as well as the level of audience identification. From this it is apparent that the aesthetic experience no longer involved the contemplative lure of the traditional, auratic work. It no longer addressed the beholder, or viewer, in the same, private and authoritative fashion. In fact, it no longer addressed the same kind of viewer at all, since the scrutiny and absorption demanded by traditional works related to an individual subject, whereas film consciousness, as Benjamin saw it, took hold through the collective, in the mass audience. The film spectator "is no longer the one single viewer ... it is a collective subject from the start."[81] Thus, the notions of beholder, contemplator and ultimately subjectivity came under radical revision. The spectator was now seen to be mobile and part of the dispersed collective mass, rather than the specifically located, contemplative individual.

The transformation to technological aura was introduced through the aesthetic experience of the masses in an anti-élitist way as a matter of collective self-portraiture and mass appeal. With the decline of singular aura and the individual, Benjamin's interpretation of film media as a group experience was conducive to an active mode of reception in terms of perception and cognition. In broad terms, "Benjamin characterizes the movie theatre as a sort of exercise and training ground for acquiring the transformed mode of perception required by modern life."[82]

The dispersion of technological art meant, Benjamin believed, mass participation could be both critical and instructive. In fact, the mass was never taken to be an inert conglomeration but always an uneasy, dynamic juxtaposition; a-mass-in-movement. This was a mass related to mass nature, to the "mass-like character of reproduction.... Benjamin does not speak simply of the 'mass' or 'masses' but of 'mass movements' ... it entails a dynamic element ... the result, or rather, the corollary, of that movement of detachment, 'ablosen,' that marks the decline of aura."[83] Mass movement related to a multiplicity of sites that made the unique universal, detaching the experience from its auratic encasement. This was no longer the contemplation of a unique origin but the distracted and diverted reactions of a mass audience relating to film's shock-effects. Putting a positive spin on this development, Benjamin believed that as film was an object of simultaneous collective reception, the mass could react in a more critical fashion: "The technological reproducibility of the artwork changes the relation of the masses to art. The extremely backward attitude toward a Picasso painting changes into a highly progressive reaction to a Chaplin film."[84] This progressive attitude involved pleasure and expert appraisal, one where the reactions of each individual member "regulate" and control each other in a synergy. The conclusion was that the film work finally shook off the shackles of the authority of art, liberating the audience to become critical and receptive. The impressive technology of film was ideally suited to this. Scientifically film could reveal what before went unnoticed, able to "isolate and make analyzable things which had previously floated unnoticed on the broad stream of perception."[85] This was now accomplished in optical and auditory terms by filming. By capturing the unnoticed we were, as in psychoanalysis, exploring the unconscious, the space informed by human consciousness that gave way to the space informed by the unconscious. Benjamin used the "optical unconscious" to describe this exploration of the ephemeral and unnoticed of everyday life.

With the new age there resulted an intimacy and penetration into concrete reality and a phenomenological sense of the thing-in-itself. The film experience offered a metamorphosis of perception, away from the immanent experience of the work to a cognitive attitude that led to increasing contemporary social knowledge and material involvement. The loss of aura was replaced by retrieval: "in permitting the reproduction to meet the beholder or viewer in his own particular situation, it *reactivates* the object reproduced."[86] Reactivation was the perfect way to describe dynamic upheaval from a moribund state to the reactivation that led to deepened apperception.

The nature of deepened apperception and the way it characterized film consciousness during this period is best understood through the concept of "distraction." Benjamin saw this as a widespread attitude: "Reception in distraction — the sort of reception which is increasingly noticeable in all areas of art and is a symptom of profound changes in apperception —finds in film its true training ground."[87] Benjamin believed the shock engendered by montage and unexpected juxtaposition could target the collective mass in the guise of distraction. First seen most clearly in Dadaism, Surrealism's artistic precursor, distraction was the opposite of contemplative immersion. In Dadaism it took the form of scandals that at best would outrage the public. Artworks became "missiles, jolting the viewer, taking on a tactile quality." [88] Film brought the same effect into a new technology. Early critics of film honed in on distraction as pure escapism, a diversion to avoid thinking, or mindless amusement: in other words, an excuse to categorize film as a second rate art form compared to élitist, traditional art. Benjamin found such simplifications anathema. Distraction was to be considered not as escapism but another form of perception, a positive way of reacting to the film experience. In a state of distraction there was habit and absentmindedness. Rather than hold the art-work at a distance, distraction meant absorbing it: "the distracted masses absorb the work of art into themselves."[89] Apperception, understanding new ideas in terms of previous experience, had changed because society had changed, especially through technology, "technology has subjected the human sensorium to a complex kind of training. There came a day when a new and urgent need for stimuli was met by film."[90] This again was a reference to the shock of every day life and the way film consciousness inevitably developed a symbiotic relationship to technical advances. The collective was trained to parry the shocks of the everyday by the montage construction of film. Just as authority in the traditional work of art had waned, so authority now resided with a subject who was both collective and distracted.

Benjamin believed dispersed film consciousness was connected to the inability to connect associations. In his early essay on photography, attention is drawn to fact that as the camera gets smaller it captures fleeting images "whose shock effect paralyzes the associative mechanisms in the beholder."[91] What is paralyzed is the associative train of thought with its memory links, intrinsic to the ability to form identity, both psychologically and hermeneutically, through personal narratives. Without such links viewers are literally distracted, even though they have an induced heightened attention. The absent-minded mass, "unfocused" and "incidental relating to its surroundings," display empirical consciousness, understood as consciousness which is "distracted in itself" and "unable to secure self-coherence or self-identity."[92] In other words, a marked difference both from the subject of traditional works of art, contemplative and centered, as well as the traditional, phenomenological subject, whose "transcendental unity of consciousness ... secures the thoroughgoing identity of a manifold in intuition."[93] For the most part, Benjamin saw all this as a constructive prolongation of the Surrealist project of profane illumination. Being in a state of distraction opened the possibility for the collective mass to come to terms with a totally new social condition through the edification derived from experiencing modern art forms, without any unified anchor point.

Benjamin's sanguine approach to this development is not, however, without reservation and the reason for this goes back to his antinomies, those related but dissimilar concepts and approaches that apparently cannot work in harmony together. For Benjamin, however, they are not always mutually exclusive — an either or — but become an illogical, both. Regarding experience and the aura, this emerged clearly in "On Some Motifs in Baudelaire" (1939), where Benjamin voiced consternation over the characteristics of a shock-induced consciousness that he had previously praised. These thoughts were written when Europe was already in turmoil, and had to do with a sense of history and the rise of Fascism, what Benjamin termed the aestheticization of politics; the Fascist use of rituals and spectacles to direct the masses to war.

The skewed sense of history impacted the relationship to memory that was clearly prioritized in Benjamin's explication of dialectical imagery. The phenomenon of a distracted, collective mass perturbed Benjamin as well as attracted him because disinterestedness and absent-mindedness impacted memory and remembrance. They made for an impoverished experience: "what is lost ... is the element of temporal disjunction in this experience, the intrusion of a forgotten past that disrupts the fictitious progress of chronological time."[94] On the one hand, Benjamin saw a stronger collective could erect a defensive shield against the excess stimuli of modern capitalism, where consciousness acted as a filter or screen: "The greater the shock factor in particular impressions, the more vigilant consciousness has to be in screening stimuli."[95] But this amounted to a truncated experience, or disassociation of memory "the special achievement of shock defense is the way it assigns an incident a precise point in time in consciousness, at the cost of the integrity of the incident's contents."[96] At times this presented no problem, the experience of erlebnis, traditionally closer to the individualized, intuitive experience favored by romantics, was considered appropriate to the encroaching alienation in society and found its expression in an allegorical, disruptive and fragmented mindset. But Benjamin's admiration for Proust also showed how important he considered "long" experience to be. Long experience, ehfahrung, was a richer and deeper experience where recollections stood out from time, and where past immediacy reached out to ritual and prehistory. For the collective to enact a "refiguration of experience," rather than a mere "behaviorist adaptation to the present"[97] both kinds of experience had to be dialectically drawn upon.

Returning the Gaze: Aura Transformed

Benjamin's nuanced analysis of film consciousness included notions of the look that have taken up much of modern film theory, especially the psychoanalytic. The classical lack of excess in the cinematic look had always seemed to frustrate the desire and imagination Benjamin linked to the beauty of traditional works. The original context of look exchanges related to aura as a reciprocal process: "To perceive the aura of an object we look at means to invest it with the ability to look back at us in return."[98] Here we have a look coming from the depths, unconsciously, as part of the marking of distance integral to inbuilt tradition and the urhistorical state of nature prior to individual differentiation. Again, it is Freud and the unconscious, an expression from perception experienced in an unconscious mode, a gaze that confronts us with another self, never seen before in a waking state. When experienced aura is full perceptibility, it is the fulfillment of an expectation that a look will be returned or reciprocated. The auratic object has been invested with the ability to return the look and this applies not only to the perceptual moment, but also to the past, the ability to look back corresponded to the data of mémoire involuntaire, data that has been lost to memory. Benjamin made it clear that the experience of aura rested on transposing what is a common response in human relationships, to inanimate or natural objects. There is a metamorphosis of the object into a counterpart, so a whole field of surprising correspondences between animate and inanimate nature is opened up. In this relation there is never exhaustion or completion but always something held in abeyance through the play of subjectivities. The promise is of a reactivation of looks, which are challenging and invigorating. In addition, there is also, through the other — be it person or object — an inherently unsatisfiable desire.[99] Here beauty in an artwork is what "reflects back at us that of which our eyes will never have their fill" as "what it contains that fulfils the original desire is the very same stuff on which the desire continuously feeds."[100] In the aura of the inapproachable work of art returning the gaze, there is an "investiture" of the object derivative of the spectator's originary gaze, constituting intersubjective and interpersonal exchange, and equal (inter)dependence. There is an incessant lock between the inorganic and organic gazes that cannot be ruptured, one that retrieves the beautiful "out of the depths of time."[101]

In film theory part of this discussion has been couched in terms of suturing the spectator into the dynamic of film looks, by co-opting those looks and perspectival positions according to an unfolding narrative. The result is a certain closure and fulfillment. Being sutured into a film is not the conscious decision of the viewer but the result of the imaginary production of returned gazes that play upon subject position. This offsets the threat spectators feel from off-screen looks that disturb their sense of control:

> What annuls the threat is the system of shot/reverse shot, by which a second shot shows the first to have been the field of vision of a character within the fiction. In this way the Absent One turns out to be a particular character whose point of view is disclosed ... the system of shot/reverse shot sutures the rupture ... and envelops cinematic discourse within the imaginary.[102]

Off-screen space involves anxiety that is only allayed by the reverse shot structure responding to the absence invoked by the empty space. The off-screen character denoted as the absent one, "sutures" the spectator back into imaginary satisfaction. Once sutured, the reverse shot, by which the second shot shows the first to have been the character's field of vision, no longer remains outside the system. It is incorporated into it. The threatening "absent other" is re-appropriated within the film work, and cinematic discourse is reinserted into the fullness of the imaginary. As such, this closed circuitry accords to a sense of self-reliance that would sustain Benjamin's remarks on the inherent fulfillment derived from mechanical works of art, an ability to sate desire and contain the gaze. To an extent, Benjamin's comments on the film gaze turned out to be the bedrock upon which film signification occurred. Film is able to contain and exhaust its own gazes through suture. Excess is delimited and the gaze of the absent one is recouped into an overriding configuration. However, just as aura needs to be modified in terms of mechanical reproduction, so suture must be adapted to the self-reflexive and open-ended film. On one level, suturing the gaze has the same enclosed interplay that traditional aura had. It relates the story on its own premises and locks the beholder into its realm as in traditional aura. It also plays the game of veiling and disclosure, releasing what is pertinent to the narrative and hermeneutically sealing what needs to be interpreted. The historical development of story through diegesis places and displaces the spectator under its own ruling authority. Nevertheless, with the release of aura through technological reproduction such traditional authority is lost. Especially in modern, reflexive film, without suture the spectator is multi positioned and let loose, bereft of the compensatory, satisfying return of the gaze. The circuitry of gazes is intentionally broken. This initial phase compares to the bombardment experienced by the collective from contemporary shock effects, as experience becomes "erlebnis" and the richness of tradition and contemplation dissipates. Yet, when film does become reflexive another kind of auratic depth penetrates beyond surface appeal and imaginary fulfillment. Some films do this by drawing attention to the conciliatory acts of suture and exposing discursive processes, bringing them into relief. Here, suture describes the inclusion and closure of the spectator's look but also, self-consciously, the possibility for its frustration. The play of complete-incomplete itself becomes a motif, just as it has always been a function of representation:

> Completeness ... is ... only apparent: the image is never complete in itself....
> The realization of the cinema as discourse is the production at every
> moment through the film of a subject address, the specification of the play
> of incompleteness-completion.[103]

If aura is to be retained in the film experience, it must play upon this important oscillation between proximity and distance, a distance that can be maintained both in the seamless editing of the sutured gaze and its reflexive counterpoint. The lack of fulfillment, rather than being sated by the image or experience of catharsis, maintains tensions and momentum. The network of associations, which cloaked and veiled the object retaining its beauty in distance, can be characterized through film consciousness in both cognitive and visceral terms through heteropathic identification. In film consciousness, heteropathic identification is maximized by strategies that consciously remind the spectator of his/her own productive capabilities. The spectator's love for the ideal-ego is frustrated by its absorption back into the spectator. Just as fragmentation and juxtaposition are key tools for a montage of attraction, so heteropathic identification suggests personal fragmentation and reorientation, frustrating the effort towards a coherent ego, and the falling back into passivity and complacence. Auratic distance can be sustained by affirming alterity through empathetic marking, maintaining the representational frame, "insisting upon particularity over and against standardization," and generally frustrating all parts of the film system that offer a comforting "belong-to-me quality."[104] The immediately auratic attraction of film illuminates the screen with images which "pulsate" and "dazzle" suggesting a strong affinity not with catharsis but with the traditional aura at a distance. When distance is retained, the fourth wall reinforced, and difference sustained, film consciousness becomes a force to question norms rather than accept them. Whereas in mainstream films, film suture and aura secure the narrative circuitry, the suture of alterity and the transformed aura of technology, on the contrary, demystify while still creating a fissure for mémoire involuntaire to surface, in other words an integration of both Erlebnis and Erfahrung.

Within this scenario other personal and social coalitions can emerge, drawn together by a unique consciousness that encourages active curiosity and the ability to question. In the age of mechanical reproduction the camera gave the masses a "face," a reproduction that brought the mass "face to face" with themselves. But in eyes that look at us with a mirror like blankness "a very different kind of aura emerged: that of a singularity that is no longer unique, no longer the other of reproduction and representation but their most intimate *effect*."[105] The theoretical implication is that aura has a variability that constitutes its inherent, fundamental split. Aura has not been destroyed by dispersion but has a durability and dynamic informing reproduction. There is something intrinsic to aura that brings about its fluctuation, as a rift:

> For aura has a paradoxical duality not only in the relationship of the original to the reproduction but also in its own relationship to itself. In other words, aura is always already split: it is both excess and necessity; necessity as a lingering core which characterizes the original; excess as an evanescent, fleeting, unfixable, uncontainable "other" which returns in reproduction and which in its turn is fixed, only to be split again with the advent of a new technology.[106]

Films that encourage heteropathic viewing play upon the process of disturbing identification. Like Benjamin's allegorical rejection of traditional narrative, they are capable of breaking the ideological backbone that impacts social structure and symbolic systems. The correlation of signifier and signified can be disrupted, the unified form and content of the organic artwork fractured to create an-other realism. In this way, auratic distance and impenetrability survive as the effect of a mature state of film consciousness. Benjamin sets the stage for this in the dream factory of film. Akin to the ceremony, the aura-effect of film consciousness first takes root in the emotions and the dream state. From Proust, "the only reality that is valid for the individual, namely, the world of his emotions," to Valery, "here I see such and such an object does not establish an equation between me and the object.... In dreams, however, there is an equation."[107]

As film consciousness took shape for Benjamin it no longer became the continuum engendered by tradition, but an event. This is where the dialectical image, of momentary appearance, fugitive, and fleeting, was related to film consciousness. These flashes appeared like a field of energy generated between two opposing poles. The poles were their embedded setting and condition, yet the energy process produced was tantalizingly brief and incapable of prediction. Its expression in film consciousness was as a self-constituting event, not produced by the media but events that *were* the media, happening "in places that are literally inter-mediary, in the interstices of a process of reproduction and of recording."[108] Benjamin saw film's revelatory capabilities were productively experienced as a posthumous after-shock rather than as a dependence on originary moments. The imagery of the dialectic presided over phenomenological, primary production. In the modern context, Benjamin saw the nature of the mediauratic event to be ephemeral, something that exceeded denotation and signification. Filming was to have a privileged role and share in the antipathy to rationalization that Benjamin explored in his Baudelaire essay. Reason had no privileged access to nature.

Within a Husserlian lifeworld comprising the incalculable accumulation of everyday events and situations as expressed in human praxis, objects, in their givenness, come to appearance by shattering their traditional, esoteric, auratic shell. What is striking is that this observation is equally applicable to film in its trajectory from a realist filming to an expressive art form. Filming suffers a comparable fate, from its original, almost pristine moment of capture through spatio-temporal embodiment. It differentiates itself from nascent duplication to the various disseminated forms that simulated imagery adopts, but without shaking off its auratic background, the shadowy echo origin of its historical encrustation. Benjamin brought together the equipment-free aspect of reality, film's heightened artifice, and the inapproachability and distance of aura on several levels of synthesis. From the fluctuating mystique that carried over to the transformed aura of technology, there was a forward looking narrative rather than an archaic search for origin associated with the similar. This impetus, where the telos of fulfillment vies with the resonance of origin, was not to be identified with organic narrative or closure in any sense of the word. Rather, it was the result of an expression in language that was directly experiential, directly connected to film language and the lifeworld: "The smashing of the aura suggests not the loss but the shock of profane illumination, that is, the revealing of heretofore hidden, profound correspondences in the world. Arguably the aura is not lost in its destruction but transcended."[109]

Ultimately, aura must survive in the age of technical media and deal with the mundane, in the sense of both the ordinary and the worldly. For profane illumination to be effectuated, film consciousness found allies in the materialistic and the anthropological, but also the mysterious. Just as the historical, dialectical image was to be read, or unraveled, by the materialist histiographer as a multi perspectival monad, so film imagery had to be recognized as having the multidimensional quality of aura combined with the immediacy of the moment. This was only possible, however, in the mature film consciousness of the time-image. Filming had to, firstly, in its embedded sense, pierce or penetrate the lifeworld through its demiurgical eye in a way that transcended human capability. Secondly, as pure apparatus, it suspended meaning and fractured the self. As Benjamin described it, to preserve the clinical act of penetration, and rely on instrumentation, there had to be an effacing, a literal turning away, "the surgeon abstains at the decisive moment from confronting his patient person to person...."[110] Were this to take place only through the movement-image, perceptual necessity, narrative wholeness and object modulation would be retained. But for Benjamin, to remain faithful to the immobilization of time in the spatial image, aura, in the form of the data of mémoire involuntaire, must emerge in a medium in which time, intrinsic to film, comes to a standstill. For this to happen, it cannot be within the movement-image, but must be within the time-image, where time is not immobilized but reconfigured, from indivisible moments to the simultaneity of points of the presents, from the indirect image of time to the coexistence of sheets of the past in a world memory. It is only through such a coexistence of temporal dimensions that Benjamin's non-progressive notion of historical unfolding can be expressed. As Benjamin put it in "On the Concept of History," the material histiographer admits messianic time into the present as a constellation, "he establishes a conception of the present as now-time shot through with splinters of messianic time."[111] The aura that belonged to the ubiquitous image had to carry this through even in technological reproduction;

it had to release the latency of the past, by making the future of the past relevant. In eyes that return the gaze, the messianic cessation of happening, or
the rift in time, dislocated temporal flow and emptied the future of fulfillment,
in order for it to be positively reassembled in the ultimate montage.

Benjamin and Surrealism

Surrealism served the ideal purpose of collecting the various strains in
Benjamin's thought and gave vent to them through an art form that was both
radical and political. The surrealist movement combined extreme aestheticism, which looked at the self-referential dimension of art works — the means
of their own artistic production — with the politicization of the same art form.
Surrealism was a strong reaction against bourgeois art, its institutionalization,
and all the concomitant philosophical rationality that went with it. There was
instead to be a fusion of art and life. Indeed, Surrealism took to the streets
by using everyday objects and situations as grist to its expressive mill. The
creative tension between the autonomy of art and the surrealist reappraisal of
that autonomy proved irresistible to Benjamin. Around and within the movement, Benjamin detected the same themes he had pursued and often criticized throughout his analysis of Marxism, the traditional work of art, and
early Romantic criticism. Many aspects of the surrealist movement acted as
counterpoints to traditional art theory and offered the hope of serving as a
conduit for the social upheaval Benjamin hoped for. In similar fashion to the
fragmentation of allegorical form, Surrealism attempted to deconstruct and
penetrate beyond the notion of a coherent totality of the artwork. Above all,
it looked at the mythic forces and ideology that enshrouded modern society
and offered strategies for demystification. Its relevance for film consciousness
emerged both from its influence over the means of expressing technical reproduction, as well as its repositioning of subjectivity.

Surrealism's phenomenology placed the subject within a subject-object
correlate rather than ensconcing it within a positing, transcendental ego. By
using bits of reality, fragments of society and parts of nature, the surrealist
called attention to the artificiality of the work and its own construction. In
the process it reduced society to nature: "The Surrealist self seeks to recover
pristine experience by positing as natural the world man has created."[112]
Society was seen as a ready given state of nature, where the surrealist "moves
as primitives do in real nature: searching for a meaning...."[113] Unlike the
symbol and similar to the allegory, meaning does not lie beyond but is immanent and to discover this, the inorganic work comes into its own. The procedure for accomplishing this was montage, "the fundamental principle of

avant-gardiste art."[114] Montage was used in many different art forms but the surrealist intent was to draw attention to the arbitrariness of material objects and to the fact that their meaning was contingent on context and relation. The intent was that through juxtaposition and surprising combinations objects would speak for themselves or become revelatory in a way that does not occur in everyday, taken-for-granted social life. Both history and popular culture could be scavenged for facts. Objects could be removed from their natural context and given a second breath of life after they had faded into obscurity, or passed by unnoticed on the capitalist conveyor belt. It was somehow expected that surrealist montage would let images speak for themselves, even with the strong construction process involved in finding material in the first place and its subsequent repositioning. Surrealists attempted to overcome preconceived messages with an array of ideas and techniques to promote spontaneity, including pure chance and automatic writing. The mindset they set out to promote was akin to dreaming and intoxication. At best, there was a conviction that the ultimate product, though a constructed one, could bring about results through the tension inherent in the relationship between fragments. For Eisenstein, the result was to be new thought patterns, and for Benjamin, new interpretations of material culture.

"Dreamkitsch," Benjamin's early, 1925 text on Surrealism, first suggested its potential power to be a liberating influence over the "compulsions of mythic forces."[115] It was significant for pointing out the importance of dreams, which Benjamin saw as being related not only to the psyche of individuals but in general to historical experience: "Dreaming has a share in history ... dreams have started wars, and wars, from the very earliest times, have determined the propriety and impropriety — indeed, the range — of dreams."[116] Just as Deleuze is troubled by the empty clichés of habit, so Benjamin saw outmoded objects and modes of behavior in society "worn through by habit and patched with cheap maxims."[117] It is this that dreams pick up on in the form of kitsch, dreams have become the shortcut to banality. The psychoanalytic model of "surface delusion and hidden significance," uses the rebus' dream pictures and puzzles as a model, "to decipher the contours of the banal."[118] Dreams pointed to everyday banality and to its drift, with kitsch the quintessence of that banality. The interrelationship of dreams and the waking world was pivotal since, in a remarkable turnaround, our waking state turned out to be the unconscious realm of involuntary projections. There was a conviction that the artifacts of capitalist culture, conscious products of a rational system, could be deconstructed to reveal that they were in fact unconscious, dream-like projections.

The Surrealists were most concerned with the manifestations of the psyche rather than the latter's own working. Benjamin observed that "picture puzzles, as schemata of the dreamwork, were long ago discovered by psycho-analysis. The Surrealists, with similar conviction, are less on the trial of the psyche than on the track of things."[119] The artistic endeavor in "the track of things" was directed to overturn the experience and perception of traditional works of art and replace it with experiences that were close, intimate and all consuming. This is also the experience of film and mechanical reproduction that Benjamin analyzed in his later essays: "What we used to call art begins at a distance.... But now, in kitsch, the world of things advances on the human being; ... and ultimately fashions its figures in his interior."[120] We come to see the banal as revelatory since it is the fodder of every day conversations and transactions as well as dreams.

The Surrealist film movement differentiated itself from the Avant-Garde, in fact, in principle it was opposed to many of the latter's tenets. In French silent cinema Impressionist cinema was the dominant film movement of the time. With Epstein, L'Herbier and Delluc at its helm, Impressionist cinema was "pure cinema," prizing the "autonomy of the visual language of cinema" and its formalism.[121] But for the surrealists, the vanguard of impressionists was reactionary, overly subjective, and clung to the tradition of psychologi-cal drama, though not averse to depicting "disturbed states of subjectivity, such as madness or nightmare."[122] Politically, there was a rift between the more conservative, even authoritarian convictions of the impressionists and the outright revolutionary declarations of Breton. As for Dada, there was cer-tainly an overlap between it and Surrealism, with artists such as Man Ray, contributing to both. Dada had the same goal of disturbing the spectator, debunking accepted norms and defamiliarizing the ordinary. Both movements readily dissected the human body "cutting it into fragments" and "dissolving it into fluidity."[123] The general thrust of Dada films, however, was to use more abstract imagery than the socially recognizable ones of Surrealism. It also looked in a self-reflexive way at the art form itself, an over-indulgent approach for the surrealists. It failed to enliven the every day with every day images or relate these images to the dream work. Surrealist film set out to penetrate surfaces to encapsulate moments of shocking in-sights in the phys-ical and sensual universe. It allowed for a superimposition of dreams and everyday reality, suturing it into a seamless visual experience.[124]

In the 1929 essay on Surrealism, we find support for the early years of the movement "as an inspiring dream wave," where "life seemed worth liv-ing only where the threshold between waking and sleeping was worn away" and where the dream state "loosens the self" by intoxication.[125] Dreams were taken to be the harbor and sanctuary of utopian visions, which were frus-trated by the ideology and false consciousness of contemporary life. The absurdities many irrational thinkers pursued to promote the promise of the not-yet thought may have seemed far-fetched in "civilized" society, but they were an accepted part of the dream world. In the consciousness engendered by the surrealist approach there were elements of intoxication and escape through dream or drugs, but they were in no way intended to be associated with avoiding reality. For Benjamin, they had practical application, on one level, a turning away from a preoccupation with the ego, and, on another, as an exemplary template to experience profane illumination, one which had a "materialistic, anthropological inspiration."[126]

The question posed was just how revolutionary this consciousness could be. Deleuze saw in film consciousness a fundamental shift in our experience of space and time within the movement-image, but it was to take the more radical time-image to shake the foundation of thought into genuine change. Likewise, Benjamin saw the surrealist application of the fusion of Freudian psychoanalysis and Marxist materialism to everyday behavior as being a major and genuinely revolutionary contribution to desired change. But for it to res-onate through consciousness, the wishes of the collective had to become a political reality: there was a need for "transfiguring the immaturity of the social product" and overcoming "the inadequacies in the social organization of production."[127] There had to be significant political expression, and, at the very least, an acceptance by the surrealists of the need for profound change to both individual and collective alike. This was no easy task since the surrealist movement itself was quite small and turned out in the end to be short-lived.

It was not only the potentially potent, theoretical foundation of the movement that attracted Benjamin. Film in general was a new art form and as-yet "had not been 'putrefied' under layers of tradition and aesthetic pre-tension."[128] In the early years of film, surrealists saw what mainstream films there were more as an ally than adversary, in that they bore none of the pre-tensions of the avant-garde. Films were a "perfect anti-culture" phenomenon and already the appeal to the mass rather than the bourgeois individual was evident. Using poetry and analogy, the intention was to break through the rational order of Capitalism and taken-for-granted complacency of bourgeois individualism. Film's proximity to the lifeworld and to found objects, com-bined with Benjamin's co-opting of the psychic topography, evoked what Breton saw as the natural ambiguity of film "where all events — the dream as much as the document — can be presented as equally real."[129] As Brunius put it describing the impact of film on both subjectivity and objectivity:

[T]he film enjoys incomparable facility for passing over the bridge in both directions, thanks to the extraordinary and surreptitious solidity that it con-tributes to the creations of the mind, objectifying them in the most con-vincing manner, while it makes exterior reality submit in the opposite direction to subjectivization.[130]

Breton referred to an absolute reality or "surreality," describing it as the resolution of the two apparently contradictory states of dream and waking life, eased by the flow of film images and editing which presented them equally in indiscernible verisimilitude. In this resolution, desire was paramount, incorporating affectivity and understanding through "figured analogies" in an attempt to transcend traces of dualism of subjectivity and objectivity, or thinking and feeling.[131] As an activity of artistic response, early film spectatorship was set up as a parallel experience to Benjamin's fringe, city dwellers — a dynamic, peripatetic form of spectatorship made for an equally "anarchic medium."[132] Before Breton's founding Manifesto in 1924, there already existed a prototype surrealist spectator:

> A decade before there was Surrealist cinema, there was Surrealist spectatorship: Breton and his friend Jacques Vaché used to wander from one picture-house to another, buying tickets without even consulting the program, entering and leaving on a whim — relishing the visual collage thus put together in their heads as if it were a single film.... At once passive and voluntarist, the Surrealist as spectator put himself in the same state of lyrical availability in front of the screen as when, as flâneur, he walked though the crowded metropolis awaiting the solicitations of chance....[133]

The reference to the flâneur was appropriate. Benjamin's flâneur, the bourgeois man-about-town, walked the city streets to read its signs. A displaced intellectual, he was at home in crowds or department stores, observing all manner of social expression and empathizing with those market commodities that bore the mark of desire. For Benjamin: "The definition of flânerie as a state of intoxication is fully developed, together with its links to Baudelaire's drug experience,"[134] as a condition of experiencing the city intoxicated, equivalent to the "staccato projection rhythms" of early, silent film with their "hypnogogic piano accompaniment."[135] Benjamin's flâneur roamed the labyrinth of commodities as he had roamed through the crowded labyrinth of the city, displaying the same curiosity and empathy, the same intoxication lauded as a part of dreaming, the surrealist condition for encouraging profane illumination.

The revolt implied by intoxication and ecstasy was genuine, but there had to be political commitment to overturn existing conditions. The means to accomplish this was not through more extreme experiment or creating public scandals but by looking at everyday life, "no face is more Surrealistic to the same degree as the true face of the city."[136] Recognition of the mysteries of life was well and good, but we "penetrate the mystery only to the degree that we recognize it in the everyday world, by virtue of the dialectical optic that perceives the everyday as impenetrable, the impenetrable as everyday."[137]

The banal may have been dull and ordinary but this was not to overshadow the fact that it provided the surreal with much that could be deciphered. Ultimately, the unconditioned truth Benjamin sought in the idea could only be aspired to if the reassembling of banality was treated as seriously as the constellations of dialectical images. Here, Benjamin's optical unconscious, as discerned through the camera, related to the desiring unconscious of the spectator. It was most clearly expressed through an affinity with the close-up of what was already in existence. The mere passage through the lens tangibly changed the world.

The film work could visualize the surreal impetus to disclose the customs and rituals that encompassed material phenomena, yet without, Benjamin insisted, escaping the pragmatics of daily life. Benjamin's phenomenological leanings rejected moves away from the independence of phenomenal being and insisted on an ethnomethodological immersion in the concrete particularity of the everyday, as evidenced by the Arcades Project. Benjamin was a sensitive micrologist who saw possibilities for utilizing montage and shock-effect as a way of remaining faithful to its subject matter. For Benjamin, assemblage and juxtaposition of imagery were not designed to help reach a transcendent truth but rather elicit a fidelity to being-in-itself. By resting in the moment, the nunc stans of history, we come to experience the pristine quality of the created world. The transformed aura of technology brought out the exoteric rather than the esoteric and Surrealism helped uncover the most concrete qualities of the epoch. Shock effect was intended to directly impact the influence of commodification and defetishize objects, proving in the process that the rationalized capitalist world was no natural phenomenon but just as irrational as any extreme surrealist image could be.

The surrealist impact was related to the power of imagination, bringing opposites together, a playing off of the actual and the possible, or the real and the surreal. In phenomenological terms, this was based on the immanence of singularities, on the "showing" of the transcendental, and a demand for absolute presence. Surrealist film offered the chance to occupy multiple positions, ultimate variations on the real world through concrete singularity: "We have no direct access to the amazing world of singulars except through some sort of show, in life or in movies."[138] With the world of film visualizing singularity without recourse to concepts, we intuit visible singulars in a purer form than concrete reality. Defamiliarization and the aesthetic become relevant to situation and emotively specific, showing the way we experience objects as they are configured affectively. The immanent power of discrete objects became fully present through film's filter, disrupting the hold of personal agenda, "not seeing the optical data through which we see the world ... but seeing the singular itself in all its beautiful nudity."[139] This made film consciousness multi-perspectival, embracing a wider configuration of the real and the possible than any immediate, personal intentionality could produce. In the process it undercut rational pretensions by exposing the nerve of mass hallucination based on the control of desire and the perpetual deferral of its satisfaction.

Surrealism could fulfill its goal if it brought about similar effects to those of intoxication. To do so would fire imagination and rejuvenate perception, but specifically in those ways Benjamin related to constellations: the grouping of experiences that conflate the past and present through processes of mimesis or similarity. The constellation marked a cornerstone of Benjamin's thoughts, literally "a group of stars each with a particular point in time and space," they have then to be recognized and configured by the viewer into a gestalt pattern.[140] For Benjamin the emergent quality of truth as something that manifests and disappears fits this relational patterning: "Every idea is a sun and is related to other ideas just as suns are related to each other. The harmonious relationship between such essences is what constitutes truth."[141] As truth emerges from the constellation it can infuse the viewer or just as easily withdraw as the constellation is refigured, or as perspectives change. Truth is "bodied forth in the dance of represented ideas,"[142] it is contingent and relational, it cannot be appropriated in the same way as data or knowledge and is, therefore, elusive.

Imagination has an intimate relation to the past, but for Benjamin it was a process that demanded concrete materialization not mere intellectual abstraction. What Benjamin suggested with regards to Surrealism was precisely its ability to evoke, or set in action, Bergson's independent, or image memory, the memory of image space, rather than automatic memory. Automatic memory is linked to motor activity, habit and pragmatic action. Whereas image memory is the past that may not be immediately practical but which, nonetheless, holds the key to change; for Benjamin the prerequisite for successful surrealist expression. As soon as normal perception is interrupted, or experienced in a different way "this memory merely awaits the occurrence of a rift between the actual impression and its corresponding movement to slip in its images."[143] Such memories which are "slipped in" through the mimetic faculty and correspondences cause dislocation but also rejuvenation.

Referring to Baudelaire's writing, Benjamin described the medium of memory as dense, so that the sensory data that emanate seem "to have arisen not from this life at all but from some spacious 'vie anterieure.' It is this prior existence that is intimated by the 'familiar eyes' with which such experiences scrutinize the one who has them."[144] This pre-established center of vision, similar to Bergson's description of memory, is something that does not exist within us but which we inhabit, and looks at us to deliver an already developed photograph:

By what happy chance could we just hit upon on a growing number of intercalary recollections? The work of localization consists, in reality, in a growing effort of expansion, by which the memory, *always present in its entirety to itself,* spreads out its recollections over an ever wider surface and so ends by distinguishing ... the remembrance which could not find its proper place.[145]

For Benjamin, Surrealism could effectuate change if it pursued the correlation between the dream world and contemporary life, by exploring the mechanics of dreams and thus the mechanics of desire in society. It should do this, not by pursuing the abstract for its own sake but rather by utilizing a focused form of narrative discourse with recognizable material. It had also to incorporate Bergson's luminosity in the density of memory within the individual psyche and the collective consciousness. This would work through delving rays of attention within liminal areas, where the individual melds into the collective and the mind projects outwards into the explorable life-world. This meant utilizing the play of looks and gazes that film consciousness is most at home with: "We are both looker and looked-at, explorer and explored. And if the screen is a mirror to our look, it is one which can only reflect the unreflectable, for it is mirror turned threshold, and it is through this threshold that inner and outer realities collide and contradiction destroyed."[146]

Benjamin included in the ambit of film styles that supported his critical attention several additions to Surrealism, including comedy and animation, especially the characters of Disney. Benjamin saw Mickey Mouse as a direct creation of collective dreams, one that assumed utopian significance.[147] These films were directly related to the "psychotic" tendencies technology introduced in the masses at large. Benjamin believed they could serve as a therapeutic balm to the psychoses brought about by industrial and military technology. The early films of "Mickey Mouse" drew direct attention to the fragmentation and disassociation that was linked to industrialization, in particular, regarding body and subjectivity. The characteristic of animated creatures, in general, is one of hybrid, the "blurring of human and animal, two-dimensional and three-dimensional, corporeal and neuro-energetic qualities."[148] The dislocation and morphing quality of the characters paralleled Benjamin's reference to the historical experience of mutilation and fragmentation in technological warfare and industrial production. In his fragment, "Mickey Mouse" (1931) Benjamin admitted:

[F]or the first time it is possible to have one's own arm, even one's own body, stolen ... a creature can still survive even when it has thrown off all resemblance to a human being. He (Mickey Mouse) disrupts the entire hierarchy of creatures that is supposed to culminate in mankind.[149]

Depictions of bodies in parts, dislocations and transmutations, were not merely physical violations of the human shape, but they also addressed the way mankind had fantasized the projection of its psychosocial body in the form of prosthetic body armor.[150] As Benjamin pointed out, through technical media, a healing escape from contemporary psychosis presented itself: "[T]echnologization has created the possibility of psychic immunization against ... mass psychosis ... American slapstick comedies and Disney films trigger a therapeutic release of unconscious energies."[151] Collective reception was a possible antidote to self-alienation if it worked with a film experience that was modeled on reflected shock experience. Even laughter was both a physical and mental reaction, one that could infectiously spread through the collective audience. There was a process of:

> [T]ransference by which individual alienation can leap into collective, public recognition. Such transference is brought about by a series of staged shocks or, if you will, counter shocks.... In the stimulation of involuntary and collective laughter, the Mickey Mouse films affect their viewers in a manner at once physiological and cognitive.[152]

Benjamin saw the rebellious potential in a cartoon figure could surrealistically achieve its ends against overwhelming odds: "where everything is solved in the simplest and most comfortable way, in which a car is no heavier than a straw hat and the fruit on the tree becomes round as quickly as a hot-air balloon."[153] This malleable, labile imagery transcended notions of immutable substance by visually disintegrating borders. Using humor, parody, and irreverence for authority, the stakes for mankind were high: "In these films, mankind makes preparations to survive civilization."[154] Benjamin suggested it was the laughter from animation and in-sight through bizarre, surreal images that acted, not only as a safety valve, but also a powerful debunking force against the oppression of society. Disney characters blurred the boundaries between the human and the animal, the real and the surreal. Technology and technical media raised questions concerning the concepts of what was natural and non-natural, perceivable and perceptible, acceptable and representational. This resulted in a reappraisal of their defining qualities and a fracturing of their delineating boundaries. In this way, they could serve as a reminder of humankind's deficiencies but equally argue for a liberated film consciousness to advantageously probe and discover the world in an original, and potentially rejuvenated way.

Distraction and Innervation

Benjamin's view of the collective and its relationship to film consciousness was inexorably connected to his interpretation of technology, or "technik," both in the sense of technique and technology. Technology had always been at the cusp of mankind and nature, or the cosmos. Already in the 1920s Benjamin differentiated between the potentially harmful use of technology as a tool of mastery of everything under heaven and earth and its liberating potential. Its most telling negative expression emerged after a World War that raped, pillaged and desensitized Mother Earth and its people, where "multitudes, gases, electrical forces were hurled into the open country ... new constellations rose in the sky ... aerial space and ocean depths thundered with propellers, and everywhere sacrificial shafts were dug in Mother Earth."[155] All this was carried out in the name of militarization in the spirit of technology. But such instrumental misuse was more due to the lust for profits in a capitalist society than to anything inherent in technology. Benjamin felt that putting technology in its rightful place meant considering it not as mastery over nature but rather in terms of the relation *between* nature and man, as "interplay between nature and humanity."[156] Technology was changing the face of reality and in the process created a space for a new relationship with nature and the cosmos. This involved relating it to the collective place, or image-space, and exploring new ways of seeing, feeling, and framing time into new velocities. It involved a new physis — the new body for collectivity that was beginning to flex its muscles.

The relationship between mankind, nature and the cosmos had changed substantially since antiquity. At one time it was ecstatic and collective, "man can be in ecstatic contact with the cosmos only communally"[157] while in modern times it had become individual, poetic and "detached."[158] War, however, had reintroduced the antiquity notion of the collective approach, but its communing with the cosmos was "a *perverted* attempt to reenact the ancient ecstasies of cosmic experience."[159] Rather than drop control over nature in favor of imbibing its majesty it reinforced its ideal of mastery and control, albeit in a new guise. All artistic gratification through sense perception had been irrevocably altered by technology. Due to technology, humankind's "self-alienation has reached the point where it can experience its own annihilation as a supreme aesthetic pleasure."[160] In this connection, Fascism seemed to accord an expressive freedom to the masses, but it was an empty, impotent freedom. Property and social rights remained out of proletarian hands. The freedom of expression allowed to the collective was termed, an aesthetic freedom, it was overtly noticeable, or exhibited, but lay beyond the reach of social change, corresponding to an art for art's sake that institutionalized art at a distance from political activism. For Benjamin, modern conditions promoted such an impoverishment of experience that there was a need not merely to open one's eyes or renew acquaintance with tradition and remembrance, but to restore the very ability to perceive at all. In seeing so much, or being bombarded by stimulation, eyes ended up seeing nothing at all.

Benjamin saw that the technology of industrialization and urbanization wielded a double-edged sword. Consciousness protected itself by shutting off from being over stimulated, and isolated present consciousness from past memory. It engendered a perverse relish in participating in spectacles, which in the age of Fascism was expressed through rallies, parades and warlike preparation. The response to the threat of instrumental power was to project the body collective into a fantasized, mobile stronghold that epitomized what Benjamin meant by self-alienation:

> In the great mirror of technology, the image that returns is displaced, reflected onto a different plane, where one sees oneself as a physical body divorced from sensory vulnerability — a statistical body; the behavior of which can be calculated, a performing body; actions of which can be measured up against the "norm"; a virtual body, one that can endure the shocks of modernity without pain.[161]

Once inured against the threats from outside, the collective body could enjoy images of its own mass movement with disinterested pleasure. The implication of this phenomenon, however, was that technology posed a threat to mankind's synaesthetic system, the expansive processes of perception also described by Bergson and Deleuze. The synaesthetic system is indicative of extended subjectivity, a circuitry where the decentered subject communes with forces greater than any individual, a process that takes place psychologically as well as physiologically:

> The nervous system is not contained within the body's limits. The circuit from sense perception to motor response begins and ends in the world. The brain is thus not an isolable anatomical body, but part of a system that passes through the person and her or his (culturally specific, historically transient) environment.[162]

One of the overall effects of technology was seen to be a paring down of experience, its devaluation where the "synaesthetic system is marshaled to parry technological stimuli"[163] and where, in its worst manifestation:

> [T]he cognitive system of synaesthetics became one of *an*aesthetics ... the motor responses of switching, snapping, the jolt in movement of a machine have their psychic counterpart in the "sectioning of time" into a sequence of repetitive movements without development. The effect on the synaesthetic system is brutalizing.[164]

In order for humanity to "return to its senses," in every sense, Benjamin looked to film consciousness to undo the fundamental alienation the corporeal sensorium experienced in late capitalism. There was a need to restore the mimetic faculty and the free flow of innervation to rekindle future revolutionary praxis. Benjamin's notion of innervation, also related to synaesthesia, had roots in Freudian psychoanalysis. As it carried over to the surrealist movement, its relevance for film consciousness was undeniable, "innervation referred to a neurological process that mediates between internal and external, psychic and motoric, human and mechanical registers." Physiologically it defined the transmission "generally in an efferent direction, of energy along a nerve-pathway."[165] For Benjamin, the wide circuitry of innervation — activities between mind and reciprocated bodily expression "vitalized the will"[166] and supported pictorial imagination, as evidenced by Surrealism. There was a strong sense here of implication, associated with Leibnitz:

> The faculty of imagination is the gift of interpolating into the infinitely small, of inventing, for every intensity, an extensiveness to contain its new, compressed fullness — in short of receiving each image as if it were that of the folded fan, which only in spreading draws breath and flourishes, in its new expanse, the beloved features within.[167]

As with innervation, imagination and implication, the represented world and perceiver are encompassed within the all-pervasive monad:

> The world exists only in its representatives as long as they are included in each monad.... It is as if the depths of every monad were made from an infinity of tiny folds (inflections) endlessly furling and unfurling in every direction.... Microperceptions or representatives of the world are these little folds that unravel in every direction....[168]

The fold, as a fan, spreads out spatially into places that exponentially take on significance and temporally activate experiences of the past in the present. Film consciousness was thought to produce the requisite heightened awareness that pierced the structures of common sense, releasing connections, propelling disjunctions and short-circuits in the mind to break through the fence encircling present residence. Breaking through this fence meant, for Benjamin, the disruption of everything that smacked of stasis or origin. Even the phenomenological filming of the lifeworld was couched in terms of detaching the reproduced object from the sphere of tradition rather than nature. The positive form of film was emphasized as being "inconceivable without its destructive, cathartic side."[169] In terms of innervation, perception and reception, there was a circuitry composed of elements that relied on each other to manifest a constellation and help make sense of its contours. Film's shock effects worked because they replaced traditional art forms by giving the collective heightened attention, breaking individual associations for those associations created by montage. Breaking associations yet still having enough control to be productively creative was central to Benjamin's notion of distraction, to sustain the reoccurring process of breakdown and assemblage, "distraction and destruction as the subjective and objective sides, respectively, of one and the same process."[170]

Distraction, or zerstreuung, variously came to include dispersion and entertainment in the pantheon of Benjamin terminology. In essence, it was a form of reception in distraction. The meaning that needed to be supported in all its versions was one that overcame jejune notions of non-thinking and escape, in favor of active participation. For example, comparing the distracted act to the improvisation of jazz musicians, Eiland describes it as both an individual and collaborative affair:

> The musician must have at his disposal a set of (variable) moves, to paraphrase Benjamin, in order to perform his task, which involves equal measures of spontaneity and knowledge, or receptivity and productivity. The deflection of attention here is manifold and concentrated, for the player is both carried away and in control. [171]

The suggestion was to come to grips with technology, working with it and through it, but not under its control. The leverage exerted on technology produced film consciousness in its most productive form, where the mass-in-movement as "producers ... continually disperse any singular symbolic meanings."[172] Dislodging symbolic meaning and unity in favor of plurality, instability and disjunction are traits, once again, of the allegorist pursuit. This was to be carried out by a joint member of a group who in reciprocity was part of mass reception. The motor that generated distraction was allegorically inspired montage, which in its ability to shock and jolt underpinned distraction as a physiological process. Benjamin noted that "distraction, like catharsis, should be conceived as a physiological phenomenon."[173] The distracted, in the sense of absent-minded mindset was, therefore, transformed by Benjamin into a state similar to the intoxication of the gambler or the fanatical collector, a state of heightened rather than numbed apperception, a state of involvement rather than absence, one that involved physiologically the whole sensorium, through touch, behavior and interaction.

Benjamin spelled out in an unequivocal way the fusing of human and machine consciousness in a note to his artwork essay. Here the intimacy between the collective and technology was unmistakable. The historically unique collective now had "its organs in the new technology."[174] Technology, with a "mind" of its own, as an interpenetrated consciousness, "asserts its claims vis-à-vis society" and "aims at liberating human beings." This sanguine view was in distinction to the effects of "first technology" based on domination and individualism. With contemporary "second" technology that included film and technical media, the image-space for the collective was

driven by innervation that set out to change the world. The freeing of innervation into a more fluid, two-way process between the psyche and somatic
was intrinsically connected to filming's mimetic function, a function concretized by the optical unconscious, the ultimate anthropomorphic charac-
terization of the apparatus and film consciousness. The optical unconscious
opened up Husserl's lifeworld, the consciousness of the world, together with
"the secret lives of things"— objects with their own history and temporality.
The process related to phenomenology's two faces of film, filming and filmed
representation, or, as Hansen put it, the technology of inscription and the
collective, space/time of reception.[175]

The optical unconscious began its trajectory in still photography as a
forgotten archive, able to find the inconspicuous spot where in the immediacy of the long-forgotten moment the present was perpetually open to the
past. With the productive integration of the optical unconscious into the film
experience, film consciousness took on the shape Deleuze later described in
the time-image. Individual subjectivity became the trans personal collective,
together with a sense of disjunctive temporality. Benjamin encouraged the
use of tools that could help dislodge staid forms of thinking. Indeed, any
form of fixed thought was reactionary as it conflicted with thought processes
intended to strip away veneers. When things simply are, they stop becoming, and it is in the in-between, or at the threshold, where things are not yet,
that energy exudes its powers: "The possibilities for change are located in the
movement between the sacred and profane ... in the activities of consecration
and deconsecration. Power and meaning are not found in the thing itself, but
in its margins, in the passage between art and reality...."[176] The obverse to
distraction and dispersion is collection, "sammlung," that establishes a peculiar kind of in-between stasis. There is stasis but also excess or residue that
prevents closure and true completion. For filming, no matter how closely it
corresponds to its subject matter, there will always be difference, and no matter how well constructed montage expression is, its message will float somewhere between the experience and its collective reception. The events that
emerge here are auratic flashes and their penumbra, appearing between the
process of recording and reproduction, occurring in the movement of dispersal and collection Benjamin found fundamental to film consciousness. The
step is now a small one from camera consciousness to the virtual realization
of mature film consciousness, where both the represented world reveals hitherto unperceived qualities and subjectivity too reveals an "entirely new structural formation."[177]

6

Deleuze and Cinema

Montage and Movement-Image

Deleuze's first category of film imagery, the movement-image, is constructed around Bergson's notion of duration. By opposing the idea that images represent objects, that there exists an analogy between objectivity and its representation, we are left with the notion that the movement-image *is* the object. With movement we have modulation, a perpetual passing from one state to another, a relentless restlessness and transformation that makes immobility impossible. Film is imagery in movement and movement-images are intrinsic to Bergson's description of the virtual and the cross over between matter and perception.

Deleuze uses Bergson's description of movement to deconstruct the components of film movement through editing and montage. In the process, we find the way movement-images are expressed in classical film and their application to the more experimental film varies considerably. Deleuze first applies his definition of the movement-image to classical cinema. In doing this he invokes the world of resemblance, a system of representation relating to pre-existing reality based on a mechanistic picture of the world. In terms of film reproduction and representation, the classical movement-image presumes the independence of its objects, the substantiality of things, a profilmic space that stands for a reality pre-existing filming. With the classical movement-image we identify a narration best described as organic, with an inbuilt, transcendent presumption of truth:

> The will to power of organic narration seeks to confirm itself in an
> image of Truth as the selfsame, or repetition as resolution rather than

differentiation.... The truth-seeker wants to "correct" life by making it conform to an atemporal, systematic and transcendent image of thought....[1]

In this approach, judgments require a transcendent system that protects
thought from error by isolating or extrapolating it from life. The organic
movement-image projects through rational, sensorimotor divisions a notion
of truth in relation to totality. Its pregiven affinity to extraneous images of
truth is an attempt to:

> [E]ncompass and subsume the world as image and to make life conform to
> the "laws" of the open totality: differentiation and integration ... the open
> totality in movement aspires to the creation of an ideal world, one that
> overcomes and transcends life and against which life must be judged.[2]

Organic representation brings with it a sense of transparent intelligibility,
coherence, perfect vision and an idealisation of the real. Once the case for
organic representation and the movement-image is made we find an order of
thought that centers on dialectic comprised of differentiation and integration.
Although Deleuze acknowledges the importance of the classical movement-
image, he also explores its insufficiencies. By doing so he sets up a unique
tension between the dialectic of the movement-image with its differentiation
and integration, and the indeterminacies of the higher order time-image.

The ground is laid here for the remarkable restructuring of time we find
with the time-image, one that re-examines notions of presence, repetition and
the now. Nonetheless, within the movement-image the ghost of the past we
find in the present is the same ghost of movement we find in the more mature
time-image. It is the same echo effect of retentional consciousness phenomenology finds in the temporal continuum as a simultaneity of presences, and
the same point Bergson made in claiming the psychic state contains the whole
virtual past as well as the present of being.

In the movement-image, Deleuze recognizes the importance of the
Whole but has reservations: "The Whole can only be thought, because it is
the indirect representation of time which follows from movement."[3] Thinking the Whole is not a neatly rounded resolution but a productive complex
of image and metaphor. At the movement-image stage, film consciousness
still seeks the Whole, to be at one with the object and confirm the givenness
of substantiality. It is subsumed by the delineation of past, present and future
and the logical contradictions of absence and presence, or visibility and invisibility. But even here the Whole cannot be seen as mere totality; it is also an
openness of promise, an active concept that can be added to and subtracted
from, a structure capable of contradiction as well as comprehensiveness. For
Bergson, perception in the interval opens out into the Whole of duration that
is always virtual: "It is actualized according to divergent lines; but these lines

do not form a whole on their own account, and do not resemble what they actualize."[4] In fact, the Whole is the force that itself creates what creates it.

The same notion of the Whole discussed in terms of the movement-image can be appraised in terms of a permanent resistance to closure, it is "not a closed set, but on the contrary that by virtue of which the set is never absolutely closed, never completely sheltered, that which keeps it open somewhere as if by the finest thread which attaches it to the rest of the universe."[5] This is the "precursor" seen as "a thread which traverses sets and gives each one the possibility, which is necessarily realised, of communicating with another to infinity."[6] Film assemblages are related to each other as units but they are infiltrated by the Whole as the promise of its expansion because the Whole, qualitatively, is of a different kind. It is spiritual, duration, built upon the *relationship* of parts rather than a dependence on substantiality. It is also indicative of difference itself, likewise sustained as openness. For Deleuze, the vision of the Whole cannot be directly apprehended but its presence is forever at work as force ensuring the movement of duration, a guarantee for change as the basis for the movement-image. Deleuze has described the propulsion of movement as a force that runs through all life, disrupting immobility and preventing closure. Movement is immanence, "established between the parts of each system and between one system and another, (it) crosses them all, stirs them all up together and subjects them all to the condition which prevents them from being absolutely closed."[7]

There is multiplicity within the open Whole but it does not yet accede to the fluid multiplicity and shifting parameters we find in the time-image. Specific images, either in montage juxtaposition or within their own compositional power of expression, evoke specific meaning as well as overall theme, isolated expression as well as universal emotion, situational dilemma as well as abstract, social judgment. This is an encompassing circuit, vital and inclusive yet open, mutually referential yet expansive: "The Whole forms a knowledge, in the Hegelian fashion, which brings together the image and the concept as two movements each of which goes towards the other."[8] Consciousness always relates to the Whole, keeping both reciprocally open, this is its nature, to be constantly changing and to be open.

Such vitality and dynamism, however, also reaches a limit point with the movement-image, so that a qualitative shift is needed to reach another dimension. In relating this to the ontology of film and social circumstance, we are reminded of Benjamin's views on the status of film and society during the 1930s:

> Cinema is dying ... from its quantitative mediocrity ... the mass art ... has degenerated into state propaganda and manipulation, into a kind of fascism which brought together Hitler and Hollywood, Hollywood and Hitler. The spiritual automaton became fascist man.[9]

Deleuze's ambivalence to the Whole and subsequent support for the time-image takes shape through argument and counter-argument, represented by theorists and film makers such as Eisenstein, representing the organic movement-image and Artaud, apologist for the time-image. Artaud, with a similar mission to Eisenstein, wanted to bring cinema "together with the innermost reality of the brain." However, for Artaud "this innermost reality is *not the Whole, but* on the contrary, *a fissure or crack.*"[10] Before we can understand this tension between the movement-image and the Whole, and the time-image and the fissure, we must look more closely at the way movement-images, in terms of coherence and subsequent fragmentation, lie at the heart of the film experience.

Eisenstein Montage

In Deleuze's description of the movement-image, Eisenstein figures prominently as the key transitional figure. Reflecting Deleuze's intricate account of the emergence of film consciousness, Eisenstein's influence can be felt both in the classical movement-image and in the thought-provoking time-image. Deleuze begins with Eisenstein because it is with montage that we take up the original challenge to film's formative years — to move away from the static photogram and create dynamic assemblages. Primitive film recording was considered photographic and rigid, resulting in a need to release it from its immobile straightjacket and use montage and the mobile camera for "the emancipation of the view point."[11] For Deleuze, basic cutting or editing is a question of distribution, of how to organize variables within a set. But montage, which encompasses diverse forms of film editing, raises the level of film expression through flexible perspectives and relates to the Whole. All choices of combination and discrimination take place in postproduction but they are dependent on previous artistic decisions in initial filming and the natural expression of phenomenology's prepredicative, what Deleuze calls "life as it is": "Montage, it must be said, was already everywhere.... It precedes the filming, in the choice of material, that is, the portions of matter which are to enter into interaction, sometimes very distant or far apart (life as it is). It enters into the filming, in the intervals occupied by the camera-eye (the cameraman who follows, runs, enters, exits; in short, life in the film)."[12]

Time is implicated in all forms of montage, from the Griffith school of classical editing to the Soviet school of dialectical montage. As the vital act of cinema, montage expresses the totality of a film through a series of continuities and false continuities. The journey to reach an overall or dominant theme in film is a process of the interaction of parts and whole where meaning is created from implicitly related parts. Even though the kind of films Deleuze includes in his examination of montage differs vastly in style and content, montage techniques are similar in that they include relations of parts to the whole, juxtaposition, alternating rhythms and convergent actions. Though all film narrative has a continuity of discontinuity, the techniques of classical film narrative have their own forms of continuity, many of which differ from Eisenstein's more discontinuous armature. The temporality of the movement-image, incorporating classical and montage editing, includes an expanding arche and telos; the universal, temporal spiral that extends into both past and future.

Eisenstein made it clear that his strategy of montage was one calculated to oppose conventional editing techniques.[13] Editing and continuity cutting would reproduce the way an ideal observer perceived events, maintaining a naturalistic and seemingly uninterrupted flow. Such seamlessness perpetuates an intended reality-effect, allowing nature to speak by sustaining the indexical link between reproduction and reality, in both spiritual and universal contexts. This basically non-dialectic view is to be contrasted with Eisenstein's dialectical montage that combined showing the actual together with what the actual means, an image-concept correlation. Using the language of the dialectic, Eisenstein fragmented and deconstructed in order to fabricate and reconstruct. Shots come into collision with each other through conflict, for Eisenstein, the main characteristic of all effective art. The precision of the exercise does not go unnoticed. Eisenstein worked with fragments in order to be scientific and ease the predictability of calculations. Calculations were evident with Eisenstein's five methods of montage, metric, rhythmic, tonal, overtonal and intellectual as a hierarchy of affective responses. The lower four levels worked according to Pavlovian reflexology but the fifth level, intellectual montage, did not. Intellectual montage juxtaposed two concrete images to bring about an abstract concept not contained fully in either of two images. The intent of these quantifiable units and emotional synergy was to bring the spectator in consonance with the historical meaning of reality. This was to be accomplished by minimizing the spectator's own creative unconscious and bring recognizable images from concrete reality in defamiliarized and unexpected contexts. For Eisenstein "the artist does not create meanings 'ex nihilo,' but produces them from a nature that is nonindifferent"[14], which is to say, a nature already infused with dialectical movement, a nature embodying a unique, emotional landscape. For Eisenstein, the dialectic principle of dynamics was embodied in conflict, and it was possible to consciously reproduce this tension in every artwork.

The 1924 montage of attraction set up a direct relation between film and human response. Eisenstein saw theatre and film as art forms capable of having calculable influences on the psyche. Through Eisenstein's efforts in this area the very nature of film consciousness began to change. The montage of attraction introduced special images, directly or indirectly associated with the main action, to bring about a calculated effect on the spectator. There was emphasis on the play of associations linked by the spectator to particular phenomena. As yet, the theoretical concern was somewhat piece-meal, reflexive and thought-provoking but without the overall, organic unity Eisenstein would later develop.[15] In practice, however, all of Eisenstein films employed visual contradiction and vertical montage as the incorporation of images from different systems into the film flow. Most significantly, the concern was with a total, all-embracing perspective. There was a continuous progression, an embedded spiral, from the physiological to the emotional and, ultimately, to the cognitive:

> The gradational quality is determined by the fact that there is no difference in principle between the motion of a man rocking under the influence of elementary metric montage and the intellectual process within it, for the intellectual process is the same agitation, but in the dominion of the higher nerve-centers.[16]

This physiological correlation of thought and emotion was most fully developed in Eisenstein's later organic work. The goal became "fusion (rather) than friction, synthesis rather than analysis."[17] The point was now to consider the overall effect and acknowledge that the whole was an anticipated result that also predetermined individual elements.[18] The sense of unity in variety came to predominate over fragmentation.[19] At the same time, montage experiments meant Eisenstein walked a thin line between the inculcation of ideas as the conviction of a committed filmmaker and the input of spectator writerability as a free act of responsive creation. Eisenstein argued that rather than reflect natural perception, film created a unique, filmic fourth dimension, also reminiscent of Bergson's emphasis on the all-pervasive image. The "felt" experience of the filmic fourth dimension resulted from the merging of the physiological and the psychic, in that the physiological was taken as an other form of the psychic, "'psychic' in perception ... is merely the physiological process of a *higher nervous activity*."[20] The physiological becomes the felt vibrations of the stimuli at work within the shot and between shots, arranged according to dominant themes and directly affecting the cortex of the brain as a gestalt whole. The way this emerged was purely in a fourth dimensional temporal zone where sound and vision became physiological sensations of affect working off of each other in a non synchronized manner. In a far more sophisticated way than the early Kuleshov experiments, Eisenstein explained there was no direct correlation between a dominant stimulus and the thought intended to accompany it. Both the film experience and hybrid thought became a complex and nuanced film consciousness, vitalized by visual stimuli comprising a whole range of dominant, subordinate and accompanying variables. Thought was enriched and expanded, even if somewhat programmed.

Imaging Thought Process

We have moved on from the Whole as a separate idea, pure intellectual montage inspired physiologically, to one in which we find the working of the thought process forefronted, imbued with affectivity. Circuits are opened between the highest degree of consciousness and the deepest level of the unconscious. For Eisenstein, the interpenetration of these polarities and the tensions they produced constituted film consciousness. The contemplator, as part of organic nature, was to feel holistically bound to the film work, in the same way as with the surrounding milieu. Eisenstein's pre-logical thought was connected to the dialectical movement of image and concept as it forged out new brain patterns of film consciousness. For Eisenstein, film consciousness found expression both as a personal, private language and as a universal, collective one. It touched on the relation of the individual to the collective, "apart from this there are no true art-works."[21] The notion of "inner speech" was essentially concerned with this pre-logical condition. Unlike the logical formation of uttered speech, inner speech constituted a "flow and sequence of thinking unformulated into the logical constructions in which uttered, formulated thoughts are expressed ... a special structure of its own ... a quite distinct series of laws ... which lie at the foundation ... of the form and composition of artworks."[22] Inner speech was mythical and universal. It saw language as imagistic, primitive, sensuous and alogical. The image as human creation and the object in nature coincided with the dialectic of human intervention in nature. In its affinity with materiality, film was especially suited to pre-logical thought: "This imagistic communication inherent in the dialectical use of film was an automatic, unambiguous communication."[23] In contrast, Eisenstein's "inner monologue," was more particularized and personalized. At the apex of montage, it reconstructed the course of thought as if in a stream of consciousness. With its roots in literature, it found "full expression ... only in the cinema ... to listen to one's own train of thought ... *to catch yourself, looking at* and listening to your *mind.*"[24] Inner monologue grappled with intellectual montage to break down subject and object distinction, absorb outer action and combine synchronized and non-synchronized sound and speech. Film images could direct the process of perception and associative understanding by filling out imagery through sensuous thought. Only film could express this dynamic.

It is clear that the notions of inner speech and inner monologue, with their sense of singular immanence and exploration of consciousness, form a bridge between Deleuze's movement-image and the time-image. As such we are forced to question the limiting reflexology of physiological reactions and start redefining the ambit of the open totality. Eisenstein freely pursued intellectual cinema through concept formations. By an adroit combination of sensory thought and emotional intelligence, affectivity was encouraged to accompany thought, containable, effective and aligned with reason. The supportive rather than combative relation between emotion and thoughts in the arts has been widely recognized, "emotions can themselves be rational or irrational ... emotion can be rational because it has the ability to guide reason, to make salient what needs attending to in a specific situation, and to initiate a response."[25] The connection between intellectual cinema and emotional intelligence was most conspicuous in terms of the pathetic. It brought with it a pervasive, interconnecting orbit of experience and opened up the possibility for distending the organic Whole: "The whole is no longer the logos that unifies the parts but the *drunkenness*, the pathos which bathes them and spreads out in them.... This is a primitive language or thought, or rather an *internal monologue*, working through figures, metonymies, synecdoche, metaphors, inversions, attractions...."[26] The break with realist illusion created a surge that lifted film consciousness to a higher plane of self-transformation. In the composition of the famous Odessa Steps sequence, for example, Eisenstein described caesurae in the action, like transferring to something new, up to a limit and beyond; a leap into opposition, resulting in ecstatic sensibility. Change was not simply evolution but a leap through revolution, a move into the opposite. The dialectical changes in nature occurred in leaps and bounds, suggestive of the collision and friction characterized in all Eisenstein's film montage. Pathos was in accord with this extremity of action and reaction, though still within a practical, political setting. The impetus of the work of art, working through pathos, was to let concrete reality speak itself but via the transfigurations of film, "the work of art takes control of the viewer's perceptive functions (physiological and, hopefully, intellective) until that spectator begins to act in consonance with the logic of objective reality."[27] The consistency of individuation was overcome in favor of involvement in a larger process. Ultimately, pathos should force the viewer from his seat, make him "clap or cry out, it is everything that forces the viewer to be beside himself."[28] As a projection of self, a leap beside oneself engendered a new quality of disposition and shock to the system.

Eisenstein's use of shots-in-conflict and play of contradictions were designed to set up a balance between existing forms of nature and the mind, a rhythmic correspondence between organic nature and creative reason. In true dialectic fashion, existing conditions were given a dynamic that played on contradiction and conflict, resulting in a boost to spectator perception. For Eisenstein, the shock resonating through film consciousness was sustainable through dominant and subdominant themes, through movement within the frame and movement between shots. Shock was to be the effective form of image communication.

Jean Epstein made a similar point with his "photogenie" approach to film. Paying little attention to linear continuity, film was allied to instability and displacement. For Epstein, the defamiliarizing moment came when mechanical reproduction depicted the external world in terms of repetition within difference, "in the reiteration of the object, its soul and essence float to the surface and accost our jaded perceptions."[29] Space and time were yoked together producing dynamic hesitation, pregnant pause, the stagger and recoil:

> Even more beautiful than a laugh is the face *preparing* for it. I must *interrupt*, I love the mouth which *is about to* speak and holds back, the gesture which *hesitates* between right and left, the *recoil* before the leap, and the movement *before* landing, the *hesitation*, the taut spring, the *prelude*, and even more than all these, the piano being tuned before the overture. Photogenie is conjugated in the future and in the imperative. It does not allow for stasis.[30]

This is a duration where "there are no inactive feelings that is, not displacing themselves in space, there are no invariable feelings, that is, not displacing themselves in time — only the mobile ... aspects of things, beings, and souls can be photogenie."[31] Only certain images, elusive and irrational, have the potential to create such emotional, sublime and shocking reactions in the spectator. Deleuze concurs, "you can't escape the shock that arouses the thinker in you."[32] Being shocked into a process of thinking, the "nooshock" activating thought, is the same shock by which film images "think" themselves in Eisenstein's dialectical method. "Montage is in thought ... that which under the shock, thinks the shock."[33] The dialectical method decomposes the nooshock, the imperative to think, into "well-determined moments" where we move from the image to thought, from the "percept to the concept"[34], a trajectory later developed by Deleuze into a move from the outside to the inside. The key is that the process is an automatic one, communicating directly with vibrations to the cortex, opening up to, or thinking the Whole. Previous to this various tactics associated with the need to shock and rejuvenate thinking were carefully orchestrated. Within diverse film movements, through Avant-Garde to Surrealism, the shock-effect was used to disrupt the passively accepted, submissively contained drift of everyday experience. Experiences of epiphantic moments and revelatory insights were intended to create moments of awareness within an otherwise unaware state. The totality of existence was seen in terms of contrasts and polarities. On the one hand, an undifferentiated acceptance of the drift of everyday experience passively accepted and submissively contained. On the other, the interruptions, moments of awareness as the necessary concession to what was a lethargic acceptance of the status quo. Arrested action created the hiatus necessary for Epstein's *photogenie*, feelings of alienation in Brecht's epic theater, and Benjamin's dialectical images in the now of recognizability, but automatic communion with the brain would come only later with Deleuze's time-images.

Affectivity and the Interval

In pinpointing the mechanics of montage, Deleuze relates its dynamic and disruptive impact to affectivity in the interval. Taking Eisenstein's lead, he relates the shock to thought created by collision montage as beginning with vibrations to the cortex that touch the nervous and cerebral system directly. "[T]he shock wave or the nervous vibration ... means that we can no longer say 'I see, I hear,' but I FEEL ... it is this set of harmonics acting on the cortex which gives rise to thought, the cinematographic I THINK."[35] This echoes Eisenstein's combination of hearing and seeing: "For the musical overtone (a throb) it is not strictly fitting to say: 'I hear.' Nor for the visual overtone: 'I see.' For both, a new formula must enter our vocabulary: 'I feel.'"[36] Indeed, feeling, affects and passion are the "principle characters of the brain-world," which is also the film world.[37]

Affectivity acts as the precursor for thought thinking itself just as much as thinking the Whole does. The arena for this experience is the interval. Bergson describes the interval as a field involving a relation between received movement, excitation, and an executed movement, response. In film terms, there are different intervals according to which category of image we are dealing with. Movement-images that take place in the interval relate to action. They are most characterized by realism, the melodramatic and heroic with classical developments of growth, crisis and resolution. This is the cinema of representation, "behavior must be truly structured ... the situation must permeate the character deeply and continuously ... and ... the character who is thus permeated must burst into action, at discontinuous intervals."[38] Deleuze finds three major expressive forces occupying the interval and relates them to constituted subjectivity:

All things considered, movement-images divide into three sorts of images when they are related to a centre of indetermination as to a special image:

perception-images, action-images and affection-images. And each one of us
... is nothing but an assemblage of three images.[39]

Already in the interval associated with the movement-image's sensorimotor
schema we find roots for the creativity that will transform into the time-
image. The interval offers the possibility for enactment of action as well as a
potential for thinking otherwise. It is here we find interlacing between the
making of rational process in the movement-image and the creative indiscernibility of the time-image:

> The interval in movement, expressed through the moment, offers the free-
> dom to choose and the temporal disjunction between perception and mem-
> ory informs the freedom to think. This makes the interval the moment of
> creativity at the interface between matter and memory.[40]

This most clearly emerges with the third category of image, the affective-
image, related as it is to emotion in intuition. Deleuze notes that when emotion in the interval is tied to representation, or mobilized by society to carry
through "story-telling functions," it remains impure. On the other hand, pure
emotion as affectivity is a catalyst, even when not directly actualized it "precedes all representation, itself generating new ideas ... an essence that spreads
itself over various objects, animals, plants and the whole of nature."[41] To
make his point, Deleuze draws attention to the body, especially the face. The
face serves as a fulcrum for the affective-image to find expression. By attending to, or lingering on, the face we arrest representative actions. They are
unfulfilled. If actions were fulfilled as in the succession of movement, or pure
qualities were carried over to the spatio-temporal state of things, they would
become the "quale" of an object, resulting in the loss of affectivity. With the
face, however, there is no such loss. We have an immobile surface supporting the emission of micro-movements of expression. Close-ups of the face are
images with a life of their own, with the power to halt action by a focus on
the purely optical, "it puts forward a peak of attention, a clarifying instant
of insight, a detached moment of defamiliarization."[42]

The close-up encapsulates the investigation and exploration of the
momentary in what Epstein also called "magnified space," an elongated present; a centripetal regulation of spectator attention with the close-up as the
soul of cinema. Blowing up image size engulfs sight and through sight cognition increases.[43] By bringing things close "pain is within reach. If I stretch
out my arm I touch you, and that is intimacy.... Never before has a face turned
to mine in that way.... I consume it."[44] Deleuze extends the affect of face in
close-up to a general envisaged condition, one that applies to any part of the
body, or indeed any object. Clearly, the gamut of expressions that can be read
off of an envisaged object is broad and wide-ranging. What is most significant

is that the envisaged embodies a pure quality unfettered by spatio-temporal limitations. The means of expression and the affect expressed are mutually reliant; their unity forms the icon of the affective-image. As Epstein put it, "this face of a fleeting coward, as soon as we see it in close-up, we see cowardice in person, the 'feeling thing,' the entity."[45] Though apparently individually centered, the affective-image is no such thing; it is impersonal, non-individualized and free from the constraints of sensorimotor activity.

Affectivities can only be known through concrete singularities and can never be exhaustively shown. Each state will be a particularized expression of an emotion, as read on the face or body; a non-personalized singularity. The self-consistency and independence of affectivity is unlike the personalized expression of emotions in the individual that are usually expressed in terms of the state of things, as part of the representative world. By giving the affective-image independence it becomes possible to integrate each expression of affectivity into a montage construction "singular combinations or conjunctions with other affects."[46] This liberates it from a familiar, pre-established variety of moods or qualities and brings it to a level of consciousness that is more than mere automatic repetition. There is constant scope for change and innovation creating possibility for expression within unlimited contexts. Affective-images, and their inherent potentiality, mirror that part of film consciousness not yet tied down by the experience of action, the non-subjective aspect of affectivity, and therefore anticipate the time-image.

Deleuze expresses the notion of affective-image through the power quality presented in Auge's "any-space-whatever." His original definition of the envisaged and the iconic affective-image is extended into any-space-whatever to become the qualisign:

> Space itself has left behind its own coordinates and its metric relations. It is a tactile space. Space is no longer a particular determined space, it has become *any-space-whatever*, to use Pascal Auge's term.... It is a perfectly singular space ... so that the linkages can be made in an infinite number of ways. It is a space of virtual conjunction, grasped as pure locus of the possible.[47]

Any-space-whatever begins with a certain open specificity that can be infinitely linked with other specificities, the same independence as the affection-image, transcending succession and chronology. This is a space of singularity, relating to the virtual, the pure locus of the possible, with openness for links with other spaces or times, or no space at all. With the impression of rain, for example, we return to a phenomenological description:

> *Rain* is not a determined, concrete rain which has fallen somewhere. These visual impressions are not unified by spatial or temporal representations. What is perceived here with the most delicate sensibility, is not what rain

really is, but the way in which it appears when, silent and continuous, it drips from leaf to leaf, when the mirror of the pool has goose-pimples, when the solitary drop hesitatingly seeks its pathway on the window-pane, when the life of the city is reflected on the wet asphalt.[48]

Object, place and person appear in a multitude of guises and situations, each aspect pushing the envelope of contextualization to unravel embedded associations. Further into any-space-whatever, reveals the void, or better, a world devoid of any human coordinates. This extends the affective-image from the close up and envisaged to a more diffuse and penetrating system of emotion that can be elicited from an infinite compound of staggered, temporal layers and spatial associations. The substantiality of shadows comes into its own here, the shadows of life, of nature and the luminous shadows of film. The Gothic and Expressionist make the chiaroscuro space "something unlimited."[49] Shadow, light and darkness play around any-space-whatever to presentify metaphysical struggles for survival, oppositions between good and evil, struggles between mankind and nature. The depths of these struggles can be visually depicted because they can be pinpointed in a specific historical milieu while at the same time affectively disconnected from their roots. They reach a spiritual space, "space becomes any-space-whatever and is raised to the spiritual power of the luminous."[50] Characters and situations come to epitomize phenomenological modes of consciousness tinged with various emotional states. Feelings take on a life of their own in their qualitative singularity by breaking the resistance of the past and the aporia presented by an irretrievable unconscious. Film consciousness shows affectivity in action by visualizing the breakthrough of feelings through sheets of the past and their interaction with the present. In this localized, unfreezing of past strata we utilize mechanical reproduction as automated consciousness, just as we convert feelings to thoughts within the human cerebral mechanism. The movement of affectivity is clear as it takes shape through the determinate events of motor activity to the indeterminate auto-affection of the subject experiencing from inside. There is a motor effort but it is on an immobilized plane, one concerned with potentiality, choice and depth. Movement within indetermination does not complete any predetermined trajectory but rather eddies through any-space-whatever as a feat of artistic exploration.

Vertov and the Machinic

For Deleuze, one of the filmmaker who comes closest to expressing the philosophical impetus behind Bergson's notions of duration, and the indeterminacy of the subject, is Vertov. Vertov was pivotal for manifesting the machinic aspect of film consciousness. Deleuze directly compares Vertov's system in "cine-eye" to Bergson's description of universal variation, "the world before man," aggregate of all images that vary and interact without privileging the human eye ("I"):

> Vertov himself defined the cine-eye: it is that which couples together any point whatsoever of the universe in any temporal order whatsoever.... The materialist Vertov realizes the materialist program of the first chapter of *Matter and Memory* through the cinema, the in-itself of the image.[51]

Vertov believed in the experimentally expressive camera eye's magical powers, its "mechanical imagination," "automatic subjectivity," "lens with personal vision," machine with a "subjective language" and commitment through "biased, active qualities."[52] Vertov set up a mimetic relation between the mechanical and human eye, or technology and humanity, weighting the balance in favor of technology. The "kino-eye" challenged the human eye's visual representation of the world with its own visuality, resulting in a less partial, less corrupted and more genuine experience of life: "The machine makes us ashamed of man's inability to control himself, but what are we to do if electricity's unerring ways are more exciting to us than the disorderly haste of active men and the corrupting inertia of passive ones?"[53] The argument for the superiority of the instrument was couched in terms of a qualitative leap: "The kino-eye ... gathers and records impressions in a manner wholly different from that of the human eye ... the camera ... since it is perfected ... perceives more and better."[54] This was tantamount to extending the camera's magical powers into a fetish, an object of "reverence" far more powerful than the human, as if "enchanted" or possessed of a "power independent of us."[55]

The human and machinic body were originally drawn together by late nineteenth century thinking which espoused the authority of the natural sciences, especially the new energeticist conception of the human body, fixing an identity between the human, mechanical and natural forces, "considered to be systems of production, subject to the same objective and universal law of energy conversion and conservation measurable by science."[56] This re-enchantment of technology, kinship between man and technology, harmonized the expansion of production and was intended, politically, to lead to the "perfection and ultimate salvation of humankind."[57] Vertov's paean to the mechanical eye managed to elevate the mechanical world to a Kantian aesthetic, a kinship between human beings and machines even when "human beings are entirely absent" from the scene.[58] Objects with purposiveness without purpose derive their status from their harmonizing with the cognitive powers of the mind. Such harmony over tension, and a Kantian contribution of the common sense of the faculties, only partly explained Vertov's unique contribution to film consciousness. He attempted to bring to light objects beyond perception, exceeding the limits of human subjectivity, and raise the transcendental empirical to a viable realm of activity.

With Vertov, the liberation of imagery into any-point-whatsoever and the circuit of decomposition between subjectivity and objectivity became materially manifest. Vertov's materialist montage of the interval was an expression of Bergson's acentered universe. Just as Bergson's open totality; it anticipated the transition from indirect to direct time-image. Shots were juxtaposed according to the direction of movement within the frame. Scale, volume, depth, graphic design and lighting cumulatively built to form the quantity of intervals determining the pressure of tension. As Deleuze explains it, the originality of Vertov's theory of the interval was that the interval is returned to matter, a projection of dissemination, carving out distance between two consecutive images and then filling that distance as if matter itself had *usurped* human choice by making the impossible choice. Eisenstein used intervals to intensify montage structure but Vertov "considered them elements of the art of movement and contributed to the poetic impact a constructivist attitude ... drawing attention to film's own techniques — baring the device."[59]

Vertov superimposed the camera or the cameraman over other images. The human eye and the mechanical eye become one as literalizing Bergson's intermediate image "a unification of the human eye with the 'machine eye' in order to create a more substantial, more dynamic and more revealing version of reality."[60] Vertov wanted to reshape spectator's perception and thus participate in exploring the external world through the "penetration of its internal structure."[61] More so than Eisenstein, Vertov was interested in film's mechanics, the phi-effect, the stroboscopic nature of cinematic projection where forms are transformed by the alternative projection of images, and hypnotic effects induced subliminally. Vertov cut the intervals between otherwise adjacent shots, creating collision movement, conflicting graphic forms, antagonistic angles, and inserted subversive shots into sequences that thematically were the antithesis of their general meaning. Shooting life unawares in documentary fashion, the kinoks fostered a non-dramatized cinematic presentation of reality, one restructured through montage, images interactively conscious as matter, emerging from the friction of collision, sparking a relay of perspectives on the world beyond the delimiting condition of human perspective. This worldview was to be re-viewed or re-cycled by the spectator and reconstituted as an other force of vision leading to a higher form of consciousness. The force that revolved around the interweaving of movement reinforced the labile experience of everyday life: "The orchestration of movement is complex to the point that it is difficult to determine where one movement begins and another leaves off. Each movement is inscribed and defined within the context of another, so that a constant flux is created."[62]

Vertov's version of experimental montage, a montage that discarded harmony or similitude, approximated Bergson's objective perception where all images vary in relation one to another, a revolutionary experience of the singular perspective: "Kino-Eye uses every possible means in montage, comparing and linking all points of the universe in any temporal order, breaking when necessary, all the laws and conventions of film construction."[63] We find shifting vibrations of pure matter, centered on a vortex of movement; aparalletic and interactive: "[W]hat can be closer to a materiality made up of luminous wave and molecular interaction?"[64]

Deleuze describes the manner Vertov brings together the upsurge of matter and its perceptual realization in film consciousness in terms of the "gaseous." Gaseous is the level of film consciousness that has passed beyond the solid state of materiality. We begin with landlocked objectivity, a prisoner to earth's gravitation pull. Up to this point, perception-images have still expressed relative immobility but with camera-consciousness and mitsein we have the first major breakthrough to genuine, flowing perception. But it takes the reume-image to experience the molecular rather than molar and go beyond the delimiting strictures of formalized thought. Reume-images are most associated with the movement of water and can be discerned in the French School of filmmaking that included Renoir, Epstein and Grémillon's documentary work. However, this state of perceptual liquidity, which breaks frameworks and allows for alternative visions, only does so in terms of a mitsein, as the peak of the movement-image. Its transversal quality is retained through a floating, peripatetic sensibility but we are not yet peering into the minutest workings of matter. Only with the deconstruction of matter do we begin the ultimate journey of the mind through regions of gaseous perception.

Under consideration is both the deconstruction and refiguration of movement, together with its own reflexive analysis. Penetration of internal structure takes place on all levels, not merely the breakdown of the everyday but also the internal structure of time, montage and film itself. Nothing escapes the act of reflexivity. Vertov's compositions and use of the camera eye took liquidity beyond human spirituality to a machinic equivalence of material energy. It was through the level of machinic expression that one could enter into all levels of vital energy. This qualitative move goes beyond perception into the molecular condition associated with the gaseous, understood as the "genetic," "to reach 'another' perception, which is also the genetic element of all perception."[65] There is a complete dismantling of process to enter into what constitutes process, a meta-reflexivity honing in on components. Components become the apprehension of creativity in action, the sign of film's genesis through its gaseous state, "defined by the free movement of each molecule ... the particle of matter or gaseous perception."[66] Taking the photogramme as the photographic unit, we delve deeper into the gaseous beyond perception, into the energic element of movement. Here we discover units of montage and the photogramme turned inside out, showing its innards, the pulsation of its life force: "[F]lickering montage; extraction of the photogramme beyond the intermediate stage ... vibration beyond movement ... re-filming or re-recording and extraction of a particle of matter."[67]

Put together, "all these procedures act to form the cinema as machine assemblages of matter-images."[68] This breaking down of image and perception in the sense of unraveling their constituent parts bears testament to the intractability of the image, a defiant indomitability because we cannot escape the image no matter what level we penetrate to. Like Antonioni's *Blow Up* (1966), the image resists closure and the definitive: "The image is not a symptom of lack, but an excessive residue of being that subsists when all should be lacking. It is not the index of something that is missing, but the insistence of something that refuses to disappear."[69]

With Vertov's materialist montage we delved into universal variation and ubiquitous perspective. This is not transcendental vision but images themselves being expressed in the maelstrom of any point whatsoever. Without essence, the film image still makes sense, or is caught in the act of making sense on the molecular level of non-rational linkages. Image in movement and the movement of matter coalesce in the realm of life. How deeply we delve into the constituents of the machinic life force is unclear. The various expressions and diverse nature of the film image set the ground rules for what series is established between the moving machine and the psychological automaton. Once the interval is transferred from being the characteristic point at which centers of indeterminacy separate a reaction from the action experienced into the correlation of images themselves, it exceeds human perception. The shift is from spirit to matter. Only after this takes place can the direct time-image come into play for film consciousness to reach a stage conducive to thinking otherwise.

Through Bergson, the machinic eye becomes the intuition that makes up the new cine-brain: "Bergson is not one of those philosophers who ascribes a properly human wisdom and equilibrium to philosophy. To open us up to the inhuman and the superhuman (durations which are inferior or superior to our own), to go beyond the human condition: This is the meaning of philosophy...."[70] This inhuman dimension of duration, the spiritual reality, "is both atheist and mystical, inasmuch as it exists as entirely material 'cerebral vibrations'....This spiritual movement is imparted through the perceptual process of intuitive thought — the process of the cine-brain — that returns to things their living becoming in duration."[71] The question is whether the cine-brain that supersedes the human eye is still connected to the duration of the open totality; can it fulfill the conditions of expressing duration itself? "The brain screen of cine-thought thereby attains new ontological conditions ... conditions that retain a Bergsonian duration but one no longer thought within the conditions of the movement-image."[72] With regards to Vertov, Deleuze explains, even with the machinic eye, we have still not reached a "non-human world where movement equals matter" or even "a super-human world which speaks for a new spirit." The movement-image still "remains primary," even though perception is carried over into matter, and "action is universal interaction," we are still dealing with "a negative of time as the ultimate product of the movement-image through montage."[73] Vertov has gone beyond what had hitherto been achieved in terms of a non-human world to a degree that he "attains the sublime"[74] of the movement-image, a unique machinic consciousness. But "in overcoming the sensorimotor," Vertov's films "remain within the classical regime ... they erect a machinic interval ... which re-invents, without leaving ... the philosophical conditions of the movement image."[75]

Liquid Subjectivity

Deleuze asks how is it possible to speak of images in themselves that are not for anyone and are not addressed to anyone. "How is it possible to speak of an Appearing, since there is not even an eye?"[76] With image-in-movement, an image is what has become out of the gaseous. The plane of immanence comprises light in the form of diffusion. It spreads out and transmits. In the movement-image there are not yet bodies or rigid lines, but only figures of light. Blocks of space-time are such figures. If we take perception as an awakening, an en-lightening, recognition of being, then the most primitive state is light imagery as blocks of space-time. This flow of light is already a photograph, already vision, already an eye, but not an "I." Light and the eye come from matter; they are imagery, illumined from within without the factoring of a subjectivity illuminating them from without. From Deleuze we see a move away from an exterior, phenomenological ray of attention being directed or projected to en-lighten through object-subject correlation. Rather, matter already has illumination:

> The whole difficulty of the problem (representing matter) that occupies us comes from the fact that we imagine perception to be a kind of photographic view of things, taken from a fixed point by that special apparatus which is called an organ of perception.... But is it not obvious that the photograph, if photograph there be, is already taken, already developed in the very heart of things and at all the points of space?[77]

Deleuze makes clear that the propagation of light so fundamental to film cannot be understood without accepting some opposition between Bergson and phenomenology. This, even though it is clear the phenomena of phenomenology have the same coming-to-light Bergson described. Phenomena come to-light through phenomenological intuition: "The phenomenon gives itself by itself and on the basis of its own visibility, far from being reduced to presence for a consciousness (there is) ... an initiative of the phenomenon to enter into visibility."[78] Without acknowledging his common ground with phenomenology, Bergson saw things as inherently luminous, consciousness was "diffused everywhere and yet does not reveal its source: it is indeed a photo which has already been taken and shot in all things and for all points, but which is 'translucent.'"[79] When Deleuze appropriates this he directly relates the projection on the screen and its luminosity to the brain, "The brain is unity. The brain is the screen. I don't believe that linguistics and psychoanalysis offers a great deal to the cinema. On the contrary, the biology of the brain — molecular biology — does."[80] Related as they are to movement, images form part of matter, they are matter in a constant state of change, renewal — universal variation. The "infinite set of all images constitutes a kind of plane of immanence"[81] and images exist in themselves here. To say the body is matter and that it is an image is one and the same thing. The plane of immanence is forever open, in movement, as movement. There are emergent states that persist, bodies that perdure and centers of action, but before this there is identity of image and movement which "stems from the identity of matter and light. The image is movement just as matter is light[82] and cinema's movement-image is the perfect conduit for the consciousness of this. Film consciousness is one with the perpetual movement of light, though its expression differs according to different schools of film making.

According to Bergson's account even though there is inseparability of mind and object consciousness, those moments of the subjective or emerging centers of indetermination, are not source points but rather blockages or backdrops to the flux. What is lacking "behind the plate (is) the black screen on which the image could be shown. Our zones of indetermination play in some sort the part of the screen. They add nothing to what is there."[83] This relocation onto the screen allows for undifferentiation in that there is no longer a source point, or projection from one source as in the film projector, but fluidity depicted in the movement of images on the luminous screen. Within this orchestration of movement, a fluid state of human detachment is established. Deleuze calls this stage of film consciousness, "mitsein," the intricate placing and displacing of human subjectivity before it becomes the intersubjectivity of mature film consciousness. The mitsein of camera consciousness is most accessible through the work of Pasolini, though Jean Mitry's film theory has earlier attested to its presence.

In this connection, Deleuze uses the notion of the spiritual automaton of film, its psycho-mechanics, to consider an objective sense of vision. Already in the basic shot we find "the sole cinematographic consciousness is not us, the spectator, nor the hero, it is the camera — sometimes human, sometimes inhuman, or superhuman."[84] Camera consciousness is not the consciousness of any one person, nor the viewpoint of a centered subjectivity, nor the transcendental expression of an ultimate truth as captured by technology. It is rather a consciousness partly found in all of these and in none. More than anything else it is a consciousness expressed through the flux and transformation of an ever evolving temporal art work that assimilates all centers and incorporates them into an indivisible flow. Camera consciousness is most closely aligned with the director/artist's vision, though it is an assumed version of this vision. The emergence of camera consciousness as an anonymous point of view is expressed independently of particularized subjectivities, it is likened by Mitry to a "semi-subjective" image and, by Pasolini, to a "free indirect discourse"; in either case there is no equivalent in natural perception. In the notion of free indirect subjectivity, we have the viewpoint of a character on screen simultaneously with the camera that sees him, another vision in which the first is transformed and reflected. This vision sees the character's world from another point of view, transforming the viewpoint of the character into a meld of simultaneous visions and sounds. Elements are introduced which the character is unaware of and in the process that includes the optical unconscious, perspective is expanded. From this Deleuze forms his category of the dicisign, which is a perception of a perception, "the camera 'sees' a character who is seeing; it implies a firm frame, and so constitutes a kind of solid state of perception."[85]

Making sense of this reflexivity and meta-perception comprises the transition from time being reliant on motion to time being manifested directly. It changes the sense of meaning that emanates from the imposition of a subjective center to one that is a result of virtuality. Establishing camera consciousness breaks through the split between the ego and the "I," the subjective and objective, the self and other, to present an alternative machinic perception of the world. Vertov's cine-eye makes visible what the spectator cannot see, as more than human, as part of Bergson's intellectual intuition, as intuitive knowledge that establishes itself in moving reality as part of the life of things. This is where science and metaphysics meet and where philosophy is the effort to go beyond the human state.[86] The non–human mitsein stretches the vision of human perception to the limit and beyond, a shadowy accompaniment to the impermanence of materiality, haunting it, reflecting it and ultimately reconstituting it.

Deleuze's analysis of Eisenstein and Vertov is the culmination of his survey of the movement-image's impact on film consciousness, but to support empirical findings he uses the theories of Peirce, the founder of semiotics. For Peirce, signs were conceived on the basis of phenomena; images and their combination rather than through the determination of language. This appeals to Deleuze because, like Bergson's movement-image, signs are related to matter itself and not linguistically dependent.[87] Thoughts pick up movements and their concomitant signs.

Peirce had a tripartite system of signs. Firstness had to do with imagery that was new in experience, fresh but eternal. These images were self-sufficient, enough unto themselves, tantamount to the transcendental condition for what is; an immediate consciousness as a foundation for all consciousness. In terms of affectivity, to which it directly related, it is not a sensation or feeling, but the quality of a possible sensation or feeling: "Firstness is thus the category of the possible."[88] As we have seen, this is what the affection-image is, singular, self-contained, expressive, but unactualized potentiality. Secondness had to do with actualization and individuation, within "determinate space-time, geographical and historical milieux," through, "collective agents or individual people."[89] This refers the affective link to physical conditions and action, and is recognizable as the action-image. Of special interest to Deleuze is Peirce's third kind of image, the "mental," or Thirdness, which Deleuze uses to discuss the crisis of the action-image as a prelude to the time-image. Thirdness is a mediation and relation-image: "The point of Thirdness was a term that referred to a second term through the intermediary of another term or terms."[90] The characteristic of Thirdness, its mental coloration, is a figure of thought. It takes the form of logic in that it is more abstract than direct actions and more symbolic, giving rise "not to perceptions but to interpretations which refer to the element of sense."[91] These interpretations have a transformative effect on aspects of the movement-image, since they can be seen as a chain of semiotic relations, an endless semiosis. Even the affection-image deepens into an intellectual "feeling" of relations less tied down to situation and circumstance, with a closer affinity to abstract coordinates, and metacriticism.

This is not to say the affection-image and the action-image have nothing mental about them in the first place, but images of Thirdness, relation-images, explicitly make the mental an *object* of the image. Thirdness unequivocally relates thought to the movement-image, not to perceptions that are manifested in the interval, but to interpretations of those intervals. As we will find in the time-image, it is the outside, as a third term, of what becomes the inside. In keeping with mature film consciousness, Deleuze sees the relation-image as a step closer towards a new way of thinking; it has as objects of thought "objects which have their own existence outside thought."[92] As a relation-image, then, Peirce's Thirdness had to do with symbolic acts and abstract relations, and, most of all, interpretation and reasoning. Different kinds of images make matter as movement signaletic material, and signs are the expressive ways of combining images and recreating images.

However, Deleuze only goes so far with Peirce: "We take the term 'sign' in a completely different way from Peirce.... We could no longer consider Peirce's Thirdness as a limit of the system of images and signs."[93] The reason for this is to return to the need for a cine-brain that as image breaks through representation and cliché. To go further than Peirce we must acknowledge there is something hiding in the image as a force that "constantly attempts to break through cliché, to get out of cliché." [94] Like Benjamin, it is necessary to break down in order to rebuild, "it is necessary to make holes, to introduce voids and white spaces, to rarify the image...."[95] What is needed is the "seer or visionary ... to go beyond the sensorimotor without reconfirming its movement in a sublime outside.... The figure of the visionary ... recurs in Deleuze's discussions of art and is always associated with a resistance to cliché."[96] This will be the turning point into the time-image, where vision denotes, in a Bergsonian way, a "mystical understanding of art" that combines the new optical-sound image with a "profound, vital intuition."[97] As direct visions, the seers' images will be genetic, without a beyond, without an outside, indeterminate, a mystical aesthetics that is the "'creative and artistic' essence of the vision of the seer."[98] This again is a return to Nietzsche and the artist-philosopher, which corresponds in cinema to the spiritual automaton, "the seer whose visions exist 'flush with the real' and whose automatic image-thought is the appearance of the moving matter of duration in a nervous-cerebral shock." [99] To this extent the seer as spiritual automaton is all-seeing, part of the imagery of screen luminosity but also implicated into viewer sensibility and creativity to override the limitations of sensorimotor thought.

7

Marking Time

Thinking Otherwise

In order to think otherwise attitudes derived from special narratives and montage must be in place. Though Deleuze takes the Second World War and the horrors of the Holocaust to be the cut-off point for a different kind of imagery, it is worth emphasizing that the potential for change was already present in cinema's earlier years. As we have seen, Deleuze recognized that Eisenstein's organic and montage experiments, Surrealism, Avant-Garde and the experimental documentary work of Vertov were all groundbreaking developments in the evolution of film consciousness to its modern form. Though the way of looking at things in natural perception as a centered equilibrium of forces came to be overturned, Deleuze reminds us that the movement-image was itself aberrant and abnormal to begin with. Epstein's comments in the 1920's described how spectators experienced non-rational, "slowed down and reversed sequences ... the non-distancing of the moving body ... constant change in scale and proportion ... and false continuities of movement."[1] Later, Jean-Louis Schefer noted that the movement-image does not reproduce a world but constitutes an autonomous world that has no centre and is observed by a spectator "who is in himself no longer centre of his own perception."[2] Clearly, Deleuze's dark precursor was already at work on the movement-image from the outset:

> It took the modern cinema to re-read the whole of cinema as already made up of aberrant movements.... The direct time-image is the phantom which has always haunted the cinema but it took modern cinema to give a body to this phantom.[3]

168

With mature film consciousness we focus on aberrant time and establish a temporal experience subordinating movement to both multiplicity and invention. In this way we create philosophic concepts:

> One must be capable of thinking the production of the new, that is, of the remarkable and the singular ... this is a complete conversion of philosophy ... cinema ... has a role to play in the birth and formation of this new thought, this new way of thinking ... the organ for perfecting the new reality.[4]

The new structures Deleuze uncovers in modern narratives comprise images that no longer refer to a globalizing or synthetic situation. They even surpass the indulgence of the open totality to become dispersive: "The cinema is always narrative, and more and more narrative, but it is dysnarrative in so far as narration is affected by repetitions, permutations and transformations which are explicable in detail by the new structure."[5] The adversary has been, and still is, the cliché—a floating image circulating in the external world; penetrating all our thoughts. Gridlocked in a tunneled vision of limited perspective, we discriminate in favor of what is functional, instrumental and self-fulfilling. The cliché has been refined to meet perceptual demands and pragmatic contingency. It sets up a series of associations and self-fulfilling expectations to accompany the image, driving its core ever more distant, as if suffocated by increasing numbers of concentric circles. It is only when our consciousness experiences the defamiliarization of shock effects and distraction that sensorimotor actions are replaced by a denuding of the image that allows us to face it pristine, as a thing-in-itself.

The time-image takes over the pristine image, shatters its cliché-ridden palliatives and effectuates another kind of density, one that encourages openness from a multiplicity of viewpoints. It is diffuse, caught in suspension, endlessly referential, unconstrained, a correlate freed of encoded meanings. Divested of predictability, it is mindful with diverse modes of consciousness relating to fractures that allow in pure recollection. This is a system of film narration marked by difference. Bergson's open totality has given us difference within systems and between systems, sustaining openness. But genuine indeterminacy and experimentation comes only with difference in-itself. In a sense this is a special kind of communication and reciprocity permeated by the immanent dynamics of forces and intensities; series characterized by multiplicity, the perpetual change of the now, various time syntheses of past in present, retention and protention, and the alternating virtual and actual-image.

The expression of difference in film imagery is through connecting linkages that are not the successive formulations of movement-imagery but direct and without mediation. Difference needs to be articulated:

[D]ifference must be articulation and connection in itself; it must relate different to different without any mediation whatsoever by the identical, the similar, the analogous or the opposed ... the difference is gathered all at once rather than represented on a prior resemblance.[6]

Two systems vying with each other, difference and representation, and the conflict between them played out by subterfuge, sophistry and deception. Difference in-itself is concealed by the system of representation from which it must find release, "it is under the same conditions that the in-itself of difference is hidden, and that the difference falls into the categories of representation."[7] Coalescence is needed between what is within series themselves and the subjectivities, or areas of indetermination, through which systems are expressed. For Deleuze, priority lies not in the originary idea and the particulars that relate to the universal but to originary difference that only gives the impression of similarity *after* the event. The dynamics and tensions of heterogeneous systems, fired by the couplings within series, are to be sustained by combining "passive selves" and "larval subjects," the genuine movers of systems:

> [I]t is not even clear that thought, in so far as it constitutes the dynamism peculiar to philosophical systems, may be related to a substantial, completed and well-constituted subject, such as the Cartesian Cogito: thought is, rather, one of those terrible movements which can be sustained only under the conditions of a larval subject.[8]

Larval subjects, on the borders of the livable speak through the systems that they help to sustain as dynamic. In any other form they would serve only as a blockage rather than a conduit. Differences in a system relate to each other but they cannot do so by a conscious effort of comparison. They do so only under the impulse of a force brought about by a "differenciator," the result being an internal resonance within the system and an external coupling between systems. The force that does the linking is not a centered subjectivity dragging everything into a common likeness. There can be no guiding hand or privileged point relating systems under an overarching concept; this would introduce an unnecessary dualism. Nor do we have absolute difference since systems consistently *do* link up or couple. From coupled series to dynamic systems forces of intensity bring about a movement of "pure spatiotemporal dynamism." The differenciator force is varied with hidden faces:

> Thunderbolts explode between different intensities, but they are preceded by an invisible dark precursor, which determines their path in advance, but in reverse, as though, intagliated. Likewise, every system contains its *dark precursor* which ensures the communication of peripheral series ... this is fulfilled by quite diverse determinations.[9]

Phenomenologically, the dark precursor rejects noetic correlates because it is without a continuity of subjective identity, likewise noematic correlates, since there is no constitutive similarity through its acts of constitution. The only consistency is retroactive. The precursor recognizes its own fiction and the series to which it relates has only the illusion of retrospective resemblance. To enable this, the differenciator is where it is not, it is "the self-different which relates different to different by itself."[10] It lacks its own identity, a Sartrean *pour soi*, with no mirror image for it to deceptively fill any absence. We cannot, then, presuppose any identity for the agent bringing together these heterogeneous systems since to do so would make it foundational and carry over functions of comparison, analogy and likeness, all of which would be to replace qualitative difference by quantity and measurement. Differences cannot be calculated in this way. The way difference emerges, especially in its temporal expression, will be according to its possibility for "fractionation," according to the disguises of the differenciator and the attractive forces of coupling and resonance.

The film spectator, as a centre of indeterminacy and part of indeterminate imagery, is sucked into the process as a force field, sustaining the system as dynamic and vital and preventing sedimentation and habitus. Systems are meaningfully structured while simultaneously transmuted and fluid. The precursor presages what is to come like a kinetic charge but does not specify details, only momentum. If the dark precursor lingers in the wings, a shadowy presence alertly negating itself for the sake of systematic renewal and difference, centers of indeterminacy, as subjectivity, must be inventive enough to speak these changes. They must be affectively vulnerable, openly vital and self-effacing to explore the singularities of the time-images found within dysnarrative contexts.

This power of change deters the conscious prioritizing of any one system over another. It is repetition but the "clothed" repetition of disguises and masks that retains difference. However, film is more than this since, in addition to levels of repetition that move away from representation to difference, there is a constant ungrounding process, underscored by the time-image. This finds its expression in Deleuze's third synthesis which has frequent recourse to Nietzsche's philosophic position of ontological repetition: "Beyond the grounded and grounding repetitions, a repetition of *ungrounding* on which depend both that which enchains and that which liberates, that which dies and that which lives within repetition."[11] Art is especially conducive to expressing forms of repetitions that prevent closure:

Each art has its interrelated techniques or repetitions, the critical and revolutionary power of which may attain the highest degree and lead us from the sad repetitions of habit to the profound repetitions of memory, and then to the ultimate repetitions of death in which our freedom is played out.[12]

By making difference in life apparent, art is part of the life force. The film work's own series constituted by sets, assemblages and sections taken from the series that is life, can be part and parcel of the same repetitious, singular return of the same as difference, if time-imagery is accented. Without a referential origin there is no talk of primacy but only types of repetitions with their own vital procedures. The dark precursor is the invisible upholder and guardian of difference and change. The interaction between systems, driven by the shadow force, sheds light on each as a marking of time that comes to settle, and then elusively move on.

The differences that come to form the character of film's time-image are now more clearly delineated. Organic representation is finally overcome and with it specific difference in the identity of the concept. The process has been sealed by Nietzsche, where the death drive merges with the movement of life itself, overflowing all series, opening them up eternally to chance and chaos. Nietzsche has already rejected received notions of representational and transcendent truth implicit in classical narrative, "the self-contained infinity of God is thus replaced by the open infinity of human interpretation."[13] With Nietzsche, vital ideas and their inspirational attraction exist in an endlessly relational and mobile way:

> If one now goes on to consider that, not only a book, but every action performed by a human being, becomes in some way the cause of other actions, decisions, thoughts, that everything that happens is inextricably knotted to everything that will happen, one comes to recognize the existence of an actual *immortality*, that of motion.[14]

The challenge to the symmetry of organic completion is infused by Nietzsche's eternal return with its insistence on movement, change and difference: "The idea of eternal recurrence shakes us from thinking of the ideal of eternity in terms of something remaining always the same, in favor of a new focus on transience — *a delight in what passes* ... eternity itself is to be thought of in terms of movement."[15] Reference to the eternal recurrence here helps us fix the elusiveness of the present by thinking of the present in the mode of the past. By suffusing it with the ontological past that it already is, the present can be "articulated." On the other hand, the ontological past that suffuses the present is itself opened up and made less determinate by the thought of the eternal return. Movement has become the perspective of time and "in thinking of the eternal return, we break down the barriers between past and present, thinking each in the mode of the other" as a way of affirming diversity and becoming.[16] As Deleuze points out, in terms of a "memory of the future" the eternal return, contra Plato, retains the theory of becoming:

> The eternal return is a force of affirmation, but it affirms everything of the multiple ... of the different ... of chance.... If there is an essential relation

with the future, it is because the future is the deployment and explication of the multiple, of the different and of the fortuitous, for themselves and "for all times." It concerns ... excessive systems which link the different with the different, the multiple with the multiple, the fortuitous with the fortuitous, in a complex of affirmations always coextensive with the questions posed and the decisions taken.[17]

Forks of Time

To understand the importance of the eternal return it would be apposite to reiterate Deleuze's observation on the true and the false, since it is this distinction that courses through Deleuze's demand for new imagery. In a compact and complex section in Cinema 2, Deleuze looks at the status of narration in the modern era in terms of the true and the false:

It is the power of the false, which replaces and supersedes the form of the true, because it posits the simultaneity of imcompossible presents, or the co-existence of not necessarily true pasts. Crystalline (or falsifying) description was already reaching the indiscernibility of the real and the imaginary, but the falsifying narration which corresponds to it goes a step further and poses inexplicable differences to the present and alternatives which are undecidable between true and false to the past. The truthful man dies, every model of truth collapses, in favor of the new narration.[18]

The new status of narration is one that no longer has the pretension of truth, indeed it becomes basically "falsifying"; there is now a "power of the false." As Deleuze explains it, Leibnitz illustrated the difficulty of conceiving a direct correlation between truth and the force of time. Leibnitz posited the infinity of possible worlds, even though the world we live in, acknowledged as relative, is the chosen one. If an event is to take place next week, from the vantage point of today, there is still a possibility it may not take place. But once the event has taken place it retroactively affects that earlier presupposition, that the event possibly may not take place. In the future, the realization of an event affects its previously possibility. Yet, can we accept the impossible; something not happening, that has happened, as a follow up to the possible? For Leibnitz an event may or may not take place but this eventuation does not take place in the same world. If it does "in fact" take place then its "not taking place" belongs to a different world, these two worlds are possible, but are not compossible.[19] This is because God chooses between the infinity of possible worlds which are "incompossible" with each other. Though we can argue the existence of these worlds, they do not in fact come *into* existence because God has not chosen them. Mere possibilities do not exist, as such, they are rather of the ideal order. What follows from the possible is not its contradiction, the impossible, but rather the Leibnitz notion of the imcompossible: "The past may be true without being *necessarily* true."[20] Leibnitz's notion of a central harmony and divine thought complexes, however, come under scrutiny from Deleuze, who takes up the notion of imcompossibles claiming they *can* belong to the same world rather than be excluded from it. In Borges, for example, the labyrinth of time, or the power of the false, is a straight line that becomes a forking line, which passes through "*imcompossible presents*, returning to *not-necessarily true pasts.*"[21]

Much of what Deleuze argues with respect to indiscernibility and truth has its roots more in Nietzsche than Leibnitz, "it is Nietzsche, who, under the name of the 'will to power,' substitutes the power of the false for the form of the true, and resolves the crisis of truth, wanting to settle it once and for all, but, in opposition to Leibnitz, in favor of the false and its artistic, creative power...."[22] In fact, "the power of the false" in terms of the will to power, and "how the 'true world' finally became an error" is developed "within the domain of cinema ... substituting for each stage in the Nietzschean commentary a particular director — e.g. who Welles, Robbe-Grillet, Lang, Godard, Cassevetes, Perault, Jean Rouch and Alain Resnais — who works over the concept of the 'will to power' under the name of the power of the false."[23] It is such a pantheon of directors and creative artists that utilize technical aspects of cinema narration to explore problems of truth and falsehood, with each providing their own particular, partial resolution. Film consciousness enters into the crisis of truth through film narration and the experience of time. With Nietzsche underpinning this account it is natural to look at "appearance" itself; cinema is after all images-in-appearance:

> [T]he character of Zarathustra represents the twilight of the concept of truth, the death of the "truthful man," and the collapse of every model of truth ... his appearance also marks the dawn that breaks into a long night of insomnia and promises the return of good sense and a spirit of happiness and joy.... With the vanquishing of the true world the world of appearances vanishes as well.[24]

Film consciousness is the attempt to solve this problem of truth, but one which eliminates appearance in order for it to return as difference. Its final breakthrough comes not in the movement-image, which is still connected to sensorimotor descriptions and the open totality, but in the time-image that finally disconnects from the real and true world: "Description becomes its own object and narration becomes temporal *and* falsifying at exactly the same time."[25] As a result of the new time-image the most ubiquitous character that inhabits this imagery is the Borges' forger, "the forger becomes *the* character of the cinema: not the criminal, cowboy, the psycho-social man, the historical hero, the holder of power, etc., as in the action-image, but the forger pure and simple, to the detriment of all action ... the unlimited figure which permeates the whole film."[26] By becoming the universal figure, or personage, who inhabits the time-image, the forger puts into relief all the elements that go towards thinking otherwise in film consciousness; undecidable alternatives, inexplicable difference and indiscernibility. In this way, time is finally freed from the control of the true and "cinema discovers a new means of producing description," a "means of disconnecting itself from the 'true world,' to become again as a return — but now in an immanent sense — 'a pure world of appearances.'"[7]

The time-image is drawn out by its crystalline character, an image that is indiscernible, read through the understanding of memory, the perceptively actual and the subjectively virtual. Deleuze describes the choices made from within the complex of the time-image, based on a series of forks, as temporalized junction boxes leading to further splitting and the establishment of tiered levels of actions. Events come together causing repercussions that open up questions, re-route the significance of the past and emit a whole series of shock waves reverberating through the present, living at the limit. The time-image as crystal presents "the vanishing limit between the immediate past which is already no longer and the immediate future which is not yet ... mobile mirror which endlessly reflects perception into recollection."[28] What we see in the crystal is the split of time.

The switching exchange between the actual and virtual of the crystal is categorized by Deleuze as "limpid" and "opaque," a reversibility of light and dark indicative of uncertainty. The result is paradox: "Paradox displays the element which cannot be totalized within a common element, along with the difference which cannot be equalized or cancelled at the direction of a good sense."[29] Actuality and virtuality in the time-image are conveyed by a paradoxical film image in a state of constant fracturing. As a break up of sequential or logical action, the time-image is mental, reliant on the acts of recollection-imagery as an entrance into the past that splits the past (already constituted as a split). This is not to say the dualistic range of actual-virtual, organic-aberrant, action-description and physical-mental is redundant or aporetic. Rather, they positively feed off of each other; reflecting each other and ultimately become each other in their own particular (dis)guise. At one and the same time the actual is always present but a present marked by an absence that changes it. The present image is still present and already passing and the fact that the past coexists with the present means there is persistent duplication of matter and mind, of present perception and virtual memory, primal impression and retentional consciousness.

The virtual, after being expressed in whatever form available through actualization, will differ from the source point, the original point (phenomenology's primal impression) where real and virtual images reflect each other, producing an ever-widening circuit, like a dazzling hall of mirrors. It is a circuit with roots in the prepredicative, still containing the sedimentation of alternative significance to the instrumentality of choices adopted. Such circuits will be soldered over so that the retention of the just-having-been may refer to the circuit of virtual imagery or, just as feasibly, to the immediacy of the actual image. The integrity of each circuit cannot be secured because splitting takes the form of specularity, an inevitable, unpredictable parting of the way.

Thus, when bringing the virtual into actualization we are not repeating the same process as the creation of virtuality. The creation of virtuality takes place automatically, through durational unfolding as part of perpetual flux, the complex process of image-matter as the perpetually open. Only the present is psychological, the past is pure ontology and its only access is by a genuine "leap" into its being. Once the leap is taken we find that the contraction of perception can be seen not in terms of diminution but in the light of potential expansion, as intuition in phenomenology and multiplicity in duration.

When we reach into the past we are wresting what has concealed itself from memory. This bank of memory in the form of layers and sheets of the past, both originary and non-psychological, becomes apparent in diverse ways according to the fulfillment of the interval. It also serves as a phenomenological, descriptive tool for understanding the workings of the time-image. Each time a virtual image is called up in relation to an actual description, the object is de-formed and created anew, widening and deepening the mental picture it inspires. An expansive process is created, a multidimensional circuitry with layers crisscrossing each other. The time-image entices the spectator into constituting new meaning by combining sedimented action with a fresh sense of context in a chosen region of the past. This justifies an intricate hermeneutic that pushes the envelope of its phenomenological roots as an interpretive act, risking the very time line which the past is meant to elucidate.

What is significant here for film consciousness is that the ontology of film takes effect through the powers of a reconstituted spatio-temporal reality with a marked shift of perspectives, centers of dispersion and shapeless distortions giving a *positive* meaning to difference. In that shift, the role of spectator moves from an extraneous centre of projection and identification to an immanent cog in the unfolding realization of a past unconscious, through to a crystallizing force of prismatic manifestations. This deeply implicated role of the spectator comes strongly to the fore in Resnais' *Last Year in Marienbad,*[30] which looks at the interplay of the past and present, and the repetition of the same, through a series of multiperspective visions. These visions are presented through a film consciousness that is constantly split, only brought together as an identity through the spectator's hermeneutic grounding, as a search for meaning. There is no one particular, subjective consciousness but a fragile intentionality that works through the eclecticism of material drawn upon by unique film consciousness. Without a reassurance of objective reality there is only the reality of externalized thought. In *Marienbad* phenomenological consciousness and Deleuze's lines of departure and flight come together. The leaps of temporal disjunctions and fractured identities mean that we are no longer in the realm of commonly accepted subjectivity but rather within a machinic series emanating from a molecular level of process. This is the formation of realities and objects through assemblages that absorb the brain and body within the indiscernibility of matter and memory.

Marienbad is relevant to both the phenomenological and Deleuzean approaches because it highlights the difficulty and frustration in finding suitable criteria for judging truth-values, so that ultimately truth is "falsified." It opens up questions of foundation and reflexively directs us to both Husserl's search for a presuppostionless method and Deleuze's questioning of the tools one uses for questioning. There is a sense of nihilism here that presents both the absurdity of the belief in nothing, a philosophical cul-de-sac, and a necessary erasure of existing beliefs before new ones can take their place. If the mind wishes to understand itself as creator it must recognize in that act of creation a play with the death of time. Through Deleuze's transcendental empiricism the notion of reality as merely subjective projection is subverted by a lifeworld tenacity that gives a voice to objecthood. In his literary as well as film work, scriptwriter Robbe-Grillet looked to the very surface of materiality, "to describe things, as a matter of fact, is deliberately to place oneself outside them, confronting them ... no longer a matter of appropriating them to oneself, or projecting anything on to them."[31] The material upsurge of being seeps through inanimate objects, topographic configurations and fractured centers of materialized consciousness. This is in keeping with Deleuze's insistence that the eye of matter lies within matter itself, within the stream of materiality.

This combination of the material upsurge of being and the forking of time cements the independent development of the aberration of movement. No longer tied to invariability and truth, false movement finally liberates time and transforms thought. Especially in writers like Robbe-Grillet, standards based on traditional precepts of legal connections in space, and chronological relations in time, in other words, organic, truthful narrative, are discarded. The system of judgment that forms the backbone to traditional narration disappears in the false, "the power of the false ... affects the investigator and the witness as much as the person presumed guilty."[32] Constant modifications ensue not based on subjectivities or centers of indetermination but as in *Marienbad*, on disconnected places and de-chronologized moments which now come to characterize film consciousness. The fundamental reason for this is because the power of the false is linked to multiplicity.

In the final analysis both truth and the figure of the forger, even with its multiplicity, come out second best to the false and its power of transformation. Change is locked in a time warp for the former two but with transformation there is metamorphosis and only with the genuinely creative artist does film consciousness result in genuine change. Neither camera consciousness nor the open totality is sufficient to mark the difference.

Aberrance and Problem Ideas

When the past is not reducible to a former present, and when the future comprises an eternal recurrence of change, we are in the realm of Deleuze's crystalline time and we can look at the questions posed and the decisions taken. This allows for connections and constructions not based on any assumed coherent narrative in life. The combination of linkage and connection with perpetual movement means formed connections retain openness, a lack of teleology, whether they relate to events of external moments or personal (self) histories. This narrative model frequently shows protagonists themselves impelled by chance rather than motivating actions:

> This declining belief in totalizing or organic ideologies and global situations throws into question the narrative foundations and logic of the action-image. Indeed, the aimless wanderings of modern cinema's protagonists is itself a deterritorializing figure.... Protagonists no longer act, they rather wander and observe.[33]

It is with the sense of aberrant movement that time comes to express the fact that we finally have time-images beyond movement itself. "Opsigns" and "sonsigns" subordinate movement to "a purely optical and sound situation (which) does not extend into action, any more than it is induced by an action.... It is a matter of something ... which henceforth outstrips our sensory motor capacities."[34] There is a force of dispersal, a "void that is no longer a motor-part of the image ... but is the radical calling into question of the image.... *False continuity becomes the law*."[35]

The idea of continuity in classical editing has not merely involved the movement-image but also the way it is contextualized with reference to the real world and the out-of-field. Implicit in every visual image is the continuity of the unseen and the unheard giving perspective to the seen and heard and acting as its invisible foundation. But now there is inclusiveness, no more out-of-field: "The outside of the image is replaced by the *interstice between the two frames in the image*."[36] As Deleuze explains it, film narrative is no longer images in a chain but the method of "between two images, the method of '*and*,' this '*and*' then that."[37] With this new conception of cinema montage, movement changes its form from being perceptually sequential to mentally simultaneous as an affirmation of the coexistence of the past, present and future. The change in modern montage is a new version of montage's vertical shifts, not from one series to another but revolving round the single shot; no longer montage but "montrage,"[38] not how images are linked but what images show.

Time-images involve an interpretation of situation that is a far greater fine-tuning of the exploration of the stratified moment than the movement-image. Reminiscent of both Benjamin's flâneur and Kracauer's anteroom, the modern behavioral mode is manifested within a specific kind of space and with a particular kind of attitude: "A state of strolling, of sauntering or of rambling ... the determinate locations blurred, letting any-space-whatever rise up where the modern affects of fear, detachment, but also freshness, extreme speed and interminable waiting were developing."[39] Deleuze's analysis of post Second World War film is not the dialectical montage Eisenstein used to engender shock effects. In later films, lack of meaning as a conscious strategy constitutes the requisite shock to sensibility. Moreover, the same techniques favorably referred to by Bazin as alternatives to Eisenstein, deep focus and depth-of-field, are praised by Deleuze for bringing out the thinking of imagery and the possibility for moving in time rather than space, "depth of field ... opened up a new direction for the cinema ... it makes the unrolling of the film a theorem rather than an association of images, it makes thought immanent to the image."[40] There is movement akin to the movement of formally linked thought, "deductive" and "automatic" and what breathes life into this movement comes from the outside. Visual imagery as thought's catalyst seems unmotivated, unexplained and irrational.

Deleuze questions any simplistic and correlative approach to hermeneutic questioning trapped within a representational impasse. For Deleuze, subjectivity should posit objects as they are by recognizing they are multiple and differential with an inherent reciprocal relationship to other determinations. These posited determinations are informed by a complex propositional experience. Answers are returned to propositions from the posited objectivities and problem-ideas. They relate to the attitude that comes from the context of situations that question them in the first place. "Positings" are characterized by multiplicity and difference and the affirmations that are returned will also be made up of multiplicity and difference. The process is the dynamic for understanding perceptual awareness and attitudinal shifts and becomes an alternative to representational facticity. There is a provocation of thought through question and disjuncture. The interchange between posited questions and positing answers is one of non-correspondence and ultimately emancipation from organic representation and the hermeneutic circle.

For Deleuze, spectator relationship to film is characterized more by these non-equivalencies of problems-ideas than it is by pursuing phenomenological predelineations and horizons that may already be immanent in a representational work. In terms of film imagery, there should be freedom to explore a perceptual rediscovery of problems-ideas.

What ignites the actual from the virtual is based on a circuitry but it is not the circular movement of a negative dialectic. What is significant here is that problems-ideas are objectively characterized and by nature unconscious, in keeping with virtuality and duration. They further challenge the status of a positing subjectivity. What is posited is activated by unconscious propositions that do not match subsequent affirmations:

> For problems-ideas are by nature unconscious: they are extra-propositional and sub-representative, and do not resemble the propositions which represent the affirmations to which they give rise. If we attempt to reconstitute problems in the image of or as resembling conscious propositions, then the illusion takes shape, the shadow awakens and appears to acquire a life of its own.[41]

The awakening shadows all too easily become part of the Platonic cave and inadequate representation, but problems-ideas can sustain the unexpected, meandering movements within uncut depth-of-field, dispersals and labyrinthine explorations which "take time" to resolve. Ultimately, thought coincides with the relation of non-relation, loosening the shadow of representation. With the new time montage there is disruption opening up the show of time to pre-subjective and impersonal sensibility.

The Split Self

The approach to cinema where film consciousness achieves the independence to think otherwise is entirely the result of seeing the world as image, image as movement, and time as shown. Deleuze's philosophy of difference combined with Bergson's creative intuition are not dissimilar to phenomenological description that includes a fractured "I" and self-thinking thought.

We see this echoed in Poulet's phenomenological comments on literary consciousness:

> Whatever I think is a part of my mental world. And yet here I am thinking a thought which manifestly belongs to another mental world which is being *thought* in me just as though I did not exist ... this thought which is alien to me and yet in me, must also have in me a *subject* which is alien to me.[42]

The "as-if" conceit of the film experience may likewise suggest a schizophrenic condition in the spectator but it is rather a question of the release of an other consciousness in itself, a thinking imagery. This includes and transcends artist, work and spectator, going on to become a consciousness channel, "a work of literature becomes ... a sort of human being, that it is a mind conscious of itself and constituting itself in me as the subject of its own objects."[43] If there were a problem here phenomenologically it would center around the birth of consciousness in terms of evolutionary growth, ("it may be that cinema had to go through a slow evolution before attaining self-consciousness"[44]). It must be asked, consciousness of what, since consciousness cannot be empty in an intentional sense. Thus, Deleuze's position and the phenomenological differ on this since there is no intentional or intended sense of mediation in Deleuze, nor dialectic resolution. Phenomenologically, the experiencing subject is the concrete self and the transcendental observer, thinker and thinker of the thinker, enmeshed in an intricate web of spectator interpretation and autonomous vision, inclusive positions of reflective thought and passive ego:

> [T]wo different egos one of which, conscious of its freedom, sets itself up as an independent spectator of a scene which the other would play in a mechanical fashion. But this dividing in two never goes to the limit. It is rather an oscillation of the person between two points of view on himself, a hither-and-thither of the spirit.[45]

For Deleuze, "the essence of cinema — which is not accessible in the majority of films — has thought as its higher purpose, nothing but thought and its functioning."[46] Film consciousness as the route to thought thinking itself, or better, thinking the unthought, starts in the same way as reflexive films, by frustrating identification. The same move towards negating objective meaning means a fracturing of the phenomenological subject and challenge to identity. Identification in the movement-image is strong, vicarious experience, dream-imagery, escapism and voyeurism have all been charted in film through psychoanalytic film theory. Moreover, the sense of the organic tends to recoup or co-opt dispersed spectator identification, albeit in a complex manner. The time-image, however, frustrates such co-option using a wide array of strategies to do so.

Contrary to Eisenstein's movement-images, also intended to make thought visible, the thought of the time-image provokes a suspension of the world. It is effectuated by indiscernible images acting as a reminder of the fact that we are not yet thinking. Imagistic power somehow beyond thought. What become suspended in the world is the present-at-hand, as well as the return of the transcendental to the prepredicative, a return itself disturbed with a reminder that there is always difference in self-thinking thought. If thought is incoherent and disjointed then indiscernible and uncertain imagery will be its appropriate avatar. In an intolerable world full of cliché and banality thought can no longer think a world or think itself. By making the unthought in thought the motor for a return to the world, we can remake ourselves, create the false and be at one with a world which can do thought justice. This return to the world, a belief that we are inherently linked to it, da-sein cannot be otherwise, is exemplified by the characteristics of the signs of the time-image, the descriptions that constitute opsigns and sonsigns, and the interpretations attainable through "lectosigns" as the way film images can be read. Creative reading centers on films with aberrant movement, non-sequencing and decentering, all of which may become issues in themselves. In the lectosign, powers of interpretation are brought to bear and images read (but not linguistically) as well as seen, "readable as well as visible, it is the 'literalness' of the perceptible world which constitutes it like a book."[47] Reference and movement are subordinated to depth interpretations relying on difference rather than identity. Again, Merleau-Ponty's presence is felt. Depth interpretation comes through image and body im-pli-cated in the world, enfolded and interlaced. Both speaking and reading are part of a directional sense (meaning) that only makes "sense" through the body's directedness. As with the notion of the outside, the readability of images in the time-image régime is not based on a fresh cohesiveness, semiotic references or bodily self-containment but rather on a unique visual-sound, present-past disjunction; a dehiscence denoting a higher evolution of film consciousness.

Time Out-of-Joint

The theoretical base for these observations lies with Kant's notion of subjectivity, and his description of imagination and the sublime. This is an analysis only briefly referred to in Deleuze's cinema work but it pervades Deleuze's thinking on the nature of time-image narration, characterized as it is by splits, disconnected places and de-chronologized moments. The sublime is a starting point in Eisenstein's dialectic, based on the shock effect and the eventual overcoming of opposition to think the Whole. With intellectual montage there is a second movement infusing the interval with affectivity as it goes from the concept to the affect; what returns from thought to the image. Kant's "*Critique of Pure Reason* related the ego to the 'I' in a relationship still regulated by the order of time."[48] At issue was the giving of "emotional fullness" or "passion" back to the intellectual process. But this was only a precursor to the later development of the sublime "in which the sensible is valid in itself ... a Pathos which leaves (the Ego and I) to evolve freely ... to form strange combinations as sources of time."[49]

Deleuze's does not relate the transcendental to the metaphysical but to time: "But in modern cinema ... the time-image is no longer empirical, nor metaphysical; it is transcendental in the sense that Kant gives this word; time is out of joint and presents itself in its pure state."[50] The process of confronting the unthinkable in thought is philosophically arrived at through the split self, "the presence to infinity of another thinker who shatters every monologue of a thinking self."[51] According to Deleuze, beginning with Kant the question is, what is it that determines the otherwise undetermined "I am." How can the determinable I think determine what is undeterminable, "I am." In one's sense of self, "nothing in myself is thereby given for thought."[52] Kant makes the link, establishes a determinable between thinking and being through difference but not by a difference which separates thinking and being, which would be "an empirical difference between two determinations" but "in the form of an internal Difference which establishes an *a priori* relation between thought and being. Kant's answer is well known: the form under which undetermined existence is determinable by the 'I think' is that of time."[53]

We begin to think in time, that is, in the fracture of the split "I." If thought "is" anywhere it is with the determinable as a force between the determining and the determined, within time. Thus, when cinema finally shows time it is showing thought of a kind which becomes discernible in the intermediate and interstice, as a visible force emanating (from) temporality. The characteristic of this visibility cannot be pinpointed. It takes different shapes but will appear as both mirror imagery and disturbance as it disassociates and fragments the pretensions of representation as determinable agency. The sense of self only takes on substantial form in the flow of time, as the existence of a phenomenon appearing as passive and receptive. This makes what seems to be the active self, making spontaneous thought, in fact a *passive subject*, the "I think" is "exercised" in it and upon it, but not by it. Thus, according to Deleuze, the I think and the I am, thought and Being, are discovered by Kant to be a transcendental but inner difference (not reliant on God).

For Deleuze, thinking about thinking can never be transparent, that is, achievable through reflection, though there is a temptation in phenomenological terms to equate these observations with intentionality, relating the heightened state of awareness to a thetic thinking and the nature of the time-image in the interstice to the noema. Deleuze would resist this in keeping with an anti-dualistic and anti-transparent approach. When Deleuze asserts that I am separated from myself by the form of time he is arguing that the ego cannot constitute itself as a unique and active subject. The subject is split because thinking takes place only when the passive ego feels the effect of an active thinking. This is how the mind qualifies itself as the affectivity of a passive ego — not as the activity of an agent:

> [T]he spontaneity of which I am conscious in the "I" think cannot be understood as the attribute of a substantial and spontaneous being, but only as the *affection of a passive self* which experiences its own thought ... being exercised in it and upon it but not by it.[54]

This fundamental difference between the "I" and ego is as different as sequential and serialized time; not the movement of a spiral coursing in on itself but the "and plus and," the "thread of a straight line." "The 'I' and the Ego are thus separated by the line of time which relates them to each other, but under the condition of a fundamental difference."[55]

Deleuze's main criticism of Kant is that after setting up a revolutionary turn in thought he did not go far enough. By following through in the *Critique of Pure Reason* the fracture of the "I" and the disappearance of rational theology and psychology as a result of the speculative death of God, Kant "did not pursue this initiative" but "resurrected God and the I."[56] The fractured "I" is filled by a new identity with the passive self remaining receptive without power of synthesis. Kant maintained variable models of recognition applicable in the form of a harmony between the faculties and ends up in the opposite camp to Deleuze: "It is impossible to maintain the Kantian distribution, which amounts to a supreme effort to save the world of representation."[57] Yet Kant's influence through to the time-image survives in Bergson and Proust:

> Bergson is much closer to Kant than he himself thinks.... Kant defined time as the form of interiority, in the sense that we are internal to time. It is Proust who says that time is not internal to us, but that we are internal to time, which divides itself in two, which loses itself and discovers itself in itself, which makes the present pass and the past be preserved.[58]

The process of fracturing is somewhat transformed in film consciousness as a consciousness which is conscious but does not rationalize its consciousness, instead showing it. In the confluence of the intermediate image, where film and spectator consciousness merge, the relation of the two automata in the film experience can lead to the unthought in thought without destroying it in reflection. It is rather sustained in sensation. Split subjectivity is still a force since it comprises part of spectator consciousness. As I contemplate thought it changes to the matter of my contemplation not what I was thinking. Thus, thought's central contradiction is a Heisenbergian impossibility to think itself without changing itself, an essentially quantum theory of life.

To reach film's time-image, realist film theory and the relation of raw materiality to filmed representation must be transcended by the interiority of time so that time moves in the subject, an immutable form of constant change that keeps the subject split through infinite modulation. This should also be considered in terms of the other half of the equation, not only thought thinking itself through the split "I" but thought thinking itself as thinking the Whole. "This is the very definition of the sublime."[59] In relationship to Eisenstein, we are still exploring movement-image and shock produced by montage which allows thought to think the shock, to be at one with thought as a thought of the Whole. For Eisenstein, in particular, and for many pre-war theorists, the unity of nature and man, the non-indifferent, was a goal that expressed itself as an appeal to the mass; the individuation of mass. Deleuze re-envisaged the Kantian sublime, understood in terms of "the violence experienced by the faculty of the imagination, when confronted by a formless and/or deformed immense power and, as a result, is thrown back on itself as upon its own limits."[60] The notion of "being thrown back on itself" represents the "uniqueness of Deleuze's intuition around the function of the imagination in the Kantian analysis," where he resolves the impasse by replacing the "principle of representation" with Bergson's definition of "the brain as a pure interval (or 'gap'), opening onto a virtual whole that is actualized according to divergent lines...."[61] The sublime "opens a gap" in experience through which the idea of the "subject as Whole" is engendered. As Deleuze puts it:

> In the sublime there is a sensory-motor unity of nature and human, which means that nature must be named the non-indifferent, since it is apparently Nature itself that issues the demand for unification of the Whole within the interiority of a subject and it is by reacting to this demand that we discover that which is fundamental to our destiny.[62]

Kant described two kinds of the sublime, mathematical and dynamic, the former immense and powerful, the latter, measureless and formless. Both decomposed organic composition. The former overcomes imagination but gives way to a thinking faculty that "forces us to conceive the immense or the measureless as whole."[63] The latter arouses terror in us but arouses a thinking faculty by which "we feel superior to that which annihilates us," a domination and sense of empowerment in which our spiritual destination appears "to be invincible"[64] and can overwhelm organic life. This is the source of a liberation that supersedes both nature and organic individuality to create a non-psychological life of the spirit where we are alone with God as light. Expressionism, too, breaks with the organic relation of the sensorimotor, "only to discover a sublime world," but now "ideal rather than material" in which we find a "spiritual redemption, but this only confirms the organic conditions of the movement-image."[65] It will take the various strategies of modern art to bring about a "negative apprehension" of the idea of the Whole.

For Deleuze, Artaud also made clear the way thought is not yet seen to be thinking; it is still "impowered." Artaud was exemplary for film even though he was skeptical about its capacity for change. He believed the harmonics and "vibrations" of film imagery harbored the "hidden birth of thought" and "resembled and allied itself with the mechanics of a dream without really being itself a dream."[66] For Artaud, the point was not transparency but the *occasion* of thought, its functioning as a coming to be: "Thought has no reason to function than its own birth, always the repetition of its own birth, secret and profound."[67] What is characteristically film consciousness, the bringing of imagery to thought and the combination of conscious thought and the unconsciousness within it, attaches itself to various models of expression. The spiritual automaton that becomes the "Mummy," "paralyzed," "petrified," "frozen," heroes who cannot think, like incapacitated and passive spectators seeing a parade of images of "frozen instances."[68]

These images that come to haunt us are not the images of surrealist dreams but rather belong to the waking world, as the unconscious within consciousness. When film comes to thought it forces thought to think the thought it is not yet thinking. Film is there at the outset, walking the pencil-thin tightrope between thought and image. This reverses Eisenstein's shock that sets trains of thought in motion within an ongoing inner monologue. For Artaud, on the contrary, there is "another thinker who shatters every monologue of a thinking self," no singular, internal monologue to latch on to but vying, recalcitrant voices in the shape of internal dialogues. The goal here is not to restore omnipotence to thought but on the contrary to recognize its condition of impasse and aporia and work with it to seek alternatives, other worldly existences within life, to return to it through whatever access points can be opened up.

The instinct of thought is to exercise all-encompassing powers to overcome intuition and dissipate ineffable imagery by appealing to logic and totality. Film's time-image puts us in touch with thought that is outside of this, not dictated by egocentricity or molded by habitual norms and rationalization. It rouses us, kindles the passion to think through the contingent, the stark encounter, the contradictory and difference-in-itself. We see time-images question foundations in much the same way as phenomenology begins with the dissolution of all assumptions and foundations in order to explore presuppositions. Like phenomenology, time-images question the natural basis of perception and then bracket it in order to relive the process by which phenomena come-to-appearance in the first place. This takes place both thoughtfully and emotionally through sensations and hyletic sensa. However, just how these access points open up is less clear. Phenomenologically the terrain has been mapped out. The prepredicative and predicative have established the domains between, on the one hand, coming-to-visibility as the being of raw experience and, on the other, the giving of meaning through significations of intentionality. When Deleuze analyses the time-image through artists such as Resnais and Antonioni, however, he finds these phenomenological categories to be insufficient.

Film Events

There will always be becoming as change. Ontologically, making of chance a necessity is the only way Deleuze sees to assure the affirmation of creation, multiplicity and a concomitant mode of thinking thought outside itself. The innermost reality of the brain must be an exteriority of thought otherwise there can be no opposition to the conformity and rigidity of truthful images of thought, which go back to Plato. Thoughts must be related to the outside and they must be "nomadic," since we are not yet thinking: "Every thought is already a tribe ... this form of exteriority of thought is not at all symmetrical to the form of interiority.... It is rather a force that destroys both the image *and* its copies, every possibility of subordinating thought to a model of the True, the Just, or the Right."[69] Time-images serve as the perfect conduit for provoking thought by disrupting certainty, taken-for-granted truths, the laziness of bland acceptance and insipid, dispassionate doubting. But first there must be a violence perpetuated on thought:

[T]he claws of a strangeness or an enmity which alone would awaken thought from its natural stupor.... Do not count upon thought to ensure the relative necessity of what it thinks. Rather, count upon the contingency of the encounter with that which *forces thought to raise up* and educate the absolute necessity of an act of thought or a passion to think.[70]

The passion to think, in film engendered by the irrational cut, raises the interval to independence and forms part of the disabling-enabling circuitry of the beyond thought. Irrational cuts, or incommensurables, play no part in linking shots or sequences sequentially but form the series as part of a connecting "and." This means that the irrational cut is the platform liberating the interval and in doing so allows for the birth of thought. In questioning its own foundations, time comes into relief in paradoxical fashion. The time-image seems to "end up" as dead time, a strange meanwhile of the yet-to-come and the "unique experience" of the past.[71] Time goes nowhere, revolving around itself as we experience a temporal depth perception, a dead-heat of time zones where no priority is gained as the genetic element of film perception, the photogramme, is forefronted. These film images of the interstice are similar to aspects of the "event" as becoming, being "in medias res," without beginning or end: "The event is the virtual that has become consistent: it neither begins nor ends but has gained or kept the infinite movement to which it gives consistency."[72] Such film events are full of promise but come to exhaust themselves in their own time, in the interstice, in simultaneity "where nothing takes place, an infinite awaiting that is already infinitely past, awaiting and reserve."[73] Yet within these seemingly idle periods, not only is nothing not taking place, there is a profundity of excess and an embracing, invisible presence. *Everything* is taking place because we are no longer in the sensorimotor schema but the power-house of affectivity, where thetic positing examines itself, where dream and recollection merge, where ego poles decompose and where the objectively determined is subjectively permeated.

The transmission of film "events" and the singularities that convey them are part of the time-image series. The series takes its dynamic by chance, the first throw of the dice, while the second throw operates under conditions that are "partially determined by the first, as in a Markov chain, where we have a succession of partial relinkings."[74] In the irrational cut, this is a "hazard" linkage, the throw of the dice, but not "haphazard," a differentiation but not association, a dynamic propulsion but not a predictable telos. As Deleuze comments on Godard:

> For, in Godard's method it is not a question of association. Given one image, another image has to be chosen which will induce an interstice *between* the two ... given one potential, another one has to be chosen, not any whatever, but in such a way that a difference of potential is established between the two, which will be productive of a third or of something new.[75]

By first isolating and then linking images in such a series we retain the singularity peculiar to them while at the same time allow them to be iterative, "a singularity is not something unique or 'sui generis,' but, on the contrary, something that can be understood only through the ways it comes to be repeated."[76] Here repetition comes to constitute meaning, by example, by review and by positing the askew. The space that is carved out in the curvature of space is the outside of thought. In the interstice, where the film 'event' takes-its-place, we have thought that pushes two incommensurables to their limit points; seeing, as the self-evident or non-discursive and, saying, as the articulate, discursive practice.

The event has a double structure; the happening that take place in what Deleuze calls, after the Stoics, state of affairs, and that dimension of the event that is out of time with the present, non locatable but making itself felt somewhere between past and future. Deleuze shows that the time-images of Welles, Resnais, Godard, Antonioni, among others, express the film event in their own specific way. Antonioni's masterpiece, *The Passenger* (1975), is a prime example and bears closer scrutiny.

On one level, *The Passenger* is a meta-critique of the cliché, an insistence on the outside of film breaking the illusory barrier of filmed representation. The doubling of realities, the doppelganger of identity, the simulacra of imagery, the duality of actor and role, stillness within movement:

> The theme of doubling penetrates Antonioni's shooting technique. In order to record the dead moment, *temps mort*, he likes to extend filming beyond the end of the scene when the actor has just stopped acting his/her character role in the film, but not quite returned to his/her own identity.[77]

In Antonioni *temps mort* wins out over *temps vivant*.[78] Antonioni's initial impact is the throw of the dice, "a fascination with chance ... the effects of chance, erratic traces, unclear trajectories, vague gestures, which are inscribed, as by a lapse, a falling asleep of the camera, on the lens, the film, the screen, the retina."[79] Above all, Antonioni's filmed "event" has affinities with Deleuze's; a happening that cannot be fixed yet contains the uncontainable within immanence. *The Passenger* creates a journey of the doppelganger, fractured identity, existentialism and death. The journalist, David Locke, replaces his look-alike, gunrunner David Robertson because he is tired of life and is attracted to taking on another persona. But ennui cannot be shaken even in disguised repetition. Locke takes up Robertson's "passage" through life and is also a passenger through Antonioni's familiar landscape of disconnected, abstract spaces which absorb characters and actions, spaces which are at one moment barren and dehumanized and at other moments areas of transience to be crossed; terminals, roads and airports, leaving only momentary traces.[80]

The film is itself an examination not only of the jaded Locke but also the jaded clichés of film. This is a gesture towards another kind of filmmaking not yet with us, a report on the status of film imagery that shows it to be coded and "locked" within the world of representation. As with any such inbuilt critique, Antonioni's own films attempt to show the way out of the impasse into a new film experience. Any pretense at escapism through identification is dissipated. As Locke's experience shows, taking on another identity in the search of fulfillment is no escape; it only leads to more of the same, in film and in life.

The memorable culmination of *The Passenger* when Locke dies alone on a bed, shows death and change to be inexorably bound to each other, as change is a kind of death from one state to another, from the individual to the generic. As Locke decomposes physically and figuratively:

> [H]e reveals the generic human hunger for transcendence and meaning ... parallel with the pilgrim or saint whose assumption is a literal elevation out of and beyond himself in an *ecstasy* which means not joy but a loss of self, passage into a larger life.... We must adapt or die, even when the adaptation means dying out of oneself, *dying into change.*[81]

We are in a world of "uncertain doubles" and "partial deaths"[82] death within life and the multiplicity of particular deaths as change. Deleuze sees more in Antonioni's films than simply themes of solitude and incommunicability. Tied down by tired colors of the world and ponderous body, they carry the weight of the past and modern neurosis. But there is a belief in renewal, a cinema of the brain revealing the creativity of the world, its colors rejuvenated by a new space-time.[83]

In *The Passenger* Locke is pulled back by the desert and the burden of the past *as* past. In a similar fashion to Resnais, time is conflated and confused. We enter into flashbacks but it is unclear to whom they belong. They appear as objective events or, just as feasibly, the vision of several characters. Notably they belong to no one other than "mitsein," Antonioni's point of view standing alongside the character. Only in the final scene of death does a lightness of spirituality make its presence felt. Indeed, this final seven-minute scene is a landmark in film and shows how Antonioni opens up to film consciousness, a "lived reality in a cinematic manner that cannot be expressed in words."[84] The long tracking scene is itself a depiction of film consciousness maturing, and the birth of the meanwhile. Here the event is death and it is shown to be double and impersonal, an event that happens to Locke yet one that is no longer about him, or his double, but an event that courses between doubles. The impersonality of the event delicately touches empirical reality as it suffuses object and subject, the apotheosis of composite life incorporating, for Merleau-Ponty, the invisible with the visible, and for Deleuze, empty, dead periods with the multidimensional, impacted time-image.

In *The Passenger* Locke has to die, as a fulfillment of the persona he has taken over, a life already endangered. The complex climactic tracking shot away from the doomed Locke into the courtyard and the final return to his now dead, assassinated body shows the release of the soul as visual continuity, "an unbroken glide through time and space."[85] This is a metaphysical change not a mystical one, Deleuze's philosophy of Nature rather than Platonic ascendance:

[D]eath as a transformation into other elements, ultimately into energy ...
the enduring organism is simply one that is consistent with its environment
... consistent motion ... this transformation of food and air into the pattern
of the organism, is what we call existence.... Nonbeing fulfills being; it does
not negate being, just as space does not negate what is solid. Each is a condition for the reality of the other.[86]

As a release, Locke's death is not merely personal.[87] Rather than his own
death, Locke is already disembodied from himself. He has turned over in bed,
turned his back to the window and the "outside." This is the death that never
happens to us as an event. Death is seen in relation to being, what comes
after death as life. Locke has been killed and no amount of technological control can change that fact. Here film shows the invisible coming to visibility,
the murmuring of being. The inadequacy of the event as some-thing that
takes place is transcended by film consciousness as part of becoming, as an
expression of Lacan's Real rather than the control of the symbolic, as the passage of the soul into the light on the unbroken luminous screen.

Outside of Film

Thought, inspired by the outside, at the "eventful opening point of the
closed," is an elucidation of the labyrinth of the finest thread that links objects
to the universe, "it is in following this thread, like Ariadne, that thought can
elucidate the labyrinth, whose portal is the dire disjunction or the (apparently) incurable fracture of all truth by the nonrelation of objects."[88] Formal
linkages of thought are automatic and deductive, they are like theorems; a
depth-of-field that makes the unrolling of film a theorem. Problems come to
"live" in theorems, they give them life and open their interiority introducing
film's "leitmotif." With the direct time-image the Whole has now to do with
the aberrant, residing in the interstice between images, "a spacing which means
that each image is plucked from the void and falls back into it."[89] We now
pass from "a simple disjunctive logic of exteriority to a *topology of the outside*
as the locus of the inscription of forces."[90]

In unraveling this, we find that once thought emerges in films of the time-
image through aberrant movement and indiscernibility, it is an automaton, an
automaton of the outside where there is no subject thinking the outside but the
singular "thought-outside." Thought is drained of its inside and is now expressed
through its outside as automaton: "Far from restoring knowledge, or the internal certainty that it lacks, to thought, the problematic deduction puts the
unthought into thought, because it takes away all its interiority to excavate an
outside in it, an irreducible reverse-side which consumes its substance."[91]

To ask what composes forms of the outside is to search for what animates it, just as what animates thought "outside-thought": "Let us call this 'element' of the outside 'force' so that the outside is only manifest as the imposition of a force."[92] The outside becomes an independence of force, thought in turmoil that does not yet think until it exerts its force of relation in the modulations rippling through the folding of an inside. The inside does not achieve independence as a result of this, as if in a hollow, but becomes the inside *of* the outside, reciprocally made possible by the acts of folding. In this light the relation of the doppelganger in *The Passenger* is even more pertinent. As Deleuze points out, the theme of the double has always "haunted Foucault":

> [T]he double is never a projection of the interior; on the contrary, it is an interiorization of the outside. It is not a doubling of the One, but a redoubling of the Other. It is not a reproduction of the Same, but a repetition of the Different. It is not the emanation of an "I," but something that places in immanence an always other or a Non-self.[93]

This is what allows for the fluidity of areas of indetermination. Their place is a site of change, becoming subject and being subjected as a process of rebirth and points of resistance as potential for reformation and reformulation. What film now shows, as a showplace and showtime, is a third dimension of imagery — one of force. Transcending content and expression, beyond that which is filmed or sculptured within time (Tarkovsky), we find the force of the outside in all its animating splendor. This is a force that sets into motion the other incommensurable yet mutually reliant elements of sight and sound, or statement and visibility. As a force it is not filmable but it is what lies beneath filming as the Being of film, as a shift from knowledge to power.

Time, too, has changed from the showing of time zones in their respective chambers to indiscernibility, not merely shorn of succession but also of simultaneity. What remains is an absolute memory, a potential of power, or a series of powers. Though not filmable as power, what is visible is exteriority as the twin elements of light and language, seeing and speaking. As an independence of force the Outside is always present, remaining distinct from the "history of forms." As a force and non-relation, the Outside allows for thinking in the interstice at the point of disjunction between seeing and speaking. Here we return to the irrational film cut between the non-linked but always relinkable images, as that which is the absolute contact between the asymmetrical outside and inside: "We move with ease from one to the other, because the outside and the inside are two sides of the limits as irrational cut, and because the latter ... appears as an autonomous outside which necessarily provides itself with an inside."[94]

In this folding and chiasm a "worlding" is (re)produced redolent of the aesthetic world of phenomenological consciousness; a force to think which is insisting and unrelenting, yet strangely self-contained and impacted. For the forms of exteriority to exert their force, a possibility filming accentuates by its mechanical reproduction, a new framing must be created that acknowledges the demise of the out-of-field and any representational connotations, "the visual image ceases to extend beyond its own frame" and the sound image too cannot be relative or explanatory of the visual but must assert its independence, "the sound image is itself framed" and this disjunction "must not be surmounted."[95] In expressing its independence the sound image is now the voice, achieving Foucault's priority of statement, extracting the pure speech act that now in film becomes "an act of myth, or story-telling which creates the event."[96] The event will emerge but as an event will sink, go deeper than any interiority. It will no longer be visible but will be like Antonioni's tensions subsuming visible traces "as an underground fire, always covered over."

For Deleuze, film's spiritual automaton is an intruder, a theft of thought. Here the phenomenon of a schizophrenic stealing of thought is referred to as a positive precursor for the Other of thought. There is powerlessness in thought which prevents it being what it is and the potential power of film consciousness is to unleash a spiritual automaton, logic of thought, which is not that of the ego but its otherness. In this way, film images becomes part of the intricate folds which comprise the membranes coursing through the space between thought and unthought, comprising, perhaps, the unique imagery of auto-affection that would otherwise be interminably distant or overwhelmingly near. Representation and the relation to the real are replaced by outside space and its relation to inside space: "This auto-affection, this conversion of far and near, will assume more and more importance by constructing an *inside-space* that will be completely co-present with the outside-space on the line of the fold."[97]

We remember that this inside-space is not the internalized integration of self-awareness we find in the changing whole of the movement-image. This is rather the inside deeper than any internal world since its profundity is independent of distance, imbricated rather into the time of virtuality, "far from showing up in space, (it) frees a time that condenses the past in the inside, brings about the future in the outside, and brings the two into confrontation at the limit of the living present."[98]

What is outside is not localizable and what is internal could not be said to relate to any foundational, self-awareness but an unthought, deeper than any internal world. The hiatus cannot be bridged by traditional forms of recuperation, integration or differentiation of identity, in other words, nothing dialectic. There is rather confrontation of an outside and an inside independent of distance. This absolute contact between the asymmetrical outside and inside is the irrational cut writ large. Between the two points we have absolute contact as we move from the one to the other. The irrational cut is the arena for this oscillation.

Deleuze, cites novelist and critic, Georges Duhamel whose antipathy for film was based on the fact that "I can no longer think what I want, the moving images are substituted for my own thoughts."[99] Where for Benjamin, who originally cited Duhamel, the inability to think one's own thoughts was described as an overcoming of the spectator's freedom for association,[100] for Deleuze this constitutes "the dark glory and profundity of cinema."[101] Film consciousness is thought as a theft of thought, so that thought is both its own agent and its own victim. We have moved some way from the inhabited and incarnated lifeworld of phenomenological art to "a strange construct we inhabit only through transmutation or self-experimentation ... from which we emerge refreshed as if endowed with a new optic or nervous system."[102] As long as the film experience is an irrelevance to thinking, full of cliché, it risks promoting the stereotype or formulaic. But when it reveals the powerlessness to think at the heart of thought, when it can return the "body's relationship to the world,"[103] it comes into its own as consciousness replete with the power of transformation.

Chapter Notes

Introduction

1. Dan Zhavi, "Merleau-Ponty on Husserl: A Reappraisal," *Merleau-Ponty's Reading of Husserl*, ed. Ted Loadvine and Lester Embree (Kluwer Academic Publishers, 2002), p. 5.

2. *Ibid.*, p. 9.

3. *Ibid.*, p. 29.

4. M. Merleau-Ponty, *Phenomenology of Perception*, trans. Colin Smith (Routledge, 1989), p. 416.

5. *Ibid.*, p. 417, and Mauro Carbone, "The Time of Half-Sleep," *Loadvine and Embree, ibid.*, p. 153, note 7.

6. Samuel Weber, *Mass Mediauras* (Stanford University Press, 1996), p. 81.

7. Martin Heidegger, "The Age of the World Picture," *The Question Concerning Technology and Other Essays*, trans. William Lovitt (Harper Torchbooks, 1977), p. 154.

8. *Ibid.*, p. 136.

9. *Ibid.*

10. Weber, *ibid.*, pp. 81–82.

11. Heidegger, *ibid.*, p. 134.

12. Hubert L. Dreyfus, "Heidegger on Technology," *Technology and the Politics of Knowledge*, ed. Andrew Feenberg (Indiana University Press, 1995), p. 102.

13. Heidegger, "The Turning," *The Question Concerning Technology and Other Essays, ibid.*, p. 48.

14. *Ibid.*, p. 49.

15. Jean-Paul Sartre, *The Psychology of Imagination* (Methuen & Co. Ltd., 1972), p. 67.

16. Suzanne Guerlac, *Thinking in Time* (Cornell University Press, 2006), p. 183.

17. *Ibid.*

18. Jacques Derrida, *Speech and Phenomena*, trans. David B. Allison (Northwestern University Press, 1973), p. 4.

19. Emmanuel Levinas, *Time and the Other*, trans. Richard A. Cohen (Duquesne University Press, 1987), p. 131, note 6, Guerlac, p. 185, note 47.

20. Keith Ansell-Pearson, "Bergson and Creative Evolution/Involution," *The New Bergson*, Ed. John Mullarkey (Manchester University Press, 1999), p. 158.

21. *Ibid.*, p. 159.

22. Richard Dawkins, *The Selfish Gene* (Oxford University Press, 1989), p. 223, and Pearson, *ibid.*, p. 159.

23. Pearson, *ibid.*, p. 159.

24. Dawkins, *ibid.*, pp. 237–8, Pearson, *ibid.*, p. 160.

25. *Ibid.*

26. Gilles Deleuze, *Cinema 2: The Time-Image*, trans. Hugh Tomlinson and Robert Galeta (The Athlone Press, 1989), p. 211 (henceforth "Time-Image").

27. Pearson, *ibid.*, p. 149.

28. Guerlac, *ibid.*, p. 178.

29. Gilles Deleuze, "Bergson's Conception of Difference," *The New Bergson, ibid.*, p. 52.

30. *Ibid.*, p. 51.

31. *Ibid.*

32. *Ibid.*, p. 52.

33. *Ibid.*, p. 51.

34. *Ibid.*
35. Deleuze, *Time-Image*, p. 119.
36. *Ibid.*, p. 121.
37. *Ibid.*, p. 123.
38. *Ibid.*, p. 124.
39. *Ibid.*, p. 125.
40. Deleuze, *Time-Image*, p. 280.
41. Paola Marrati, "The Catholicism of Cinema," *Religion and Media*, ed. Hent de Vries and Samuel Weber (Stanford University Press, 2001), p. 228.
42. Gilles Deleuze, *Difference and Repetition*, trans. Paul Patton (The Athlone Press, 1994), p. 131.
43. *Ibid.*, p. 133.
44. *Ibid.*
45. Marrati, *ibid.*, p. 230.
46. Deleuze, *Difference and Repetition*, pp. 139–140.
47. *Ibid.*, p. 167, Marrati, p. 231.
48. Gilles Deleuze, *Cinema 1* (The Athlone Press, 1986), p. 214 (henceforth "*Movement-Image*").
49. Marreti, p. 231.
50. Deleuze, *Time-Image*, p. 216.
51. *Ibid.*, p. 169.
52. *Ibid.*, p. 170.
53. Marrati, p. 238.
54. Deleuze, *Time-Image*, p. 171.
55. Marrati, *ibid.*, p. 239.
56. *Ibid.*
57. Roland Barthes, *Camera Lucida*, trans. Richard Howard (Vintage Books, 1982), p. 5.
58. Walter Benjamin, *The Arcades Project*, trans. Howard Eiland and Kevin McLaughlin (The Belknap Press of Harvard University Press, 1999), pp. 462–63.
59. Dag Petersson, "Transformations of Readability and Time," *Actualities of Aura*, ed. Dag Petersson and Erik Steinskog (NUS Press, 2005), pp. 64–65.
60. *Ibid.*, p. 65.
61. Benjamin Lewin, *Genes V* (Oxford University Press, 1994), p. 633.
62. Tim Lenoir, Foreword, in Mark B.N. Hansen, *New Philosophy for New Media* (The MIT Press, 2004), p. xiii.
63. Sue Short, *Cyborg Cinema and Contemporary Subjectivity* (Palgrave Macmillan, 2005), p. 47.
64. Allucquere Roseanne Stone, "Will the Real Body Please Stand Up?" *Cybersexualities*, ed. Jenny Wolmark (Edinburgh University Press, 1999), p. 91, Short, *ibid.*, p. 44.
65. Short, *ibid.*, p. 46.
66. *Ibid.*, p. 54.
67. *Ibid.*

68. Gilles Deleuze, *Anti-Oedipus: Capitalism and Schizophrenia*, trans. Robert Hurley, Mark Seem and Helen R. Lane (University of Minnesota Press, 1983), p. 55, Guerlac, p. 190, note 71.
69. Gilles Deleuze and Felix Guattari, *A Thousand Plateaus*, trans. Brian Massumi (Athlone Press, 1988), p. 25.
70. Gilles Deleuze, *Negotiations*, trans. Martin Joughin (Columbia University Press, 1995), p. 149.
71. Lev Manovich, *The Language of the New Media* (MIT Press, 2001), p. 302., Hansen, *ibid.*, p. 36.
72. *Ibid.*, p. 27, Guerlac, *ibid.*, p. 192.
73. Hansen, *ibid.*, p. 31.
74. *Ibid.*, p. 38.
75. *Ibid.*, p. 39; see Francisco Varela, "The Organism: A Meshwork of Selfless Selves," *Organism and the Origin of Self*, ed. A. Tauber (Dordrecht: Kluwer Academic, 1991).
76. Hansen, *ibid.*, p. 3.
77. *Ibid.*
78. Henri Bergson, *Matter and Memory*, trans. N.M. Paul and W.S. Palmer (Zone Books, 1988), p. 19.
79. Hansen, *ibid.*, p. 3.
80. *Ibid.*, p. 5.
81. *Ibid.*, p. 7.
82. Lenoir, *ibid.*, p. xxiv.
83. Hansen, *ibid.*, p. 99, John Johnson, "Machinic Vision," *Critical Inquiry* 26 (autumn, 1999) p. 39.
84. *Ibid.*, p. 144.
85. Walter Benjamin, *Selected Writings*, vol. 3, trans. Edmund Jephcott, Howard Eiland, and others (The Belknap Press of Harvard University Press, 2002), p. 120.
86. *Ibid.*, p. 117.

Chapter 1

1. With the exception of full-length studies, Allan Casebier, *Film Phenomenology* (Indiana University Press, 1993) based on Husserl's theory of representation and Vivian Sobchack, *The Address of the Eye* (Princeton University Press, 1992) based on Merleau-Ponty's theory of perception, material is in article form and only mentions phenomenology in passing. The better articles draw attention to film as a phenomenological experience but rarely offer theoretical justification, relying on generalities, "a phenomenological film theory ... proposes a mutually constitutive relationship between the viewer's life-world and the real-

ity of the filmic world." "Everyday experience and filmic experience, although ontologically different, are mutually conditioned." p. 44. Harald A. Stadler, "Film as Experience," in *Quarterly Review of Film and Video*. Special Edition on Phenomenology, vol. 12, no 3. Harwood Academic Publishers. 1990, p. 41. Stadler's article in the special edition included writers who have attempted to theorize and apply phenomenological principles to film, including the editor, Frank Tomasulo. Other major phenomenologists, such as Roman Ingarden in his phenomenological aesthetics, have an indirect bearing on film. Ingarden posited a direct ontological pluralism that avoided stiff definitions and also allowed for a Husserlian analysis, "what matters in this practical making of phenomenological aesthetics, is the realm of objects to be grasped, not the logical concepts formally structured in smooth axioms and definitions." (P.J. McCormick, *Modernity, Aesthetics, and the Bounds of Art* [Cornell University, 1990], p. 277.) Among Ingarden's four modes of being, the absolute, ideal, real and intentional, film corresponds to the intentional category, which would make it, for Ingarden, heteronomous, derived and non-actual (see Roman Ingarden. *Time and Modes of Being*, trans. R. Micheda [Springfield, Ill.: Thomas. 1964]). Ingarden acknowledged that the essence of film is not removed from its materiality in the form of a purely mental experience, nor is it a being totally dependent on its materiality. As with Husserl, intentionality makes it possible to see film as a sign possessing intersubjective meaning on both a physical and psychic plane. Ingarden's approach precluded a division into subjective and objective investigations because film reinforced the futility of considering solely an object in itself existing independently of perception. For Ingarden, as "brought into life" by the conscious acts of filmmakers and viewers, photography had a mediating function: "If it is a work of art, represented objectivities appear, not as real, but only as quasi-real; they appear only in the 'habitus of reality' ... the objects which were photographed are, so to speak not simply real objects. They perform here a function of reproduction and representation; they play a 'role.'" "The Cinematographic Drama" in *The Literary Work of Art*, trans. George Grabowicz (Northwestern University, 1973), p. 327.

2. Even though these disciplines are kept separate in their application to film, there are clear connections between them as well as with phenomenology. Christian Metz's early work was phenomenological and linguistic, *Film Language* (Oxford University Press, 1974) and later moved to semiotics and psychoanalysis, *The Imaginary Signifier* (Indiana University, 1982).

3. Siegfried Kracauer, *Theory of Film: The Redemption of Physical Reality* (Princeton University, 1997), p. 299.

4. Deleuze, *Time-Image*, p. 210.

5. Maurice Merleau-Ponty, *Phenomenology of Perception*, p. 422.

6. Maurice Merleau-Ponty, "The Eye and Mind," *The Primacy of Perception*, ed. James M. Edie, trans. Carleton Dallery (Northwestern University Press, 1964), p. 186.

7. Maurice Merleau-Ponty, *The Visible and the Invisible*, trans. Alphonso Lingis (Northwestern University Press, 1968), p. 171. See John Sallis, *Phenomenology and the Return to Beginnings* (Duquesne University Press, 1973).

8. Vivian Sobchack, *The Address of the Eye* (Princeton University, 1992), p. 136.

9. Dorothea Olkowski, *Giles Deleuze and the Ruin of Representation* (University of California Press, 1999), p. 82.

10. Henri Bergson, *The Creative Mind*, trans. Mabelle L. Andison (Citadel Press, 1946/74), p. 101.

11. Merleau-Ponty, "Bergson in the Making," *Signs*, trans. Richard C. McCleary (Northwestern University Press, 1964), p. 190.

12. Olkowski, *ibid*.

13. G.B. Madison, "Does Merleau-Ponty Have a Theory of Perception?" *Merleau-Ponty, Hermeneutics, and Postmodernism*, ed. Thomas W. Busch and Shaun Gallagher (State University of New York, 1992), p. 89.

14. Olkowski, *ibid*., p. 79.

15. Merleau-Ponty, *Phenomenology of Perception*, p. 215.

16. Temps Moderne, VIII (July 1952), p. 86, *Eugene Kaelin, An Existentialist Aesthetic* (University of Wisconsin, 1962), p. 312.

17. Gilles Deleuze, *Difference and Repetition*, pp. 49–50.

18. Michael Hardt, *Gilles Deleuze: An Apprenticeship in Philosophy* (University of Minnesota Press, 1993), p. xii.

19. Deleuze, *Difference and Repetition*, p. 263.

20. Hardt, *ibid*., p. 5.

21. Gilles Deleuze, *Bergsonism*, trans. Hugh Tomlinson and Barbara Habberjam (Zone Books, 1988), p. 44.

22. Keith Ansell-Pearson, "Deleuze Out-

side/Outside Deleuze: On the Difference Engineer," *Deleuze and Philosophy: The Difference Engineer* (Routledge, 1997), p. 3.

23. John Rajchman, *The Deleuze Connections* (MIT Press, 2000).

24. Zulfikar Ghose, *The Fiction of Reality* (London, 1983), p. 75, Frank Kermode, *The Sense of an Ending* (Oxford University Press, 1966), pp. 35–39. Wolfgang Iser, *The Fictive and the Imaginary* (Johns Hopkins University Press, 1993), footnote 4, p. 316.

Chapter 2

1. Jean-Louis Comolli, "Technique and Ideology," *Cahiers du Cinéma 1969–1972, The Politics of Representation* (Harvard University Press, 1990), p. 213.

2. Jean-Patrick Lebel, *Cinéma et Idéologie, Nouvelle Critique* 34, pp. 70, 71, Comolli, *ibid.*, p. 214.

3. Vivian Sobchack, *The Address of the Eye*, p. 166.

4. *Ibid.*, p. 219.

5. Michel Dufrenne, *Phenomenology of the Aesthetic Experience* (Northwestern University Press, 1967), p. 227.

6. *Ibid.*, p. 543.

7. Hans-Georg Gadamer, *Truth and Method*, trans. Garrett Barden and John Cumming (Sheed and Ward, 1975), p. 63.

8. Edmund Husserl, *Ideas: General Introduction to Pure Phenomenology*, trans. W. Boyce Gibson (Collier Press, 1962) § 111, Casebier, *Film Phenomenology*, p. 9.

9. Casebier, *ibid.*, pp. 11, 13.

10. Husserl, Ideas, p. 287.

11. Edmund Husserl, *Crisis of European Sciences and Transcendental Phenomenology: An Introduction to Phenomenological Philosophy*, trans. David Carr (Northwestern University Press, 1970), p. 130.

12. Edmund Husserl, *Experience and Judgment: Investigations in a Geneology of Logic*, trans. James S. Churchill and Karl Ameriks (Northwestern University Press, 1973), p. 60.

13. Husserl, *Experience and Judgment*, p. 26.

14. Natalie Depraz, "Imagination and Passivity. Husserl and Kant: A Cross-Relationship," *Alterity and Facticity: New Perspectives on Husserl*, ed. Dan Zhavi (Dordrecht Kluwer, 1998), p. 34.

15. *Ibid.*, p. 36.

16. *Ibid.*

17. Husserl, *Experience and Judgment*, p. 250 (emphasis added).

18. *Ibid.*, p. 251.

19. Siegfried Kracauer, *The Mass Ornament*, trans. Thomas Y. Levin (Harvard University, 1995), p. 118, Heide Schlupmann, "Phenomenology of Film: On Siegfried Kracauer's Writing of the 1920s." *New German Critique*, No. 40 (Winter 1987), p. 98.

20. Kracauer, *Theory of Film*, p. 299.

21. *Ibid.*, p. 31.

22. *Ibid.*, p. 302.

23. D.N. Rodowick, "The Last Things Before the Last: Kracauer and History," *New German Critique* (Summer, 1987), p. 118.

24. *Ibid.* Siegfried Kracauer, *History: The Last Things Before the Last* (Oxford University, 1969), p. 45.

25. Rodowick, *ibid.*, p. 119.

26. *Ibid.*, p. 133, Kracauer, *History*, pp. 22–25.

27. Kracauer, *History*, p. 191 (emphasis added), Rodowick, *ibid.*, p. 118.

28. Dudley Andrew, *The Major Film Theories* (Oxford University Press, 1976), p. 145.

29. Jean Epstein, "The Senses"(1921), trans. Tom Milne, Richard Abel, *French Film Theory and Criticism, 1907–1929* (Princeton University Press, 1988), vol. II. p. 242.

30. Kracauer, *Theory of Film*, p. 15.

31. *Ibid.*

32. *Ibid.*, p. 300.

33. Dagmar Barnouw, *Critical Realism* (John Hopkins Press, 1994), p. 114.

34. Miriam Bratu Hansen, Introduction to Kracauer's *Theory of Film*, p. xxviii.

35. *Ibid.*, p. xvii.

36. Kracauer, *Theory of Film*, pp. 305–6.

37. Aron Gurwitsch, "The Phenomenology of Perception," *James Edie, An Invitation to Phenomenology* (Chicago Press, 1965), p. 23.

38. Casebier, *Film*, p. 13.

39. Edmund Husserl, *Logical Investigations*, trans. J N. Findlay (Humanities Press: New York, 1970), pp. 595–96.

40. Casebier, *ibid.*, p. 39.

41. John D. Caputo, *Radical Hermeneutics* (Indiana University Press, 1987), pp. 41–42.

42. Jean-Luc Marion, *Reduction and Givenness*, trans. Thomas A. Carlson (Northwestern University Press, 1998), p. 15.

43. *Ibid.*, pp. 11–12. c/f. Husserl, *Logical Investigations*, Vol. 1, p. 340.

44. Merleau-Ponty, *Phenomenology of Perception*, p. 211.

45. Paul Ricoeur, *Hermeneutics & the Human Sciences*, trans. John B. Thompson (Cambridge University Press, 1981), p. 105 (emphasis added).

46. Ricoeur, *ibid.*, p. 101.

47. Dufrenne, *The Phenomenology of Aesthetic Experience*, p. 534 (emphasis added).

48. Ricoeur, *Hermeneutics & the Human Sciences*, p. 104.

49. Maurice Merleau-Ponty, *Sense and Non-Sense*, trans. Hubert L. Dreyfus and Patricia Allen Dreyfus (Northwestern University Press, 1964), p. 3.

50. *Ibid.*

51. Husserl, *Crisis*, pp. 374–75.

52. Wolfgang Iser, *The Act of Reading: A Theory of Aesthetic Response* (Routledge & Kegan Paul, 1978), p. 157 (emphasis added).

53. Ricoeur, *Hermeneutics and the Human Sciences*, *ibid.*, p. 182.

54. Frank Kermode, *The Sense of an Ending* (Oxford University, 1975), p. 71.

55. Iser, *Fictive and Imaginary*, footnote, pp. 316–317.

56. Hans-Georg Gadamer, *The Relevance of the Beautiful*, trans. Nicholas Walker (Cambridge University Press, 1986), p. 128.

57. *Ibid.*, p. 129.

58. Merleau-Ponty, *Sense and Non-Sense*, p. 4.

59. Gadamer, *Truth and Method*, p. 216.

60. *Ibid.*, p. 217.

61. William Schweiker, *Mimetic Reflections* (Fordham University, 1990), p. 45.

62. Gadamer, *Truth and Method*, p. 93.

63. *Ibid.*, p. 94.

64. *Ibid.*, p. 98.

65. *Ibid.*, p. 100.

66. Schweiker, *ibid.*, p. 46.

67. Gadamer, Truth and Method, p. 110.

Chapter 3

1. Merleau-Ponty, *Phenomenology of Perception*, p. 166.

2. Merleau-Ponty, *Visible and Invisible*, p. 269.

3. Merleau-Ponty, *Phenomenology of Perception*, p. 256.

4. *Ibid.*, p. 330.

5. Merleau-Ponty, *Visible and Invisible*, p. 250.

6. *Ibid.*, p. 143.

7. *Ibid.*, p. 123.

8. Merleau-Ponty, *Phenomenology of Perception*, p. 233.

9. Sobchack, *Address of the Eye*, p. 86.

10. Merleau-Ponty, *Visible and Invisible*, p. 28. See Martin Jay, "Sartre, Merleau-Ponty and the Search for a New Ontology of Sight," *Modernity and the Hegemony of Vision*, ed. David Michael Levin (University of California Press, 1993), p. 144; p. 165.

11. Merleau-Ponty, *Phenomenology of Perception*, p. xix.

12. *Ibid.*, p. 429.

13. *Ibid.*, p. 430.

14. Sobchack, *ibid.*, p. 12 (emphasis added).

15. *Ibid.*, p. 21.

16. Merleau-Ponty, "The Film and the New Psychology," *Sense and Non-Sense*, pp. 48–59.

17. *Ibid.*, p. 51 (emphasis added).

18. Merleau-Ponty, *Phenomenology of Perception*, p. 215.

19. *Ibid.*, p. 330.

20. *Ibid.*, p. 403.

21. Maurice Merleau-Ponty, *The Structure of Behaviour*, trans. Alden Fisher (Beacon Press, 1963), pp. 121–22 (emphasis added).

22. Richard L. Lanigan, *Speaking and Semiology* (The Hague: Mouton Press, 1972), p. 85.

23. *Ibid.*

24. Barnouw, *Critical Realism*, p. 64.

25. *Ibid.*

26. Roger Munier, "The Fascinating Image," *Diogenes* 38 (1962), p. 86.

27. *Ibid.*

28. *Ibid.*

29. *Ibid.*, p. 88.

30. *Ibid.*

31. Stan Brakhage, "From Metaphors of Vision," *The Avant-Garde Film*, ed. p. Adams Sitney (New York University, 1978), p. 1, Sobchack, *ibid.*, p. 92 (emphasis added).

32. Merleau-Ponty, *Phenomenology of Perception*, p. 394.

33. André Bazin, *What Is Cinema?* Vol. II, trans. Hugh Grey (University of California Press, 1971), p. 87.

34. *Ibid.*, p. 99.

35. "Bazin at Work" *Selected Writings*, trans. Alain Piette, ed. Bert Cardullo (Routledge, 1997), pp. 113–14.

36. *Ibid.*

37. Bazin, *What Is Cinema?*, vol. II, p. 37.

38. Jean-Louis Comolli, "Technique and Ideology," trans. Diana Matias, Cahiers du Cinéma, ed. Nick Browne (Harvard University Press, 1990), p. 229.

39. André Bazin, *What Is Cinema?* vol. I, trans. Hugh Grey (University California Press, 1967), p. 35.

40. *Ibid.*

41. Gabriel Marcel, *The Philosophy of Existentialism*, trans. Manya Harari (Citadel Press, 1961), p. 18.

42. Marcel, *ibid.*, p. 38.
43. Marcel, *ibid.*, p. 38.
44. Bazin, vol. 1, p. 13.
45. Gabriel Marcel, *Creative Fidelity*, trans. Robert Rosthal (Farrar, Strauss & Giroux, 1964), p. 16, George Linden, *Reflections on the Screen* (Wadsworth Press, 1970), p. 125.
46. *Ibid.*, p. 18 (emphasis added).
47. Gabriel Marcel, "Possibilités et limites de l'art cinématographique," *Revue Internationale de Filmologie*, vol. 5, Nos. 18–19 (December, 1954), p. 176.
48. Marcel, *Philosophy of Existentialism*, pp. 21–22 (emphasis added).
49. Bazin, *Introduction to Selected Writings*, p. xi.
50. Marcel, *Philosophy of Existentialism*, p. 46.
51. Merleau-Ponty, *Phenomenology of Perception*, p. xi.
52. Merleau-Ponty, *Eye and Mind*, p. 186.
53. Sallis, *Phenomenology*, p. 64.
54. *Ibid.*
55. Jean-Paul Sartre, *The Transcendence of the Ego*, trans. Forest Williams and Robert Kirkpatrick (Hill and Wang, 1960), p. 48.
56. Jean-Paul Sartre, *Being and Nothingness*, trans. Hazel E. Barnes (Washington Square Press, 1968), p. 173.
57. *Ibid.*, p. 177.
58. Merleau-Ponty, *The Visible and the Invisible*, p. 274.
59. Sartre, *Being and Nothingness*, p. 179 (emphasis added).
60. Merleau-Ponty, *Phenomenology of Perception*, p. 215.
61. Merleau-Ponty, *The Visible and the Invisible*, p. 136.
62. Edmund Husserl, *Cartesian Meditations*, trans. Dorion Cairns (Martinus Nijhoff, 1973), p. 20.
63. Husserl, Ideas, p. 140.
64. Merleau-Ponty, *Phenomenology of Perception*, p. 320.
65. Sobchack, *Address of the Eye*, p. 261.
66. *Ibid.*, p. 268.
67. *Ibid.*, p. 58.
68. Don Ihde, *Experimental Phenomenology: An Introduction* (Paragon Press, 1979), p. 46, Sobchack, *ibid.*, p. 201.
69. Jean-Louis Baudry, "Ideological Effects of the Basic Cinematographic Apparatus," trans. Alan Williams, *Film Quarterly* (Winter, 1974/5).
70. Casebier, *Film and Phenomenology*, p. 73.
71. *Ibid.*, p. 76.
72. Sobchack, *ibid.*, p. 266.
73. *Ibid.*, p. 273.
74. Baudry, *ibid.*, p. 40.
75. *Ibid.*, p. 43.
76. *Ibid.*
77. Husserl, *Crisis*, pp. 127–8.
78. John Barnett Brough, "Art and Artworld" *Edmund Husserl and the Phenomenological Tradition*, ed. Robert Sokolowski (Catholic University of American Press, 1988), p. 29.
79. Jacques Tamineaux, *Dialectic and Difference* (Humanities Press: New Jersey, 1985), pp. 133, 136.

Chapter 4

1. Robert Sokolowski, *Husserlian Meditations* (Northwestern University, 1974), pp. 161–2.
2. Izchack Miller, *Husserl, Perception, and Temporal Awareness* (Cambridge: MIT, 1984), p. 21.
3. Merleau-Ponty, *Phenomenology of Perception*, p. 407.
4. Sokolowski, *Husserlian Meditations*, p. 162 (emphasis added).
5. Merleau-Ponty, *Phenomenology of Perception*, p. 412.
6. *Ibid.*, p. 421.
7. Husserl, *Experience and Judgment*, p. 72.
8. *Ibid.*, p. 73.
9. *Ibid.*, p. 158.
10. *Ibid.*, p. 159.
11. Landgrebe, *Phenomenology of Edmund Husserl*, p. 107.
12. Husserl, *Ideas*, p. 92.
13. Edmund Husserl, *The Phenomenology of Internal Time Consciousness*, trans. James S. Churchill (Indiana University, 1964), p. 109.
14. Robert Sokolowski, *The Formation of Husserl's Concept of Constitution* (Martinus Nijhof: The Hague, 1964), p. 34.
15. *Ibid.*
16. Husserl, *Internal Time Consciousness*, p. 153.
17. Edmund Husserl, *On the Phenomenology of the Consciousness of Internal Time* (1893–1917), trans. John Barnett Brough (Kluwer Academic Publishers, 1991), p. 24 (emphasis added).
18. Jean Mitry, *The Aesthetics and Psychology of the Cinema*, trans. Christopher King (Indiana University, 1997), p. 52.
19. *Ibid.*

20. *Ibid.*, p. 53.

21. Shaun Gallagher, *The Inordinance of Time* (Northwestern University, 1998), p. 18. c/f. William James, *The Principles of Psychology* (1890, Dover Press repr. 1950), p. 609. Gallagher also points out Husserl's description of noema and noesis can be compared to the psychologist, William Stern's distinction between "zeitstrecke" and "präsenzzeit," where the former is close to the specious present, the temporally extended segment of content, and the latter to the noetic structure of consciousness, "despite Husserl's study of James, he seems to have learned more about time-consciousness from another student of Stumpf, namely William Stern: W. Stern. "Psychische Präsenzzeit." *Zeitschrift für Psychologie* 13. 1897. Gallagher, *ibid.*, p. 33.

22. *Ibid.*, p. 21.

23. *Ibid.*, p. 22.

24. *Ibid.*, p. 28.

25. Husserl, *Internal Time Consciousness*, p. 50, c/f David Wood, *The Deconstruction of Time* (Humanities Press International, 1989), p. 74.

26. *Ibid.*

27. *Ibid.*, p. 64.

28. Gallagher, *Inordinance of Time*, p. 48.

29. *Ibid.*, p. 41.

30. Husserl, *On the Phenomenology of the Consciousness*, p. 336.

31. Edward S. Casey, "Keeping the Past in Mind," in *Descriptions*, ed. Don Ihde and Hugh Silverman (State University of New York, 1985).

32. *Ibid.*, p. 42.

33. *Ibid.*, p. 52.

34. David Wood, "From Another Past," in *Descriptions, ibid.*, pp. 61–2. Both Bergson and Deleuze revise the notions of time and place.

35. Husserl, *Internal Time Consciousness*, p. 76.

36. Wood, *Deconstruction of Time*, p. 89.

37. Caputo, *Radical Hermeneutics*, p. 41.

38. Husserl, *Ideas*, pp. 124–25.

39. Merleau-Ponty, *Phenomenology of Perception*, p. 415.

40. Andrei Tarkovsky, *Sculpting in Time* (The Bodley Head, 1986), trans. Kitty Hunter-Blair, p. 14. and see Alan Wright, "A Wrinkle in Time. The Child, Memory and the Mirror." *Wide Angle*, Vol. 18. No. 1. January, 1996.

41. *Ibid.*, Wright, p. 61.

42. Vida T. Johnson and Graham Petrie, *The Films of Andrei Tarkovsky*, Indiana Press, 1994, p. 122.

43. See Deleuze, Vol. 2, p. 74 and Wright's comments, p. 52.

44. Henri Bergson, *Creative Evolution*, trans. Arthur Mitchell (University Press of America, 1983), p. 306.

45. Gilles Deleuze, *The Movement-Image*, trans. Hugh Tomlinson and Barbara Habberjam (Athlone Press, 1988), p. 2.

46. Genevieve Lloyd, *Being in Time* (Routledge, 1993), p. 100.

47. Henri Bergson, *The Creative Mind*, p. 109.

48. *Ibid.*, p. 121.

49. *Ibid.*, p. 118.

50. *Ibid.*, p. 120.

51. Henri Bergson, *Matter and Memory*, trans. N.M. Paul and W.S. Palmer (Zone Books: New York, 1991), p. 29.

52. *Ibid.*, p. 30.

53. *Ibid.*, p. 57 (emphasis added).

54. *Ibid.*, p. 36.

55. *Ibid.*, p. 104.

56. *Ibid.*, p. 102.

57. *Ibid.*, p. 103.

58. Bergson, *Creative Mind*, p. 147.

59. Deleuze, *Bergsonism*, p. 54.

60. Bergson, *Matter and Memory*, p. 67, p. 69.

61. Deleuze, *Difference and Repetition*, pp. 81–82.

62. Deleuze, *Bergsonism*, p. 56.

63. *Ibid.*, p. 57.

64. Bergson, *Matter and Memory*, p. 138.

65. *Ibid.*, p. 150.

66. Deleuze, *Bergsonism*, p. 55.

67. Bergson, *Matter and Memory*, p. 134 (emphasis added).

68. *Ibid.*

69. Lloyd, *Being in Time*, p. 100.

70. Olkowski, *Ruin of Representation*, p. 118.

71. Deleuze, *Movement-Image*, p. 57.

72. Deleuze, *Difference and Repetition*, p. 55.

73. *Ibid.*, pp. 55–56.

74. Deleuze, *Movement-Image*, p. 58.

75. Caputo, *ibid.*, p. 37.

76. James Richard Mensch, *After Modernity* (State University of New York, 1996), pp. 52–53.

77. Caputo, *ibid.*, p. 58.

78. Gary Madison, *The Hermeneutics of Postmodernity* (Indiana University, 1990), p. 34.

79. Steven Shaviro, *The Cinematic Body* (University of Minnesota, 1993), p. 31. Reference is to George Bataille, *Visions of Excess:*

Selected Writings, 1927–1939, trans. and ed. Allan Stoekl (University of Minnesota, 1985).

80. Merleau-Ponty, *Sense and Non-Sense,* p. 98 (parenthesis added).

81. Merleau-Ponty, *Phenomenology of Perception,* p. 78, and note 2.

82. Merleau-Ponty, "Bergson in the Making," *Signs,* p. 188.

83. *Ibid.*

84. *Ibid.,* p. 184.

85. *Ibid.,* p. 185.

86. Glen A. Mazis, "Merleau-Ponty and the Backward Flow of Time," *Thomas Busch and Shaun Gallagher: Merleau-Ponty, Hermeneutics and Postmodernism,* State University of New York, 1992, *ibid.,* p. 58. c/f. Merleau-Ponty, *Visible and Invisible,* p. 267.

87. Mazis, *ibid.*

88. Mazis, *ibid.,* p. 59.

Chapter 5

1. Walter Benjamin, *Selected Writings,* Vol. 2, trans: Rodney Livingstone and Others, Edited by Michael W. Jennings, Howard Eiland, and Gary Smith (The Belknap Press of Harvard University Press, 1999), p. 17.

2. *Ibid.*

3. *Ibid.*

4. *Ibid.*

5. "The Concept of Criticism" in *Walter Benjamin Selected Writings,* Vol. 1, edited by Marcus Bullock and Michael W. Jennings (The Belknap Press of Harvard University Press, 1996) (henceforth *SW1*); *The Origin of German Tragic Drama,* trans. John Osborne (Verso, 1977) (henceforth *OGTD*); *The Arcades Project,* trans. Howard Eiland and Kevin McLaughlin (The Belknap Press of Harvard University Press, 1999).

6. John McCole, *Walter Benjamin and the Antinomies of Tradition* (Cornell University Press, 1993), p. 131.

7. S. Brent Plate, *Walter Benjamin, Religion, and Aesthetics* (Routledge), p. 40.

8. Susan Buck-Morss, *The Dialectics of Seeing* (The MIT Press, Cambridge, Massachusetts, 1991), p. 236.

9. *Ibid.*; see Gershom G. Scholem, *Major Trends in Jewish Mysticism* (New York: Schocken Books, 1946), p. 26.

10. Plate, *ibid.,* p. 46.

11. *Ibid.,* p. 47.

12. Mcole, *ibid.,* p. 137.

13. Buck-Morss, *ibid.,* p. 237; Scholem, *ibid.,* pp 27–28.

14. Benjamin, *SW1,* p. 156; Jan Mieszkowski, Art Forms, *The Cambridge Companion to Walter Benjamin,* ed. David. S. Ferris (Cambridge University Press, 2004), p. 44.

15. Walter Benjamin, *Selected Writings,* vol. 4, trans. Edmund Jephcott, and Others, ed. Howard Eiland and Michael W. Jennings (The Belknap Press of Harvard University Press, 2003) (henceforth *SW4*), p. 163.

16. Mieszkowski, *ibid.,* p. 45.

17. McCole, *ibid.,* pp. 149–50.

18. *Ibid.,* p. 150.

19. Louis Aragon, *Le Paysan de Paris* (Paris, Gallimard, 1953), trans. Buck-Morss, p. 141.

20. Benjamin, *SW1,* p. 334.

21. Brent Plate, *ibid.,* p. 67.

22. Benjamin, *OGTD,* p. 45.

23. Max Pensky, "Method and Time: Benjamin's Dialectical Images," *Cambridge Companion, ibid.,* p. 182.

24. Benjamin, *Arcades Project,* p. 391.

25. *Ibid.*

26. Pensky, *ibid.,* p. 183.

27. *Ibid.*

28. Benjamin, *Arcades Project,* p. 4.

29. *Ibid.,* p. 5.

30. *Ibid.,* p. 461.

31. Pensky, *ibid.,* p. 185.

32. *Ibid.,* p. 184.

33. Buck-Morss, *ibid.,* pp 114–15.

34. *Ibid.,* p. 228, Benjamin, *Arcades Project,* pp. 916–17.

35. Sigrid Weigel, *Body- and Image-Space.* trans: Georgina Paul with Rachel McNicholl and Jeremy Gaines (Routledge, 1996), p. 4.

36. *Ibid.,* p. 18.

37. Benjamin, *SW2,* p. 217.

38. *Ibid.*

39. Weigel, *ibid.,* p. 21.

40. *Ibid.*

41. Benjamin, *SW3,* p. 117.

42. Buck-Morss, p. 210.

43. *Ibid.*

44. Petersson, "Transformations of Readability and Time," p. 56.

45. Benjamin, *SW2,* p. 244.

46. Benjamin, *Arcades Project,* p. 463, Petersson, *ibid.,* p. 54.

47. Deleuze, *Time-Image,* p. 81.

48. See Benjamin's "The Storyteller," *SW3,* pp. 143–166.

49. Benjamin, *Arcades Project,* p. 456.

50. *Ibid.,* p. 458, *Rudolph Borchardt, Epilegomena zu Dante,* vol. 1 (Berlin, 1923), pp. 56–7.

51. Benjamin, *Arcades Project,* p. 463.

52. Benjamin, *SW2,* p. 244.

53. *Ibid.,* Petersson, *ibid.,* p. 57.

54. Benjamin, *SW4*, p. 316.
55. *Ibid.*, p. 396.
56. *Ibid.*
57. Deleuze, *Time-Image*, p. 74.
58. Benjamin, *Arcades Project*, p. 462.
59. Giles Deleuze, *The Logic of Sense*, trans. Mark Lester, with Charles Stivale, ed. Contantin V. Boundas (The Athlone Press, 1990), p. 52.
60. *Ibid.*, p. 53.
61. Benjamin, *SW4*, p. 256.
62. *Ibid.*, p. 255.
63. *Ibid.*, p. 272, note 11.
64. Rodolphe Gasché, "Objective Diversions: On Some Kantian Themes in Benjamin's 'The Work of Art in the Age of Mechanical Reproduction,'" *Walter Benjamin's Philosophy*, ed. Andrew Benjamin and Peter Osborne (Routledge, 1994), p. 187.
65. *Ibid.*
66. Benjamin, *SW4*, p. 338.
67. Benjamin, *SW1*, p. 350.
68. *Ibid.*
69. *Ibid.*
70. Benjamin, *SW1*, p. 340.
71. Benjamin, *SW4*, p. 253.
72. *Ibid.*, p. 255.
73. Richard Wolin, *Walter Benjamin: An Aesthetic of Redemption* (Columbia University Press, 1982), p. 258.
74. Benjamin, *SW2*, pp. 515–17.
75. *Ibid.*, p. 517.
76. Benjamin, *SW2*, p. 508.
77. Benjamin, *SW4*, p. 259.
78. *Ibid.*, p. 260.
79. Gasché, *ibid.*, p. 193.
80. Benjamin, *SW4*, p. 260.
81. Gasché, *ibid.*, p. 196.
82. *Ibid.*, pp. 196–7.
83. Weber, *Mass Mediauras*, pp. 84–5.
84. Benjamin, p. *SW4*, p. 264.
85. *Ibid.*, p. 265.
86. Benjamin, *Illuminations*, p. 215 (emphasis added). "Reactivation" was Zohn's translation based on the early version, in both the 1936 and 1939 versions in *Selected Writings* the translation "actualizes that which is produced."
87. Benjamin, *SW4*, p. 269.
88. *Ibid.*, p. 267.
89. *Ibid.*, p. 268.
90. *Ibid.*, p. 328.
91. Benjamin, *SW2*, p. 527; Gasché, *ibid.*, p. 197.
92. Gasché, *ibid.*, p. 199.
93. *Ibid.*, p. 198.
94. Miriam Bratus Hansen, "Benjamin and Cinema: Not a One-way Street," *Walter Benjamin: Critical Evaluations in Cultural Theory*, ed. Peter Osborne, vol. II, *Cinema and Modernity* (Routledge, 2005), p. 335.
95. Benjamin, *SW4*, p. 319.
96. *Ibid.*
97. Hansen, "*Of Mice and Ducks*: Benjamin and Adorno on Disney," *South Atlantic Quarterly* 92 (Jan. 1993), p. 41.
98. Benjamin, *SW4*, p. 338.
99. See Kaja Silverman, *The Threshold of the Visible World* (Routledge, 1996), pp. 94–7.
100. Benjamin, *SW4*, p. 337.
101. *Ibid.*, p. 338.
102. Robert Lapsley and Michael Westlake, *Film Theory: An Introduction* (Manchester University Press, 1988), p. 87.
103. Stephen Heath, *Questions of Cinema* (Macmillan, 1981), p. 94.
104. Silverman, *ibid.*, p. 103.
105. Weber, *Mass Mediauras*, p. 104.
106. A. Gill and F. Riggs, "Angst of Aura" *RUA TV?* ed. Tony Fry (Power Publishing, 1993), p. 93.
107. Benjamin, *SW4*, p. 339.
108. Gill and Riggs, *ibid.*, p. 94.
109. Barnouw, *Critical Realism*, p. 28.
110. Benjamin, *SW4*, p. 263.
111. *Ibid.*, p. 397.
112. Peter Burger, *The Theory of the Avant-Garde*, trans. Michael Shaw (University of Minnesota Press, 1984), p. 71.
113. *Ibid.*
114. *Ibid.*, p. 72.
115. McCole, *ibid.*, p. 213.
116. Benjamin, *SW2*, p. 3; McCole, *ibid.*, p. 214.
117. Benjamin, *ibid.*
118. Benjamin, *ibid.*, p. 4; McCole, *ibid.*, p. 215.
119. Benjamin, *ibid.*
120. Benjamin, *ibid.*, pp. 4–5.
121. Robert Short, *The Age of Gold: Surrealist Cinema* (Creation Books, 2003), p. 21.
122. *Ibid.*, p. 22.
123. *Ibid.*, p. 25.
124. *Ibid.*, p. 12.
125. Benjamin, *SW2*, p. 208.
126. *Ibid.*, pp. 208, 209.
127. Benjamin, *Arcades Project*, p. 4.
128. Short, *ibid.*, p. 9.
129. *Ibid.*, p. 11.
130. Short, *ibid.*, p. 11; Jacques Brunius, *En Marge du Cinema Francais*, trans. Paul Hammond (Arcanes, 1954), pp. 107–115.
131. *Ibid.*, pp. 14–15.
132. Short, *ibid.*, p. 10.
133. *Ibid.*, pp. 8–9.

134. Benjamin, *SW4*, p. 208.
135. Short, *ibid.*, p. 9.
136. Benjamin, *SW2*, p. 211.
137. *Ibid.*, p. 216.
138. William Earle, *A Surrealism of the Movies* (Precedent Publishing Inc., 1987), p. 96.
139. *Ibid.*, p. 97.
140. Brent Plate, *ibid.*, p. 10.
141. *Ibid.*, Benjamin, *OGTD*, p. 37.
142. Benjamin, *ibid.*, p. 29.
143. Bergson, *Matter and Memory*, p. 95.
144. Benjamin, *Arcades Project*, p. 367.
145. Bergson, *Matter and Memory*, p. 171 (emphasis added).
146. Wendy Everett,"Scene as Threshold," *Screen* 39-2 (Summer 1998), p. 151.
147. Hansen, *Of Mice and Ducks*, p. 37.
148. *Ibid.*, p. 44.
149. Benjamin, *SW2*, p. 545.
150. Hansen, *Of Mice and Ducks*, p. 45.
151. Benjamin, *SW3*, p. 118.
152. Hansen, *Of Mice and Ducks*, p. 39.
153. Benjamin, *SW2*, p. 735.
154. *Ibid.*, p. 545.
155. Benjamin, *SW1*, p. 486.
156. Benjamin, *SW3*, p. 187.
157. Benjamin, *SW1*, p. 486.
158. McCole, *ibid.*, p. 187.
159. *Ibid.*
160. Benjamin, *SW3*, p. 122.
161. Susan Buck-Morss, "Aesthetics and Anaethetics," *Walter Benjamin: Critical Evaluations in Cultural Theory*, ed. Peter Osborne, vol. II, *Cinema and Modernity* (Routledge, 2005), p. 315.
162. *Ibid.*, p. 298.
163. *Ibid.*, p. 302.
164. *Ibid.*
165. Hansen, *Benjamin and Cinema*, pp. 337, 338.
166. Benjamin, *SW1*, p. 466.
167. *Ibid.*
168. Gilles Deleuze, *The Fold*, trans. Tom Conley (The Athlone Press, 1993), p. 86.
169. Benjamin, *SW3*, p. 104.
170. *Ibid.*, p. 141.
171. Howard Eiland, "Reception in Distraction," *Boundary* 2, Spring (Duke University Press, 2003), p. 56; Brent Plate, *ibid.*, p. 110.
172. Brent Plate, *ibid.*
173. Benjamin, *SW3*, p. 141.
174. *Ibid.*, p. 124.
175. Hansen, *Benjamin and Cinema*, p. 353.
176. Brent Plate, *ibid.*, p. 121.
177. Benjamin, *Illuminations*, p. 230.

Chapter 6

1. David N. Rodowick, *Gilles Deleuze's Time Machine* (Duke University, 1997), pp. 134, 135.
2. *Ibid.*, pp. 142–43.
3. Deleuze, *Time-Image*, p. 158.
4. Deleuze, *Bergsonism*, p. 105.
5. Deleuze, *Movement-Image*, p. 10.
6. *Ibid.*, pp. 16–17.
7. *Ibid.*, p. 59.
8. *Ibid.*
9. *Ibid.*, p. 164.
10. *Ibid.*, p. 167 (emphasis added).
11. Deleuze, *Movement-Image*, p. 3.
12. *Ibid.*, p. 40.
13. Sergei Eisenstein, *Film Form*, trans. Jay Leyda (Dennis Dobson, 1959), p. 48.
14. Dana Polan, *The Political Language of Film and the Avant-Garde* (UMI Research, 1985), p. 39.
15. David Bordwell, *The Cinema of Eisenstein* (Harvard University Press, 1993), p. 34.
16. Eisenstein, *Film Form*, p. 82.
17. Bordwell, *Cinema of Eisenstein*, p. 41.
18. Eisenstein, "Montage 38," *Towards a Theory of Montage*, ed. Richard Taylor and Michael Glenney, trans. Michael Glenney (BFI, 1992); Mitry, *Aesthetics of Cinema*, pp. 142–43.
19. Sergei Eisenstein, *Indifferent Non-Indifferent Nature*, trans. Herbert Marshall (Cambridge, 1987), p. 279.
20. Eisenstein, *Film Form*, p. 67.
21. *Ibid.*, p. 145.
22. *Ibid.*, p. 130.
23. Polan, *Film and Avant-Garde*, p. 49.
24. Eisenstein, *Film Form*, p. 105.
25. Carl Plantinga, Rhetoric and Representation in Nonfiction Film (Cambridge University, 1997), p. 378.
26. Deleuze, *Time-Image*, p. 159.
27. Polan, *Film and Avant-Garde*, p. 41.
28. Eisenstein, *Indifference*, p. 27.
29. Leo Charney, *Empty Moments* (Duke University, 1998), p. 154.
30. Jean Epstein, "Photogenie and the Imponderable" *French Film Theory and Criticism*, vol. II. 1907–39. ed. and trans. Richard Abel (Princeton University, 1988), p. 236.
31. Epstein, *Écrits sur le cinéma* (Paris: Seghers, 1974), p. 121, Charney, *ibid.*, p. 154.
32. Deleuze, *Time-Image*, p. 156.
33. *Ibid.*, p. 158.
34. *Ibid.*, p. 157.
35. *Ibid.*, p. 158.
36. Eisenstein, *Film Form*, p. 71.

37. Deleuze, *Time-Image*, p. 201.
38. Deleuze, *Movement-Image*, p. 155.
39. *Ibid.*, p. 66.
40. Olkowski, *Ruin of Representation*, p. 233.
41. Deleuze, *Bergsonism*, p. 110.
42. Charney, *Empty Moments*, p. 45.
43. Jean Epstein, "Magnification"(1921), *French Film Theory and Criticism*, vol. 1.
44. *Ibid.*, p. 239.
45. Deleuze, *Movement-Image*, p. 96, Epstein, *Écrits sur le Cinéma*, 1. pp. 146–47.
46. *Ibid.*, p. 98.
47. Deleuze, *Movement-Image*, p. 109.
48. *Ibid.*, p. 110.
49. *Ibid.*, p. 111.
50. *Ibid.*, p. 117.
51. Deleuze, *Movement-Image*, pp. 80–81.
52. Mitry, *Aesthetics of Cinema*, p. 110.
53. *Kino-Eye the Writings of Dziga Vertov*, trans. Kevin O'Brien, ed. Annette Michelson (Pluto Press, 1984), p. 7.
54. *Ibid.*, p. 15, Malcom Turvey, "Can the Camera See? Mimesis in Man with a Movie Camera," *October* 89 (Summer, 1999), p. 31.
55. *Ibid.*, Turvey, pp. 33, 34.
56. *Ibid.*, p. 35.
57. *Ibid.*, p. 36.
58. *Ibid.*, p. 44.
59. Vlada Petric, *Constructivism in Film* (Cambridge, 1987), p. 127.
60. *Ibid.*, p. 128.
61. *Ibid.*, p. 140.
62. Judith Mayne, "Kino Truth and Kino Praxis: Vertov's Man With a Movie Camera," *Cine Tracts*, vol. 1, no. 2 (Summer, 1977), p. 82.
63. *Writings of Dziga Vertov*, Michelson, introduction, p. xxxvii.
64. Deleuze, *Movement-Image*, pp. 76–77.
65. *Ibid.*, p. 85.
66. *Ibid.*, p. 84.
67. *Ibid.*, p. 85.
68. *Ibid.*
69. Shaviro, *The Cinematic Body*, p. 16.
70. Deleuze, *Bergsonism*, p. 28.
71. Stephen Zepke, *Art as Abstract Machine* (Routledge, 2005), p. 81.
72. *Ibid.*, p. 88.
73. Deleuze, *Time-Image*, p. 40.
74. *Ibid.*
75. Zepke, *ibid.*, p. 90.
76. Deleuze, *Movement-Image*, p. 59.
77. Bergson, *Matter and Memory*, p. 38 (parenthesis added).
78. Marion, *Reduction and Givenness*, p. 57 (parenthesis added).
79. Deleuze, *Movement-Image*, p. 61.

80. Gilles Deleuze, "The Brain Is the Screen," *The Brain Is the Screen, Deleuze and the Philosophy of Cinema*, ed. Gregory Flaxman (University of Minnesota Press, 2000), p. 366.
81. Deleuze, *Movement-Image*, p. 59.
82. *Ibid.*, p. 60.
83. Bergson, *Matter and Memory*, p. 39 (parenthesis added).
84. Deleuze, *Movement-Image*, p. 20.
85. Deleuze, *Time-Image*, p. 32.
86. Bergson, The Creative Mind, p. 193.
87. Deleuze, *Time-image*, p. 33.
88. Deleuze, *Movement-Image*, p. 98.
89. *Ibid.*
90. *Ibid.*, p. 197.
91. *Ibid.*
92. *Ibid.*, p. 198.
93. Deleuze, *Time-Image*, pp. 32, 34.
94. *Ibid.*
95. *Ibid.*
96. Zepke, *ibid.*, p. 96.
97. Deleuze, *Time-Image*, p. 22.
98. Zepke, *ibid.*, p. 99.
99. *Ibid.*, p. 109.

Chapter 7

1. Deleuze, *Time-Image*, p. 36.
2. *Ibid.*, p. 37.
3. *Ibid.*, p. 41.
4. Deleuze, *Movement-Image*, pp. 7–8.
5. Deleuze, *Time-Image*, p. 137.
6. Deleuze, *Difference and Repetition*, p. 117.
7. *Ibid.*
8. *Ibid.*, p. 118.
9. *Ibid.*, p. 119.
10. *Ibid.*
11. *Ibid.*, pp. 292–93.
12. *Ibid.*
13. Friedrich Nietzsche, *The Gay Science*, trans. Walter Kaufmann (New York, Vintage Press, 1974), paragraph 374.
14. Friedrich Nietzsche, *Human, All Too Human*, trans. R.J. Hollingdale (Cambridge University, 1986) vol. 1, sec 4, p. 96; c/f Lloyd, *Being in Time*, p. 119.
15. Lloyd, *Being in Time*, p. 120 (emphasis added).
16. *Ibid.*, p. 121; c/f Joan Stambaugh, *Nietzsche's Thought of Eternal Return* (Washington University Press of America, 1988).
17. Deleuze, *Difference and Repetition*, p. 115.
18. Deleuze, *Time-Image*, p. 131.

19. *Ibid.*, p. 130.
20. *Ibid.*
21. *Ibid.*, p. 131.
22. *Ibid.*
23. Gregg Lambert, *The Non-Philosophy of Gilles Deleuze* (Continuum, 2002), p. 92.
24. *Ibid.*, p. 93.
25. Deleuze, *Time-Image*, p. 132.
26. *Ibid.*
27. Lambert, *ibid.*, p. 94.
28. Deleuze, *Time-Image*, p. 81.
29. *Ibid.*, p. 227.
30. See Spencer Shaw, "At the Crossroads: Last Year in Marienbad," *Literature/Film Quarterly*, Vol. 32, no. 4, 2004, pp. 272–278.
31. Alain Robbe-Grillet, *For a New Novel: Essays on Fiction*, trans. Richard Howard (New York: Grove, 1965), p. 70.
32. Deleuze, *Time-Image*, p. 133.
33. Rodowick, *Time Machine*, p. 76.
34. Deleuze, *Time-Image*, p. 18.
35. *Ibid* (emphasis added).
36. *Ibid.*, p. 181 (emphasis added).
37. *Ibid.*, p. 180 (emphasis added).
38. *Ibid.*, p. 41. The term is Robert Lapoujade's. Deleuze note 23, p. 288, *ibid.*
39. Deleuze, *Movement-Image*, pp. 120–21.
40. Deleuze, *Time-Image*, p. 173.
41. Deleuze, *Difference and Repetition*, p. 267.
42. George Poulet, "The Phenomenology of Reading," *New Literary History*, 1 (October, 1969), p. 56.
43. *Ibid.*, p. 59.
44. Deleuze, *Movement-Image*, pp. 74–75.
45. *Ibid.*, pp. 73–74.
46. Deleuze, *Time-Image*, p. 168.
47. *Ibid.*, p. 22.
48. Gilles Deleuze, *Kant's Critical Philosophy, the Doctrine of the Faculties*, trans. Hugh Tomlinson and Barbara Habberjam (University of Minnesota Press, 1984), p. xii.
49. *Ibid.*
50. Deleuze, *Time-Image*, p. 271.
51. *Ibid.*, p. 168.
52. Deleuze, *Difference and Repetition*, pp. 85–86.
53. *Ibid.*
54. *Ibid.*, p. 86.
55. Gilles Deleuze, *Kant's Critical Philosophy*, p. viii.
56. Deleuze, *Difference and Repetition*, p. 87.
57. *Ibid.*
58. Deleuze, *Time-Image*, p. 82.
59. *Ibid.*, p. 158.
60. Lambert, *ibid.*, p. 115.
61. *Ibid.*
62. Deleuze, *Kant's Critical Philosophy*, p. 52; c/f Lambert, p. 116.
63. Deleuze, *Movement-Image*, p. 53.
64. *Ibid.*
65. Zepke, *ibid.*, p. 91.
66. Deleuze, *Time-Image*, p. 310, note 18.
67. *Ibid.*, p. 165.
68. *Ibid.*, pp. 166–67.
69. Gilles Deleuze and Felix Guattari, *A Thousand Plateaus*, trans. Brian Massumi (Athlone Press, 1988), p. 377.
70. Deleuze, *Difference and Repetition*, p. 139 (emphasis added).
71. John Marks, "Underworld: The People Are Missing," *Deleuze and Literature*, ed. Ian Buchanan and John Marks (Edinburgh University Press, 2000), p. 93.
72. Marks, *ibid.*, c/f. Gilles Deleuze and Felix Guattari, *What Is Philosophy?* trans. Hugh Tomlinson and Graham Burchell (Columbia University Press, 1994), p. 156.
73. Marks, *ibid.*, Deleuze and Guattari, *ibid.*, p. 158.
74. Alain Badiou, *Deleuze: The Clamor of Being*, trans. Louise Burchill (University of Minnesota, 2000), p. 127. Badiou uses re-concatenations rather than relinkages. c/f Gilles Deleuze, *Foucault*, trans. Sean Hand (University of Minnesota Press, 1988), p. 117.
75. Deleuze, *Time-Image*, pp. 179–180.
76. Rajchman, *Deleuze Connections*, p. 57.
77. Juhani Pallasmaa, *The Architecture of Image* (Building Information Ltd., 2001), p. 126.
78. Seymour Chatman, *Antonioni, or The Surface of the World* (University of California Press, 1985), p. 197.
79. Chatman, *ibid.*, c/f. Pascal Bonitzer, "Désir Désert," *Cahiers du Cinéma*. 262–63 (1976), p. 98.
80. Deleuze, *Time-Image*, p. 5.
81. William Arrowsmith, *Antonioni: The Poet of Images* (Oxford, 1995), p. 169.
82. Deleuze, *Foucault*, p. 121.
83. Deleuze, *Time-image*, pp. 204–205.
84. Pallasmaa, *ibid.*, p. 121. It is of interest to consider this in terms of a story, recounted by Antonioni, which took place in Nice during his wartime travels. It is the story of a bather who had drowned. The sky was white, the sea front deserted, a bathing attendant sat, the sun struggled to emerge from the mist. The only activity was the rocking of the dead body in the sea, the only sound the lapping of waves. When the bather is seen to be dead all commotion breaks loose, the atten-

dant tries artificial respiration, two children "sadistically" comment on the swollen, drooling figure about to turn blue. A policeman arrives and eventually things return to normal. For Antonioni to show this event as a series of happenings would somehow be a diminution, to distract from its import. What is included in the event, but not shown, are the tensions within Antonioni's own life that bring their own color to the scene, life in the nearby city, the duration of Being as our existential condition, the friction of the moment and the open future. To film this Antonioni "would try to remove the actual event from the scene and leave only ... that white seafront, that lonely figure, that silence, there seems to me to be an extraordinary strength of impact. The event here adds nothing: it is superfluous.... The dead man acts as a distraction to a state of tension." Michelangelo Antonioni, "The Event and the Image," *Sight and Sound*, no. 33 (1963/4), p. 14.

85. Chatman, *ibid.*, p. 189.

86. Chatman, *ibid.*, p. 190. c/f. Alan Watts, *Psychotherapy East and West* (New York, 1975), p. 23. p. 114.

87. Contrary to Arrowsmith, *ibid.* p. 168.

88. Badiou, *ibid.*, p. 85.

89. Deleuze, *Time-Image*, p. 179.

90. Badiou, *Clamor of Being*, p. 86.

91. Deleuze, *Time-Image*, p. 175.

92. Badiou, *Clamor of Being*, p. 85.

93. Deleuze, *Foucault*, p. 98.

94. Deleuze, *Time-Image*, p. 278.

95. *Ibid.*, p. 279.

96. *Ibid.*

97. Badiou, *ibid.*, p. 128. c/f. Deleuze, *Foucault*, p. 119.

98. *Ibid.*

99. Deleuze, *Time-Image*, p. 166.

100. Benjamin, *Illuminations*, p. 231.

101. Deleuze, *Time-Image*, p. 166.

102. Rajchman, *The Deleuze Connection*, p. 135.

103. Lambert, *ibid.*, p. 130.

Bibliography

Abel, Richard. *French Film Theory and Criticism 1907–39*, vols. 1 & 2 (Princeton University Press, 1988).

Andrew, Dudley. *The Major Film Theories: An Introduction* (New York: Oxford University Press, 1976).

Ansell-Pearson, Keiths. "Deleuze Outside/Outside Deleuze: On the Difference Engineer." *Deleuze and Philosophy: The Difference Engineer* (Routledge, 1997).

_____. "Bergson and creative evolution/involution." *The New Bergson*. Ed. John Mullarkey (Manchester University Press, 1999).

Arrowsmith, William. *Antonioni* (Oxford University Press, 1995).

Aumont, Jacques. *Montage Eisenstein*. Trans. Lee Hildreth, Constance Penley and Andrew Ross. BFI Publishing (Indiana University Press, 1987).

Badiou, Alain. *Deleuze: The Clamor of Being*. Trans. Louise Burchill (University of Minnesota Press, 2000).

Barnouw, Dagmar. *Critical Realism* (John Hopkins Press, 1994).

Barthes, Roland. *Camera Lucida: Reflections on Photography*. Trans. Richard Howard (Vintage Books, 1993).

Baudry, Jean-Louis. "Ideological Effects of the Basic Cinematographic Apparatus." Trans. Alan Williams. *Film Quarterly* 28, no.2 (Winter, 1974).

Bazin, André. *What Is Cinema?* vol. 1. Trans. Hugh Grey (University of California Press, 1967).

_____. *What Is Cinema?* vol. 2. Trans. Hugh Grey (University of California Press, 1971).

Benjamin, Walter. *Illuminations*. Trans. Harry Zohn (Fontana, 1973).

_____. *The Origin of German Tragic Drama*. Trans. John Osborne (Verso, 1977).

_____. *Selected Writings, vol. 1*. Ed. Marcus Bullock and Michael W. Jennings (The Belknap Press of Harvard University Press, 1996).

_____. *The Arcades Project*. Trans. Howard Eiland and Kevin McLaughlin (The Belknap Press of Harvard University Press, 1999).

_____. *Selected Writings, vol. 2*. Trans. Rodney Livingstone and Others. Ed. Michael W. Jennings, Howard Eiland, and Gary Smith (The Belknap Press of Harvard University Press, 1999).

_____. *Selected Writings, vol. 3*. Trans. Edmund Jephcott, Howard Eiland, and Others.

Ed. Howard Eiland and Michael W. Jennings (The Belknap Press of Harvard Univer-
sity, Press, 2002).
_____. *Selected Writings, vol. 4*. Trans, Edmund Jephcott, and Others. Ed. Howard Eiland
and Michael W. Jennings (The Belknap Press of Harvard University, Press, 2003).
Bergson, Henri. *Matter and Memory*. Trans. Nancy M. Paul and W. Scott Palmer (Zone
Books, 1988).
_____. *The Creative Mind*. Trans. Mabelle L. Andison, M.L. (Citadel Press, 1992).
Bordwell, David. *The Cinema of Eisenstein* (Harvard University Press, 1993).
Boundas, Constantin V. "Deleuze: Serialisation and Subject-Formation." *Gilles Deleuze
and the Theatre of Philosophy*. Ed. Constantin V. Boundas and Dorothea Olkowski
(Routledge Press, 1994).
Brakhage, Stan. "From Metaphors to Vision." In *The Avant-Garde Film*. Ed. P. Adams Sit-
ney (New York University, 1978).
Brogue, Ronald. *Deleuze and Guattari* (Routledge, 1989).
Brough, John Barnett. "Art and Artworld." *Edmund Husserl and the Phenomenological Tra-
dition*. Ed. Robert Sokolowski (Catholic University of American Press, 1988).
Buck-Morss, Susan. *The Dialectics of Seeing* (The MIT Press, Cambridge, Massachusetts,
1991).
_____. "Aesthetics and Anaesthetics." *Walter Benjamin: Critical Evaluations in Cultural
Theory*. Ed. Peter Osborne. Vol. II: *Cinema and Modernity* (Routledge, 2005).
Burger, Peter. *Theory of the Avant-Garde*. Trans. Michael Shaw (University of Minnesota,
1984).
Busch, Thomas W., and Shaun Gallagher. *Merleau-Ponty, Hermeneutics and Postmodernism*
(State University of New York, 1992).
Cadava, Eduardo. *Words of Light* (Princeton University, 1997).
Caputo, John D. *Radical Hermeneutics* (Indiana University Press, 1987).
Cardullo, Bert, ed. *Selected Writings: Bazin at Work*. Trans. A. Piette (Routledge, 1997).
Casebier, Allan. *Film Phenomenology* (Indiana University Press, 1993).
Casey, Edward S. "Keeping the Past in Mind." *Descriptions*. Ed. Don Ihde and Hugh Sil-
verman (State University of New York Press, 1985).
Charney, Leo. *Empty Moments* (Duke University, 1988).
Chatman, Seymour. *Antonioni or the Surface of the World* (University of California, 1985).
Comolli, Jean-Louis. "Technique and Ideology." Trans. Diana Matias. *Cahiers du Cinéma*.
Ed. Nick Browne (Harvard University Press, 1990).
Dawkins, Richard. *The Selfish Gene* (Oxford University Press, 1989).
Deleuze, Gilles. *Kant's Critical Philosophy: The Doctrine of the Faculties*. Trans. Hugh Tom-
linson and Barbara Habberjam (University of Minnesota, 1984).
_____. *Cinema 1: The Movement Image*. Trans. Hugh Tomlinson and Barbara Habberjam
(Athlone Press/Minneapolis, 1986).
_____. *Cinema 2: The Time-Image*. Trans. Hugh Tomlinson and Robert Galeta (Athlone
Press/Minneapolis, 1989).
_____. *The Logic of Sense*. Trans. Mark Lester, with Charles Stivale. Ed. Contantin V.
Boundas (The Athlone Press, 1990).
_____. *Bergsonism*. Trans. Hugh Tomlinson and Barbara Habberjam (Zone Books, 1991).
_____. *The Fold*. Trans. Tom Conley (The Athlone Press, 1993).
_____. *Difference and Repetition*. Trans. Paul Patton (Athlone Press, 1994).
_____. *Negotiations*. Trans. Martin Joughin (Columbia University Press, 1995).
_____. *Foucault*. Trans. Sean Hand (Athlone Press, 1999).
_____. "Bergson's Conception of Difference." In *The New Bergson*. Ed. John Mullarkey
(Manchester University Press, 1999).
_____, and Felix Guattari. *Anti-Oedipus: Capitalism and Schizophrenia*. Trans. Robert
Hurley, Mark Seem and Helen R. Lane (University of Minnesota Press, 1983).

_____, and _____. *A Thousand Plateaus.* Trans. Brian Massumi (Athlone Press, 1988).

_____, and _____. *What Is Philosophy?* Trans. Hugh Tomlinson and Graham Burchell (Verso, 1994).

Derrida, Jacques. *Speech and Phenomena.* Trans. David B. Allison (Northwestern University Press, 1973).

Dreyfus, Hubert L. "Heidegger on Technology." *Technology and the Politics of Knowledge.* Ed. Andrew Feenberg (Indiana University Press, 1995).

Dufrenne, Michel. *The Phenomenology of Aesthetic Experience.* Trans. Edward Casey (Northwestern University Press, 1973).

Earle, William. *A Surrealism of the Movies* (Precedent Publishing Inc., 1987).

Eiland, Howard. "Reception in Distraction." *Boundary 2.* Spring (Duke University Press, 2003).

Eisenstein, Sergei. *Film Form.* Trans. Jay Leyda (Dennis Dobson, 1959).

_____. *Film Essays and a Lecture.* Trans. Jay Leyda (Princeton University, 1982).

_____. *NonIndifferent Nature.* Trans. Herbert Marshall (Cambridge University, 1987).

_____. *Writings 1922–1934.* Ed. and trans. Richard Taylor (BFI Press, 1988).

_____. "Montage 38." *Towards a Theory of Film Montage.* Trans. Michael Glenny. Ed. Richard Taylor and Michael Glenny (BFI Press, 1992).

Epstein, Jean. "Magnification." Trans. Stuart Liebman, Richard Abel. *French Film Theory and Criticism,* vol. 1 (Princeton University Press, 1988).

_____. "The Senses." Trans. Tom Milne, Richard Abel. *French Film Theory and Criticism,* vol. 1 (Princeton University Press, 1988).

_____. "Photogénie and the Imponderable." Richard Abel. *French Film Theory and Criticism,* vol. 2 (Princeton University Press, 1988).

Everett, Wendy. "Scene as Threshold." *Screen* 39-2 (Summer, 1998).

Gadamer, Hans-Georg (1975). *Truth and Method.* Trans. Garrett Barden and John Cumming (Sheed and Ward, 1975).

_____. *The Relevance of the Beautiful.* Trans. N. Walker (Cambridge University Press, 1986).

Gallagher, Shaun. *The Inordinance of Time* (Northwestern University Press, 1998).

Gasché, Rodolphe. "Objective Diversions: On Some Kantian Themes in Benjamin's 'The Work of Art in the Age of Mechanical Reproduction.'" *Walter Benjamin's Philosophy: Destruction and Experience.* Ed. Andrew Benjamin and Peter Osborne (Routledge, 1994).

Gatens, Moira. "Through a Spinozist Lens: Ethology, Difference, Power." *Deleuze: A Critical Reader.* Ed. Paul Patton (Blackwell: London, 1996).

Gill A. and Riggs. "Angst of Aura." *RUA TV?* Ed. Tony Fry (Power Publishing, 1993).

Guerlac, Suzanne. *Thinking in Time* (Cornell University Press, 2006).

Gurwitsch, Aron. "The Phenomenology of Perception." *James Edie, an Invitation to Phenomenology* (Chicago University Press, 1965).

Habermas, Jorgen. "Walter Benjamin's Contemporaneity. *New German Critique* 17 (Spring, 1979).

Hansen, Mark B. *New Philosophy for New Media* (The MIT Press, 2004).

Hansen, Miriam Bratu. "Of Mice and Ducks: Benjamin and Adorno on Disney." *South Atlantic Quarterly* 92 (Jan. 1993).

_____. "Benjamin and Cinema: Not a One-Way Street." *Walter Benjamin: Critical Evaluations in Cultural Theory.* Ed. Peter Osborne. Vol. II: Cinema and Modernity (Routledge, 2005).

Hardt, Michael. *Gilles Deleuze: An Apprenticeship in Philosophy* (University of Minnesota, 1993).

Heath, Stephen. *Questions of Cinema* (Macmillan, 1981).

Heidegger, Martin. *The Question Concerning Technology and Other Essays.* Trans. William Lovitt (Harper Torch Books, 1977).

Husserl, Edmund. *Ideas: General Introduction to Pure Phenomenology.* Trans. W. Boyce Gibson (Collier Press, 1962).

_____. *The Phenomenology of Internal Time-Consciousness*. Trans. James S. Churchill (Indiana University Press, 1969).

_____. *Logical Investigations Vols. 1–2*. Trans. J. N. Findlay (Humanities Press: New York, 1970).

_____. *Crisis of European Sciences and Transcendental Phenomenology: An Introduction to Phenomenological Philosophy*. Trans. David Carr (Northwestern University Press, 1970).

_____. *Cartesian Meditations*. Trans. Dorion Cairns (Martinus Nijhoff, The Hague, 1973).

_____. *Experience and Judgment: Investigations in a Genealogy of Logic*. Trans. James S. Churchill and Karl Ameriks (Northwestern University Press, 1973).

_____. *On the Phenomenology of the Consciousness of Internal Time (1893–1917)*. Trans. John Barnett Brough (Kluwer Academic Publishers, 1991).

Ihde, Don. *Experimental Phenomenology: An Introduction* (Paragon, 1979).

_____. *Technics and Praxis* (D. Reidel Publishing Co, 1979).

_____, and Hugh J. Silverman (1985), eds. *Descriptions* (State University of New York Press, 1985).

Ingarden, Roman. "The Cinematographic Drama." Trans. George Grabowicz. *The Literary Work of Art* (Northwestern University Press, 1973).

Iser, Wolfgang. *The Act of Reading: A Theory of Aesthetic Response* (Routledge & Kegan Paul, 1978).

_____. *The Fictive and the Imaginary* (John Hopkins University Press, 1993).

Jay, Martin. "Sartre, Merleau-Ponty and the Search for a New Ontology of Sight." David Michael Levin, *Modernity and the Hegemony of Vision* (University of California Press, 1993).

Jonas, Hans. *The Phenomenon of Life* (University of Chicago, 1966).

Kaelin, Eugene. *An Existentialist Aesthetic* (University of Wisconsin, 1962).

Kermode, Frank. *The Sense of an Ending* (Oxford University Press, 1975).

Koch, Gertrud. "Not Yet Accepted Anywhere: Exile, Memory and Image in Kracauer's Conception of History." Trans. Jeremy Gaines, *New German Critique* 54 (Fall, 1991).

Kracauer, Siegfried. *History: The Last Things Before the Last* (Oxford University, 1969).

_____. *The Mass Ornament*. Trans. Thomas Y. Levin (Harvard University Press, 1995).

_____. *Theory of Film: The Redemption of Physical Reality* (Princeton University, 1997).

Lambert, Gregg. *The Non-Philosophy of Gilles Deleuze* (Continuum, 2002).

Landgrebe, Ludwig. *The Phenomenology of Edmund Husserl* (Cornell University, 1981).

Lanigan, Richard. *Speaking and Semiology* (Mouton Press: The Hague, 1972).

Lapsley, Robert, and Michael Westlake. *Film Theory: An Introduction* (Manchester University Press, 1988).

Levinas, Emmanuel. *Time and the Other*. Trans. Richard A. Cohen (Duquesne University Press, 1987).

Lewin, Benjamin. *Genes V* (Oxford University Press, 1994).

Linden, George. *Reflections on the Screen* (Wadsworth, 1970).

Lloyd, Genevieve. *Being in Time* (Routledge, 1993).

Madison, Gary Brent. *The Phenomenology of Merleau-Ponty* (Ohio University, 1981).

_____. *The Hermeneutics of Postmodernity* (Indiana University Press, 1990).

Manovich, Lev. *The Language of the New Media* (MIT Press, 2001).

Marcel, Gabriel. "Possibilités et limites de l'art cinématographique." *Revue Internationale de Filmologie*, vol. 5, Nos. 18–19 (1954).

_____. *The Philosophy of Existentialism*. Trans. Manya Harari (Citadel Press, 1961).

Marion, Jean-Luc. *Reduction and Givenness*. Trans. Thomas A Carlson (Northwestern University Press, 1998).

Marks, John. "Underworld: The People Are Missing." *Deleuze and Literature*. Ed. Ian Buchanan and John Marks (Edinburgh University Press, 2000).

Marrati, Paola. "The Catholicism of Cinema." *Religion and Media*. Ed. Hent De Vries and Samuel Weber (Stanford University Press, 2001).

Mayne, Judith. "Kino Truth and Kino Praxis: Vertov's Man with a Movie Camera." *Ciné Tracts*, vol. 1, no. 2 (1977).
Mazis, Glen. "Merleau-Ponty and the 'Syntax in Depth.'" Thomas A. Seboek and Jean Umiker-Seboek. *The Semiotic Web* (Berlin: Mouton de Gruyler, 1990).
_____. "Merleau-Ponty and the Backward Flow of Time." Busch and Gallagher, *Merleau-Ponty, Hermeneutics and Postmodernism* (State University of New York, 1992).
McCole, John. *Walter Benjamin and the Antinomies of Tradition* (Cornell University Press, 1993).
Mensch, Richard James. *After Modernity* (State University of New York Press, 1996).
Merleau-Ponty, Maurice. *The Phenomenology of Perception*. Trans. Colin Smith (Routledge & Kegan Paul, 1962).
_____. *Sense and Non-Sense*. Trans. Herbert Dreyfus and Patricia Allen Dreyfus (Northwestern University, 1964).
_____. *The Primacy of Perception*. Ed. James M. Edie (Northwestern University, 1964).
_____. *Signs*. Trans. Richard C. McCleary (Northwestern University, 1964).
_____. *The Visible and the Invisible*. Trans. A. Lingis (Northwestern University, 1968).
Michelson, Annette, ed. *Kino-Eye: The Writings of Dziga Vertov* (Pluto Press, 1984).
Mieszkowski, Jan. "Art Forms." *The Cambridge Companion to Walter Benjamin*. Ed. David. S. Ferris (Cambridge University Press, 2004).
Miller, Izchack. *Husserl, Perception and Temporal Awareness* (MIT Press, 1984).
Mitry, Jean. *The Aesthetics and Psychology of the Cinema*. Trans. Christopher King (Indiana University, 1997).
Mulder-Bach, Inka. "History as Autobiography." *New German Critique* 54 (Fall, 1991).
Munier, Roger. "The Fascinating Image." *Diogenes* 38 (1962).
Nietzsche, Friedrich. *The Gay Science*. Trans. Walter Kaufmann (New York: Vintage Press, 1974).
_____. *Human, All Too Human*. Trans. R.J. Hollingdale (Cambridge University, 1986).
Olkowski, Dorothea. *Gilles Deleuze and the Ruin of Representation* (University of California Press, 1999).
Pallasmaa, Juhani. *The Architecture of Image* (Building Information Ltd., 2001).
Pasolini, Pier Paulo. *Heretical Empiricism*. Trans. Ben Lawton and Louise K Barbett (Indiana University, 1988).
Pensky, Max. "Method and Time: Benjamin's Dialectical Images." *Cambridge Companion to Walter Benjamin*. Ed. David. S. Ferris (Cambridge University Press, 2004).
Petersson, Dag. "Transformations of Readability and Time." *Actualities of Aura*. Ed. Dag Petersson and Erik Steinskog (NSU Press, 2005).
Petric, Vlada. *Constructivism in Film* (Cambridge University Press, 1987).
Plantinga, Carl R. *Rhetoric and Representation in Nonfiction Film* (Cambridge University Press, 1997).
Polan, Dana. *The Political Language of Film and the Avant-Garde* (UMI Research, 1985).
Poulet, George. *Studies in Human Time* (John Hopkins Press, 1956).
_____. "The Phenomenology of Reading." *New Literary History*, no. 1 (1969).
Rajchman, John. *The Deleuze Connection* (MIT Press, 2000).
Rée, Jonathan. "Narrative and Philosophical Experience." *On Paul Ricoeur*. Ed. David Wood (Routledge, 1991).
Ricoeur, Paul. *Husserl: An Analysis of His Phenomenology*. Trans. Edward G. Ballard and Lester E. Embree (Northwestern University Press, 1967).
_____. *Hermeneutics & the Human Sciences*. Trans. John B. Thompson (Cambridge University Press, 1982).
Rochlitz, Rainer. *The Disenchantment of Art*. Trans. Jane Marie Todd (Guilford Press, 1996).
Rodowick, David Norman. "The Last Things Before the Last: Kracauer and History." *New German Critique* (Summer, 1987).

_____. *Gilles Deleuze's Time Machine* (Duke University Press, 1997).

Rosen, Philip. "History of Image, Image of History: Subject and Ontology in Bazin." *Wide Angle*, vol. 9, no. 3. (1986).

Sallis, John, ed. Phenomenology and the Return to Beginnings (Duquesne University Press, 1973).

_____. *Husserl and Contemporary Thought* (Humanities Press, 1983).

Sartre, Jean-Paul. *The Transcendence of the Ego*. Trans. Forest Williams and Robert Kirkpatrick (Hill and Wang, 1960).

_____. *Being and Nothingness*. Trans. Hazel E. Barnes (Washington Square Press, 1968).

_____. *The Psychology of Imagination* Trans. Philip Mairet (Methuen & Co Ltd, 1972).

Schlupmann, Heide. "Phenomenology of Film. On Siegfried Kracauer's Writing of the 1920's." *New German Critique*, no. 40 (Winter, 1987).

Scholem G. Gershom. *Major Trends in Jewish Mysticism* (New York: Schocken Books, 1946).

Schweiker, William. *Mimetic Reflections* (Fordham University, 1990).

Shaviro, Steven. *The Cinematic Body* (University of Minnesota, 1993).

Short, Robert. *The Age of Gold: Surrealist Cinema* (Creation Books, 2003).

Short, Sue. *Cyborg Cinema and Contemporary Subjectivity* (Palgrave Macmillan, 2005).

Silverman, Kaja. *Threshold of the Visible World* (Routledge, 1996).

Sobchack, Vivian. "Toward a Phenomenology of Cinematic and Electronic Presence: The Scene of the Screen." *Post Script* 10, 1 (1990).

_____. *The Address of the Eye* (Princeton University, 1992).

Sokolowski, Robert. *The Formation of Husserl's Concept of Constitution* (Martinus Nijhoff: The Hague, 1964).

_____. *Husserlian Meditations* (Northwestern University Press, 1974).

Stambaugh, Joan. *Nietzsche's Thought of Eternal Return* (Washington University Press of America, 1988).

Stein, Edith. *On the Problem of Empathy*. Trans. W. Stein (Martinus Nijhoff: The Hague, 1970).

Tamineaux, Jacques. *Dialectic and Difference* (Humanities Press, 1985).

Tarkovsky, Andrey. *Sculpting in Time*. Trans. Kitty Hunter-Blair (The Bodley Head, 1986).

Tomasulo, Frank P. "The Text-in-the-Spectator: The Role of Phenomenology in an Eclectic Theoretical Methodology." *Journal of Film and Video*, Vol. 40, no. 2 (Spring, 1988).

_____, ed. "Phenomenology in Film and Television." Special Edition, *Quarterly Review of Film and Video*, vol. 12, no. 3 (1990).

Turvey, Malcom. "Can the Camera See? Mimesis in Man with a Movie Camera." *October* 89 (Summer, 1999).

Weber, Samuel. *Mass Mediauras* (Stanford University, 1996).

Weigel, Sigrid. *Body- and Image-Space*. Trans. Georgina Paul, with Rachel McNicholl and Jeremy Gaines (Routledge, 1996).

Welton, Don, and Hugh J. Silverman, eds. *Critical and Dialectical Phenomenology* (State University of New York Press, 1987).

Wolin, Richard. *Walter Benjamin: An Aesthetic of Redemption* (Columbia University Press, 1982).

Wood, David, ed. *On Paul Ricoeur: Narrative and Interpretation* (Routledge, 1991).

_____. *The Deconstruction of Time* (Humanities Press International, 1991).

Zepke, Stephen. *Art as Abstract Machine* (Routledge, 2005).

Zahavi, Dan. *Alterity and Facticity: New Perspectives on Husserl* (Dodrecht Kluwer Academic Publishing, 1998).

_____. *Self-Awareness, Temporality and Alterity* (Dodrecht Kluwer Academic Publishing, 1998).

_____. "Merleau-Ponty on Husserl: A Reappraisal." *Merleau-Ponty's Reading of Husserl*. Ed. Ted Loadvine and Lester Embree (Kluwer Academic Publishers, 2002).

Index

215